FACING EVIL

A COP'S STORY OF MURDER, MAYHEM AND THE AFTERMATH

SCOTT J. BROWN
AND VICTORIA M. NEWMAN

ENDORSEMENTS

"Law enforcement is a special calling with a cost seldom realized by those who enjoy its benefits. It's a journey taken by sincere individuals desiring to help their fellow man... only to be confronted by his true nature ... in an ever-deepening revelation. Lies, abuse, anger, unimaginable violence and bloodshed, and at times, a direct confrontation with evil. It's also a world of tremendous beauty and privilege...the chance to bring peace to disorder, hope to despair and to see beauty brought up from ashes. Those who make this journey, together, share a special bond that only they can fully understand. This is a story of that special bond and the day two partners confronted evil ... and how triumph will continually rise out of that tragedy."

Jim Bontrager
Vice-President of International Conference of Police Chaplains
Former National Board Member of Fellowship of Christian Peace Officers
USA/Director of Warrior on the Wall

"*Facing Evil* is more than the compelling story of Deputy Scott Brown and the officers who gave their lives on October 24, 2014 protecting the community of Sacramento, California. It is a testimony to the men and women who serve our communities every day without fanfare and great reward, and the impact this can have on them, their families, co-workers, and friends. Evil destroys—and we count on those in law enforcement to shield us from these horrors. Yet, how often do we stop to consider just what we are expecting them to do, and the consequences of being asked to "face evil"? *Facing Evil* tells this story of service and sacrifice with a gripping narrative that is a powerful witness to forgiveness, healing, and hope. It humbles, inspires, and brings well-deserved attention to the physical and spiritual bravery of those who serve us.

Silouan Green
Speaker, Author, Host of The Pilgrim's Odyssey podcast

"Following the death of a police officer, the road to recovery for coworkers, families and friends is filled with challenges. Follow Scott & Liz's journey as they navigate the turbulent waters, struggles, and successfully get their professional and personal lives, and their relationship back on track as a tribute to and in honor of Danny, who gave the ultimate sacrifice."

Jack Harris
Helping Keep Good People Good

"Funerals are always difficult and are much harder for a life that was cut short—especially if the deceased was murdered. Yet, as difficult as the funeral is, it is only the beginning of the hardest work. After the service is over, loved ones have to reframe their lives, overcome their loss, and learn to forgive at a deeper level than many of us will ever know. In his heart-wrenching book, *Facing Evil,* Scott Brown vividly recounts the murder of his partner, then transparently chronicles his personal journey from massive guilt and anger to wholeness. Scott's story, which is raw, real and sometimes not easy to read, will help readers who struggle with grief, bitterness, loss, or guilt. It will help everyone who wants to live on a level where we not only survive but thrive. I recommend getting some tissues when you sit down to read *Facing Evil* and open up your heart to a great download of God's grace."

Ray Johnston
Founding Sr. Pastor of Bayside Church of Granite Bay, California

"Just as Gilmartin's book on *Emotional Survival* and Victoria Newman's books for law enforcement marriage are part of our deputy reading list, this book shall be added. *Facing Evil* is not only an enthralling, gut wrenching read for anyone interested in the work of Law Enforcement, it provides the gritty reality in the midst and aftermath of a Line of Duty Death. Regardless of where you sit in your law enforcement agency, there is absolute value in the read. Administrators have your immediate and long-term strategies in place, first-line supervisors have a plan, and road warriors, know you can survive the darkest days. Listen to Scott's words! These are lessons and insights mired in road rash and shared with a level of vulnerability rarely seen in our profession, as he navigated the aftermath of the violent death of brothers in arms."

Jeremy Kopp
Undersheriff of Gallatin County Sheriff's Office, Montana

"In *Facing Evil,* Deputy Scott Brown revisits the events leading up to a very dark day in 2014 when we lost officers to violent gunfire. Even though Scott survived that ordeal it brought its own darkness for him. Scott shares his remarkable and intimate journey from that day forward, finding strength through tragedy, and how his life will never be the same."

Sheriff Scott Jones
Sacramento Sheriff's Office

"In *Facing Evil,* Scott Brown and Victoria Newman hold nothing back. It's not an easy read because Law Enforcement is not an easy job. This book shows the nature of evil the Thin Blue Line attempts to shield its communities from. It shows the high cost "the job" exacts from officers and their loved ones. It's an honest account of what the long journey back from duty-induced PTSD requires in order to traverse and get beyond that jagged terrain. Facing Evil tells of heartbreak, community, resource, deep faith, forgiveness (the toughest kind) and healing…after the abyss has had its turn looking long back into those who stand in that Thin Blue Line."

Karen Lansing, LMFT, BCETS, aka The Cop Whisperer
Author of The Rite of Return, Coming Back from Duty-Induced PTSD

“Watching firsthand the heart-wrenching pain Scott went through as a friend, along with the way he continues to grow from it in a positive way by vulnerably sharing the true story of that fateful day along with the aftermath, has blessed me on so many levels and I know for a fact it will do the same for you.”

Jason Sautel
Retired Firefighter/Author of *The Rescuer*

“*Facing Evil* takes the reader on an incredible journey of pain, hurt, loss, and grief in a gripping tale of evil not overcoming. Victoria Newman illustrates how strength is unearthed through leaning into and embracing our own weaknesses. I feel like the final chapter of this extraordinary story of courage has yet to be written. Thank you to both Scott and Liz Brown for opening their lives for us all!”

Brad Shepherd
CEO, Warrior’s Rest Foundation

“Scott Brown takes readers to the authentic place where police officers in America live — the raw and untold sacrifices they make on the job and at home to keep us all safe. He describes in uncanny detail an event that shocked the country with the heinous headlines of a cop killer so filled with hate he couldn’t even contain his courtroom outburst years after his crimes. Scott’s story of triumph over evil implores law enforcement and civilians alike to seek out the resources available to them when facing the unspeakable traumas of life. He articulates the importance of faith, family and the grit to never give up despite unimaginable circumstances.”

Ty Steele
News Anchor

“‘*It had been a 50/50 chance for the two of us, because whoever approached that blue Mercury Marquis first, was who would die.*’ *Facing Evil* by Scott Brown and Victoria Newman speaks directly to its readers of the heart wrenching and tragic murders of two veteran Sheriff’s deputies and the pain and suffering that would lie in the wake of October 24, 2014. ’What happened this morning was of Satan, not of God.’ Guided by faith and friendship, the author recounts how he overcame the “survivor’s guilt” that had nearly destroyed his spirituality, family and career. *Facing Evil* is a must read for every law enforcement officer and significant other!”

Michael Stolzman
President of Northern California C.O.P.S.

"Every law enforcement officer's journey through their professional life is punctuated by trauma. Trauma that is in some cases life altering. Surviving deep traumas physically and emotionally intact is the victory that only some achieve. Scott's journey through hell is shared in this powerful book. The true testament to the writers, Scott and Victoria, is their ability to allow the reader to viscerally feel the emotional impact of the struggles that accompany spiritual pain. A must-read for those in law enforcement and those who care about those who serve."

Lt. Randy Sutton (Ret.)
Author of *A Cops Life*, Founder of The Wounded Blue (www.TheWoundedBlue.org)

"This is REAL—it is not a romanticized or dramatized version of a law enforcement career. *Facing Evil* represents what it is truly like to be a human being who wears a uniform and a badge. This book will punch you in the gut, touch your heart and open your eyes. Scott Brown does an amazing job of sharing the trauma, pain and growth that officers and their families experience on a regular basis, as they serve and protect the rest of us. This is a must read for officers and their families to know what resources are available to help them navigate this career. Thank you, Scott, for your courage and strength in sharing your personal journey in order to help others."

Kathy H. Thomas, PhD.
Warriors Rest Foundation, Clinical Director

"*Facing Evil* provides the reader with a raw glimpse into the intense trauma law enforcement officers can face and the ripple effects inherent in their exposures. Brown and Newman show the often-neglected perspective of the law enforcement family and the distress, intense feelings, and trauma they are exposed to through their loved one's chosen profession of service to others. The horror of this story leads to the growth that can come after traumatic exposures when those involved are guided in their journey towards overcoming the darkness and seeking light. The importance of faith and spirituality are often understated or ignored in the explorations of health and wellness and post-traumatic growth, despite the large body of research which shows positive correlations between faith systems and reduced adverse post-traumatic health outcomes. This story of post-traumatic growth and faith will serve as a beacon to those who are working towards finding light in the darkness of their own critical incidents and cumulative stress. My hope is that community members also read this book and learn about the sacrifices, trauma, and resilience of our law enforcement officers and their families."

Lt. Bill Walsh
Law Enforcement Trainer and Consultant

Facing Evil
Copyright © 2021 by Scott J. Brown and Victoria M. Newman. All rights reserved.

Published in the United States of America

ISBN #9798484003143

Front cover image was taken by SSO CSI photographers.
Back cover image taken by Randall Benton, The Sacramento Bee, used with permission.
Author images taken by Blue CHiP Photography.
Cover and Interior Design done by David Eaton.

Independently published by Scott J. Brown and Victoria M. Newman.

Dedicated to

Deputy Sheriff Danny Oliver and Detective Michael Davis, Jr.

and those in uniform who gave their lives
serving, protecting, and engaging evil
for the sake of peace

FACING EVIL

A COP'S STORY OF MURDER, MAYHEM, AND THE AFTERMATH

Foreword
Content Advisory
Introduction
Prologue: Good and Evil

PART ONE: MURDER

Chapter 1:	To Serve, Protect, and Sacrifice	29
Chapter 2:	Collision Course	41
Chapter 3:	Motel 6	47
Chapter 4:	Devastation	55
Chapter 5:	Michael Davis, Jr.	69
Chapter 6:	Consequences and Carnage	89
Chapter 7:	Surrender	99
Chapter 8:	Aftershocks	113
Chapter 9:	Danny	121
Chapter 10:	The Days After	129

PART TWO: MAYHEM

Chapter 11:	Funerals	145
Chapter 12:	Church, Scuba Diving and God	155
Chapter 13:	Returning to Work	163
Chapter 14:	Mourning and Honor	171
Chapter 15:	Line of Duty Losses	187
Chapter 16:	Circus	201
Chapter 17:	Overcoming Evil	213
Chapter 18:	Justice	223

PART THREE: AFTERMATH

Chapter 19:	Survivor	239
Chapter 20:	Getting Healthy	253
Chapter 21:	Lessons Learned	267
Chapter 22:	A New Mission	273

Epilogue: Where Are They Now? 283
Victoria's Thoughts 291
Author Page 295
Acknowledgements 299
Appendix 301

I am a warrior.

I fight not for glory or fame—for they are momentary.

I fight for those who can't.

I fight for justice.

I fight for the oppressed and the downtrodden.

And if I should lose my life for these just causes,

I have no regrets.

For I serve to protect the innocent.

It matters not where or when,

For evil knows no boundaries.

Be it fire, flood or the threat of tyranny,

I will not flee.

Justice is my weapon.

Faith is my shield.

Hope is my armor.

Cry not at my passing

For it was my honor to fight for you.

Shed not tears of sorrow, but tears of joy!

For I now stand with God.

Jon F. Hooper
Read by Sergeant Chris Guerrero at Danny Oliver's Funeral
November 3, 2014

FOREWORD

Facing Evil provides its reader with a personal view of what it was like to walk in the shoes of Deputy Scott Brown and his wife, Liz, when the unthinkable happened. On what would have been just another day at work, their good friend and Scott's co-worker was murdered right in front of him. A chain of tragic events started, and their aftershocks would last years after that day. Scott was faced with a long road to recovery. The evil actions of one person changed the lives of so many. Often, when an officer is involved in a life-altering event at work, they take the tough road of holding in their pain and sense of loss. Scott describes this in a way that will resonate with the many officers in the country who are truly affected by loss but have yet to find a way to work through their grief and pain. He uses his journey to provide hope to those who are struggling.

I was privileged to meet both Scott and Liz at a Concerns of Police Survivors (C.O.P.S.) Program when they were nearly at the beginning of their now lifetime journey of healing. On their journey, they have relied on those people and organizations that could help them, relied on their faith community, and on each other. They now speak and write about their story, using their own challenges, vulnerabilities, and triumphs to help other officers and their spouses across the country.

Scott Brown in Facing Evil, assisted by the very real and engaging writing style of Victoria Newman, is paying it forward to the law enforcement community by providing hope that there can still be joy after tragedy.

Dianne Bernhard
C.O.P.S. Executive Director

CONTENT ADVISORY

"This is REAL...This book will punch you in the gut, touch your heart and open your eyes."
Kathy Thomas, PhD.

This book contains intense recreations of violent criminal behavior that may trigger those who've had previous trauma and disturb those who have not. Strong and offensive language is used throughout the book as well. ***Reader discretion is advised.***

For members of law enforcement, there are several resources available should you find yourself adversely affected. See resources listed in the Appendix, and the How2LoveOurCops website has many resources listed as well. If, at some point, you need someone to talk to immediately, we recommend COPLINE, an international confidential law enforcement hotline. Active and retired officers and their family members can call 24/7 and have a trained listener answer your call.

CALL (800) COP-LINE

(800-267-5463)

INTRODUCTION

Facing Evil is the story of the worst day of my life. It started with a murder on a cloudy Friday morning in October and moved into pure mayhem caused by an evil man and his wife that lasted for years. This day left many people traumatized, grief-stricken, and broken in its aftermath.

So why write a book about it? Why bring it up again, all these years later? Shouldn't it be forgotten, shut away, accessed only through obscure pages of history? Believe me, I would love to forget that day ever existed.

But the truth is, for those involved in the traumatic incidents of October 24, 2014, the pain is still very much alive. I have had to be intentional in my healing—trauma and its effects don't go away on their own.

This book started in the pages of my journal. A wise therapist suggested I write my thoughts down as I moved through the trauma and grief that overwhelmed me. As I slowly worked through pain, survivor's guilt, and their effects on my mind and body, healing began. I had to face evil again, take control of my life, and stop its destruction once and for all.

Others have asked me to share my story. Doing so was hard, but it showed me I'm not alone in my struggle. Officers came to me with tears in their eyes and shared their own stories. It was good to learn we aren't alone in the way these incidents affect us. It was then I became motivated to write my story.

As my healing continued, I passed my words onto Victoria Newman, a friend who is an author and President with How2LoveOurCops. She and I had many questions. As we researched, interviewed, and poured through the nearly 7,000 pages of the investigation, we learned more than we ever wanted to know about facing evil and its aftermath. What we discovered and were trusted with became another difficult journey, but we are confident what it has become will help others.

There are several things to know before the story begins. First, I have the support of both the Oliver and Davis families, Sheriff Scott Jones, and many others who were involved in this horrific day to recount the events that took place. Our sole purpose in writing this book is to help others heal. Profits gleaned from its sale will be re-invested into the lives of law enforcement officers and their families.

Second, this book is written for adults. The murderer used a lot of strong profanity and offensive language. We did not edit it to portray his true character. His words alone require a mature reader. We also recount the deaths and injuries of several loved people; in these cases, we toned down the descriptions to honor the victims and their families.

Third, although we include the personal journeys of two other officers in these pages, I recount the story in narrative form.

Victoria and I were dedicated to accuracy in the writing of this book, but we acknowledge that our account may not be 100 percent accurate. There were minor differences in the interviews based on recollections and points of view. We tried to stay as close as possible to what actually happened, deferring to the evidence available.

Some of the names of real people involved have been changed. We did not wish to subject the civilian victims to further harm, have respected and honored others' requests for anonymity, and could not reach a few others.

We also must add a disclaimer: Victoria and I are not therapists, doctors, nor mental health experts. This is simply testimony—things we have tried on our healing journey and found helpful. We hope we can lead you to some useful resources, but everyone heals differently.

If you are a peace officer, it is our hope that you will find something within these pages to use in your own journey as law enforcement. We aim to take the mystery and stigma away from seeking help. For all others, we hope that you gain insight into the thoughts, protocols and sacrifices of our brothers and sisters in blue.

Thank you for trusting us with your time,

Scott J. Brown

A favorite photo of Danny Oliver.

Photographer unknown.

PROLOGUE
GOOD AND EVIL

"Danny Oliver was a passionate, good soul who loved being a deputy."
—Former Sacramento Sheriff John McGinness

"It's not mental illness at all; it's who [Bracamontes] is. He is who he is, and he is pure evil."
—Placer County Deputy District Attorney Dave Tellman

North Highlands, California

Sacramento Sheriff Deputy Danny Oliver was a cop's cop. He'd spent a long time on the job, didn't take crap from anyone, and at times, was as approachable as a grizzly bear.

I came to know and respect Danny on the job. We developed a friendship, maybe even a brotherhood. He became my partner, and I loved every minute with him. We stayed busy, too—there was a lot of crime in the areas we patrolled.

Once, we were conducting directed patrol in one of Sacramento's not-so-nice areas when we spotted a violation. We pulled the car over near one of our more familiar hotels. After making the stop, we identified four adults and one child in the car. Most of them were either on probation or parole, and one of the females had a no-bail felony warrant for her arrest. Unfortunately, the child in the car was her daughter, and none of the other occupants were related.

We informed the mom she was going to be arrested, but not in front of her daughter. We had the woman call her sister, who was about ten minutes away, to pick up the child. While waiting, I talked to the mother about the decisions in her life that led her to that very moment, suggesting ideas on possible change. Her activities were putting her at risk of losing her daughter—something she made very clear that she did not want to happen.

As she and I talked, Danny was trying his best to keep the five-year-old entertained and distracted. They ran around the grassy area, playing hide-and-seek around an electrical box while making funny faces at each other. I watched them out of the corner of my eye until they came to a stop fairly close to me. The little girl abruptly quit running, as if she suddenly had a thought. She turned her gaze to Danny. He froze, as if waiting for some profound statement. After a short pause, she announced, "You look like a big teddy bear!" before darting off again.

I would like to say I kept a professional demeanor, but I would be lying. Mom and I burst into laughter, and I told the little girl that she made my week. Danny half-smiled and casually asked if he would ever live it down. Not a chance!

The aunt finally showed up, and after ensuring she wasn't high or wanted for priors, we sent the little girl on her way. We then placed her mom under arrest and took her to the main jail. En route, she thanked us for being kind. She said we were the nicest cops she had ever met.

Back at the station, I told the rest of our team the story. Danny's new nickname, "Teddy Bear," took on a life of its own. We played with it mercilessly, even suggesting to others that they don't "poke the bear" when he wasn't in the mood.

****

West Valley, Utah
October 2014

In a small city over 600 miles away from Sacramento, the sale of a stolen weapon closed without a hitch. Luis Enrique Monroy Bracamontes, also known as Marcelo Marquez, hid the box that contained the AR-15 rifle in the trunk of his car. He'd obtained the firearm from a man only known as "Evil" … a known drug dealer who had connections to Sinaloa, Mexico. [1]

Bracamontes had plans for this weapon and the two handguns he and his wife, Janelle Monroy, already carried. He was convinced that his brother, Hugo,[2] and Janelle were having an affair. He'd never caught them in the act, but sensed something was off. [3]

---

[1] We refer to Bracamontes as evil throughout this book, but this man's street name was also Evil.

[2] This is a pseudonym.

[3] His suspicion wasn't unwarranted. The investigation showed that although Monroy wasn't sleeping with Hugo, she cheated on her husband with several women. She also exchanged sex for ink.

Bracamontes was 21 when he met 17-year-old Monroy. Four years later, in 2001, they married. They moved around a lot, scraping by and making trips back and forth from Sinaloa to Arizona and Utah as he got in trouble with the law. It is unknown why they were in Utah, but Monroy's family lived in Arizona. They didn't have many friends—Bracamontes didn't trust anyone—not even Hugo. The couple kept in touch with family only. Bracamontes allowed Hugo to live with them rent-free in the house they leased in West Valley perhaps to keep an eye on the suspected affair.

During this time, Monroy and Bracamontes began using methamphetamine, marijuana, and alcohol regularly. Two months earlier, Monroy was fired for not showing up to work and had not found another job. And then, they were notified that the house in which they lived was to be sold in November. They needed to find another place to live.

Bracamontes grew more and more angry, inciting arguments and fights. He began hearing voices … *"Matas policias. Kill cops. Matas los cabrones! Kill the motherfuckers!"* He bought ammunition, and lots of it.

Then, Bracamontes decided it was time to leave Utah. He wanted to get Janelle away from Hugo and make a fresh start.

****

California
1988-2014

On October 24th, 1988, a helicopter carrying 16-year-old Michael David Davis Jr.'s father and seven others struck power lines near the Mexican border.

Michael Davis Sr., an investigator with the Riverside County Sheriff's Department, was part of a multi-agency narcotics task force. All four officers and three California National Guard crewman were killed in the crash.

It wasn't a surprise to anyone when Michael Jr. followed in his father's footsteps—and several other of his family members'—eight years later. Although he tried other occupations, being a cop was what he wanted. Coupled with his strong will and deep support of the underdog, it just stuck. Michael began his career with the Auburn (CA) Police Department in 1996.

In 1999, Michael's younger brother, Jason, followed him into law enforcement, working for the Placer County Sheriff's Office (PCSO). By October of that year, Michael switched to PCSO to work alongside Jason, where both would remain for the next 15 years. Michael eventually moved to homicide.

Though he was a tough homicide detective, Michael had a heart for children. He enthusiastically coached his stepson's baseball team for years. He loved and protected his daughters. In 2007, he began to work crimes against persons, which included child abuse. In one case, Michael went above and beyond to find parenting classes for the folks of a troubled 16-year-old girl. He checked on that family for weeks afterward.

****

Somewhere on Interstate 80, West Bound

As Utah grew smaller in the rearview mirror, Bracamontes and Monroy argued, smoked crack, and discussed their future. They left the state to start over, heading for San Francisco first, and then somewhere in Oregon. Monroy held a yellow legal pad in her lap, doodling and documenting their thoughts as they discussed plans for their relationship, argued about their sex life, and compiled a bucket list of sorts.

On that list was "Kill Cops."

With the AR-15 tucked between the driver's seat and door, and Monroy's Smith & Wesson 9mm within reach, Bracamontes was intent on this new beginning. Sinaloa was a distant memory; he wasn't going back to his life in Mexico or Utah.

Cruising I-80 in Nevada near Winnemucca, both threw their cell phones out the window. They'd left everything—including several dogs and cats [4], a couple of cars, and a house full of possessions they'd accumulated—in Utah, taking only their clothes, weapons, ammunition, and identification papers (some real, some fake) with them. And Bracamontes's creepy clown masks, which were within reach on the back seat. He was obsessed with

[4] One dog died, but the rest of the malnourished pets were rescued by authorities in Utah.

them, so they had to come.

Soon thereafter, a Nevada Highway Patrol unit came up behind them on the highway. The voices Bracamontes was hearing encouraged him to begin achieving his bucket list.

In an attempt to get the patrolman's attention so he would pull them over, Bracamontes jerked the wheel back and forth and accelerated. But the patrol unit flew right past their sedan en route to a call.

Both Bracamontes and Monroy had every intention of killing that cop.

The voices grew louder … *"Matas policias! Kill cops!"*

Bracamontes and Monroy stayed in Carson City for the night, both in a meth psychosis. They planned to be in San Francisco the next day, via Sacramento.

PART ONE

MURDER

"Be sober and vigilant, for your adversary, the devil, prowls about like a roaring lion, seeking someone to devour..."
1 Peter 5:8, NASB

Danny, the Amos brothers, me, Benato and Thorns, the token fireman.

Photograph from the Brown album.

1

TO SERVE, PROTECT, AND SACRIFICE

"These brave men and women leave their homes every morning not knowing if they'll ever see their families again, yet they make a conscious choice to do so for the greater good.
To protect all of us."
—Five Finger Death Punch

Sacramento, California
November 24, 2007

Racing down College Oak Drive to a robbery in progress, I entered the crosswalk doing 60. In a flash, I saw the car, uttered an expletive, and turned the wheel hard to the right, hoping to miss it. Before I could hit the brakes, we clashed violently, metal twisting, car parts flying.

It was loud. It hurt. And everything went blurry.

When my patrol car finally came to a rest, I had spun through the intersection and smashed into a retaining wall.

****

It was Thanksgiving 2007, and my wife, Liz, was very pregnant with our first child. After enjoying a nice meal and festivities at my in-law's house, I headed out to work the night shift.

My shift started at 2200 (10:00 pm) and ran until 0800 (8:00 in the morning). I got a call about midnight for a 7-11 "stop-n-rob" in my district. This particular business was known for hitting the silent robbery alarm for basic petty theft, although they had been robbed at gunpoint a few times.

We had to treat every call seriously.

I was dispatched with one of our K-9 officers, Deputy Steve Murphy, and luckily, it turned out to be a false alarm. After leaving the store, we "940'd" in the parking lot. This is when two cops meet in different cars, window to window, facing opposite directions. We do this to get close enough to carry on a conversation without yelling while each officer watches the back of the other in case someone approaches. Plus, this way, if we need to leave quickly in an emergency, we aren't likely to hit each other.

As Murphy and I chatted, we received a new call based on a report of someone stealing a car in a neighborhood about five miles away. We both perked up and screeched out of the parking lot, trying to get to the area before the suspect got away. I made it out first and caught the green light.

It was after midnight on a holiday, so the roads were empty. I accelerated and cleared another green light, glancing behind to see if Murphy was still with me. Not seeing him, I realized he had gotten caught at an intersection, but knew he'd catch up shortly.

It was at that moment a car ran the opposite red light, and we collided.

When what happened registered in my brain, I grabbed the mic, said a few words, then realized the radio was dead. I then keyed my lapel mic and said something about an officer-involved accident. That's when I noticed the car was filled with what seemed like smoke.

I quickly unbuckled my seatbelt, shoved the door open, and exited. Not sure how I opened the door because it was so bent; it wouldn't move later on. Adrenaline, I guess, because I was out and standing on my own. Turns out, the "smoke" was actually residue from the airbag.

Murphy rolled up and assessed the situation. He had seen most of it from up the street. He went to check the other car, which was in the middle of the street on the center median. He completely sheared off a short-turn signal. Fluid and steam poured from the vehicle. There were two passengers, one of whom stood next to the car.

The adrenaline was wearing off, and my back and head started to ache. I felt a little dizzy, so sat down on the sidewalk next to my patrol car with my back against the retaining wall.

Because Murphy could no longer see me, he assumed I went down, so came over to check. As he came around the unit, the passenger in the other car took off running toward the Sienna Vista apartments, which were not law enforcement friendly. Murphy stayed with me. He notified dispatch of the runner's description, but by the time other units arrived, he was long gone.

Murphy checked the driver, who was knocked out cold, and called for a medic. I knew it wouldn't be long before they arrived, took me to the hospital, and notified Liz. I decided it was probably better she hear what happened from me. Without thinking about the time, I dialed her number. She answered after a few rings, sounding pretty sleepy.

"Hello?"

"Babe, I'm okay," I began.

Liz always keeps her phone on at night when I'm on duty. This was the first time it had ever gone off, and she was barely coherent.

"I've been in an accident. But I'm okay," I told her. "I believe they'll take me to the hospital to check things out."

"You're good?" she asked, sitting up in bed.

"Yes, I'm fine," I reassured. I knew she'd probably want to head to the hospital, but in her condition, I didn't like the idea of her driving at night. "I'll let you know if anything changes," I said before hanging up.

****

Sacramento, California

Shortly after, a California Highway Patrol officer and paramedics arrived, and I relayed my account of what happened. Going to the hospital wasn't optional, since most of my engine was firmly planted in the passenger area of the patrol unit. I wasn't a fan of the gurney, but obeyed.

I watched the road disappear behind us as we drove. Wasn't I supposed to be the one helping people, not being helped? It was a weird feeling, having people come out of the woodwork to help me. I later realized we are all in it together; when one goes down, we all feel it.

The new medic decided I needed an IV. I didn't really see why, but didn't argue … at first. Ambulances aren't as smooth as you would hope. This young man stuck and missed my vein not once, not twice, but three times. After the third attempt, I saw we were almost to the hospital.

"Stick me again, and I'll stab you with it," I threatened. "Let the nurses at the hospital do it if I need it so bad." He left me alone.

We pulled into the medic bay, and they rolled me out of the ambulance and into one of the two trauma bays of the emergency room. Lower priority rooms were full, so the other trauma bay was given to the driver who hit me. It was quickly determined that he was drunk.

Nurses and doctors came in and spoke to me, pushed on a few things, moved a few things around, and disappeared. The hospital chaplain took down my information, which included Liz's name and phone number.

That chaplain called Liz without my knowledge. One of my partners and friend, Deputy Darren Benato, picked her up and brought her to the hospital.

****

Sacramento, California
2001-2002

I became a cop in 2002 after graduating from Sacramento State University on a football scholarship. I had earned a psychology degree with a criminal justice minor, but I had no idea what to do with my life. I was bartending at Applebee's when I ran into a football buddy who suggested I go into law enforcement. Even though I had studied criminal justice, I never considered being a cop. Once he suggested it, that was all I wanted to do.

I had no idea what I was getting into.

I decided on the sheriff's department. I filled out an application and took the physical and written tests two weeks later. Then came the oral interview. I passed all tests and a background check with flying colors, so within a week, I started the academy. It was August 2001.

I really enjoyed the academy (most of it, anyway). I was in shape, so the physical stuff wasn't difficult. I loved the running, jumping, shooting, fighting, and driving. Academics weren't too hard, either, because I was still in study mode from college. As time passed, I realized I had made the right choice. I wanted nothing else than to be a cop.

I was officially sworn in as a deputy sheriff on May 19, 2002.

****

Mercy San Juan Hospital, Sacramento
Thanksgiving 2007

As Liz pulled up to the hospital, she noted several sheriff's cars. She'd never seen so many in one place in her life, so she wondered if I was actually more hurt than I had let on.

Liz had not yet experienced the true brotherhood of cops yet—that when an officer is hurt, we show up en masse. This was her first taste, and it was overwhelming.

She found me in the trauma bay with the drunk who hit me nearby. He had regained consciousness and was crying for his mom while complaining of pain.

I didn't have a lot of sympathy for him. On top of having a suspended license for a previous DUI and two warrants out for his arrest, that particular night his blood alcohol level was hovering around 0.23—almost three times the legal limit of 0.08. Although grateful that he was alive, I wasn't sympathetic to his pain.

Liz was in protective mama-bear mode. The guy was getting under her skin, and I suspect she was fixin' to crimp his IV line (or worse). Not wanting my wife to go to jail for assault, I asked a nurse to move me. She was very nice and totally understood, but regrettably told me they had no room. I suggested the hall, but that was full, too. So, we had no other choice but to sit and listen to "Drunky McStagger" while the hospital staff completed my tests.

Long story short, my injuries consisted of small abrasions on my knees from hitting the underside of the dash, a big bruise on my right hip from my gun, minor back pain, facial redness from the airbag, and two puncture marks from my badge getting caught by the seatbelt and stabbing into my arm. Not bad, considering the sad state of the car and the speed at which I was traveling. It is a testament to how well those old Crown Vics were made.

The real reason I walked away from the whole thing was because God was not done with me yet. I didn't realize it at the time, but I had so much more to do.

****

Sacramento
2002-2005

Fresh out of the academy, I immediately began patrol training in a program called Patrol First. Newly hired deputies went through patrol training before heading to the jail, so that during emergencies, they could send trained deputies from the jail to the streets to help out.

After passing patrol training, I was assigned to the Sacramento County Main Jail. I worked the housing floor and booking/intake. I became a member of the Critical Emergency Response Team (CERT), a gang intelligence team, and eventually, a Custody Training Officer (CTO). I enjoyed the jail and took every class available. It gave me time to learn in a somewhat controlled environment.

Once my number came up, I was released from the jail to undergo patrol retread training in Central Division. Once that was complete, I worked graveyard shift in the northeast division of Sacramento County with Deputy Darrell Amos.

That is where Danny and I met for the first time.

****

Sacramento Area
Thanksgiving, 2007

After I was released from the hospital, we were transported to the station to pick up my car. Although I had been in the accident, I decided I would drive rather than Liz. She was exhausted, having been sick the entire pregnancy.

On the way, Liz said she didn't feel good.

"Pull over, Scott."

I immediately did as I was told. She shoved the door open and puked on the shoulder of the I-80 freeway. As soon as she finished, she gave the go ahead. "Ok, let's go."

What a trooper!

When I finally crawled into bed that night, tired and sore, I thanked God for protecting me. I also thanked Him for giving me Liz. With all she'd been through that night, she didn't complain once. She never asked for anything for herself. She thought only of me. What an amazing wife!

It wouldn't be the last time she'd prove it, either.

****

Sacramento
2009-2014

When the economy crashed in 2009, our department laid off over 170 deputies. Several of the patrol deputies had to return to corrections. Darrell and I were taken from patrol and put back into the main jail in July 2009. I wasn't happy about it, but there were others who were let go, so I couldn't complain. I returned to patrol on October 24, 2010.

Not sure how he did it, but Darrell didn't stay long at the jail. He went back to patrol right away, and for the next three years, partnered with none other than Danny Oliver. The two loved to work together, along with Darrell's brother, Brian, who was a K-9 officer. Darrell and Danny spent hours together in the car, talking, working, and growing close. Sometime during those three years, Danny designated Darrell as his "person" who would notify his family should anything go wrong.

I have been in many crazy situations in my career, including a guy shooting at me as his sixteen-year-old daughter hugged him like a blanket, so I couldn't shoot back. The first time I ever discharged my weapon took crazy to another level. It was straight out of a movie or some bad television show, but it ended the way it was supposed to—all officers went home, and even the bad guy survived after some time in the hospital. Nevertheless, it was my first shooting, and my only frame of reference for the big one to come.

On January 7, 2012, I was working the graveyard shift in the Arden-Arcade area. This very busy region had both multimillion-dollar neighborhoods and apartment complexes cops don't go into without cover. My partner at the time and I had earned a reputation as "shit magnets"—if there was trouble to be found, we found it.

On this particular night, we were near Auburn Boulevard and Watt Avenue when the air was cleared for a felony vehicle stop in the north area of the county. This means nobody is to talk on the radio unless it is priority traffic—it has to be really important. We were too far away to respond, and they had plenty of units, so we stayed in our district.

While continuing to monitor the radio, dispatch advised that the California Highway Patrol (CHP) was in pursuit of a vehicle near Howe Avenue and a street neither my partner nor I recognized. As usual, CHP was not asking for help—it was just an FYI broadcast. CHP wouldn't ask for help unless the suspect were to run on foot and they needed to establish a perimeter. Still, we moved toward Howe Avenue just in case. All agencies run short at night, so regardless of the patch you're wearing, you back one another up.

Since we didn't know exactly where everyone was, we decided to go to Howe Avenue and Arden Way, hoping to see them. As we approached the intersection, the felony stop in the north county ended, and the air returned to regular traffic. Dispatch advised the pursuit was southbound on Howe Avenue approaching Wyda Way. I got excited, because not only was it close, but since it was a solo-unit pursuit, we could join in.

As we headed up Howe Avenue, we saw the lights and heard the sirens. I pulled into the middle "suicide" lane and waited to see if they were going to pass or turn on a side street. The suspect turned quickly into a parking lot and headed west. The pursuit included the suspect car, a CHP unit, and one of our local park units. We jumped in as third in pursuit.

We didn't have communication with CHP except through dispatch, so we didn't know why we were chasing the guy. It didn't matter—there's always a reason for running.

The suspect sped through the parking lot and out onto the street, then turned and drove through a school parking lot. As he exited, the park unit fell back, and we jumped in as secondary.

We continued behind the CHP unit, and at one point, saw him move to implement a PIT[5] maneuver. We readied for the felony vehicle stop that would follow. The CHP officer had the car stopped, but to our surprise, the suspect restarted the car and drove down a dead-end street. The CHP officer pursued him again, both vehicles ending up on residential

---

[5] Pursuit Immobilization Technique

lawns as the CHP officer hit the suspect from behind. Finally, both vehicles stopped.

My partner ran to the driver's side of the suspect's car, breaking out the window with his flashlight. The suspect started the car again and moved forward. My partner dropped the flashlight, and the glass cut his hand. Meanwhile, I positioned our car in a way that would prevent his escape again and exited the vehicle with my gun drawn. I aimed at the suspect to prevent him from running over our deputy, but I didn't have a clean shot. As the driver scraped between my car and the cinderblock wall to get around me, I got a good look at him. He was a very sweaty, medium-skinned male with dark hair, and his eyes were wide open.

This guy is high as a kite, I thought. This isn't gonna end well …

The suspect successfully maneuvered around me and raced back down the street with CHP hot on his tail. My partner and I jumped back in our vehicle and did a 1000-point turn on the narrow ghetto street so as not to hit the parked cars. We headed in the direction of the pursuit, but by this time, all units were on their way. If we would've caught up, we would've been fifth or sixth in line. Since that is against policy, we drove to a south neighborhood in case the suspect bailed. That plan changed again when we heard the suspect had been pitted again by a Sac Sheriff unit and stopped in the middle of the street. Ironically, it was the same spot the CHP officer had pitted him the first time.

We joined the felony vehicle stop to assist. As we approached, the crazy dude re-started his car and began heading up the street *backwards!* The CHP officer decided enough was enough and straight-up rammed the dude nose-to-nose. Now, both vehicles were driving up the street, one forward and one backwards! When they reached the T-intersection, they ended up on the same dead-end street we were on earlier. Both were faced the right direction by then, but their bumpers became temporarily entangled! Shortly after making a turn, they separated: the CHP officer veered to the right and hit a fat palm tree dead center, and the suspect veered off to the left and crashed in a driveway.

Next, one of our units rammed the suspect's side door as we pulled in behind. The suspect was trapped, but still trying to start his car and refusing to respond to directions to place his hands outside the window. I exited our car, which put me between the suspect's and mine—not a great idea, in hindsight. My partner headed around the front of our car, directly into crossfire. I started to warn him, but right then, the suspect got the car started and threw it in reverse. Still standing next to my door, I dove out of the way toward the other units.

As I stood up, the suspect rammed into our car before turning the vehicle toward my partner. The other units fired at the car. I fired one shot before realizing my partner was in the way. He was able to take cover behind a tree, though, and the suspect missed him, swerving back onto the street and heading back toward the cinder block wall we had been at minutes before.

In all, we had fired 17 rounds at the guy. Three bullets hit him—one in his upper right shoulder, one in his right hip, and one shattering his left femur. His car sucked up the rest of the rounds.

The dude was so high, though, he had no idea he'd been shot! So, the drama continued. We headed down Bowling Green and somehow became the primary unit in the pursuit. The suspect's car made it about halfway to the cinderblock wall and died. I pulled to a stop behind it and stood behind my open door with my gun pointed. My partner was out with the shotgun aimed, as well. I shouted commands to the suspect to put his hands outside the window, but he continued to ignore them, still attempting to start the car.

At that point, we still had no idea who he was or why he was running. As far as we knew, he could've just killed someone and been armed to the teeth. We weighed our options to end the situation. We couldn't send the K-9 if the car could still go mobile. The car started and rolled forward a few more feet before sputtering out again. I decided to sit in the driver's seat, and another officer came up alongside my open door with his rifle. My partner remained positioned outside his open door. We knew we had to end it before someone got killed, so I rolled our vehicle up to his bumper. If he started the car again, I planned to push it into the brick wall about 100 feet away.

Multiple units approached the driver's side of his car, tasing him. It didn't work. A second Taser was deployed through the broken window, because the door was so bent and jammed, it wouldn't open. When they finally wrestled it ajar, the dude had his seatbelt on and was still trying to get the car started. They cut the belt and removed the suspect from the vehicle. It was at this point we realized he had been shot. We called for a medic and rendered medical aid.

A sergeant rounded up those of us who had discharged our weapons and ordered us to stand in a driveway. We were not to talk to each other until taken to our north central division for interviews. Of course, we did say a few words to each other after the sergeant left, but not about the incident. We were driven to the station and again warned to keep silent. I obeyed the command. This was my first OIS (officer-involved shooting), and I was nervous about it. I had no idea what to expect.

At some point, someone asked if I had called Liz. I said "No." After all, I wasn't supposed to talk to anyone! The others told me not to be an idiot and call her.

I started off with "I'm okay," and told her I had been in a shooting. I relayed that I couldn't share anything yet and had no idea how long I'd be. She was calm but wanted reassurance that I was indeed okay.

As our team waited for union reps, lawyers, rangemasters, and detectives, we made small talk. Although we didn't discuss the shooting, we were sure thinking about it. I knew it was justified, but started second guessing everything anyway. I fired only one shot. That was the only shot necessary at the time. But it is policy that once a weapon is fired, those who pull the trigger are automatically off duty during the investigation. Would someone think I had only discharged my gun to get time off?

I learned later the incident was recorded on several in-car cameras and on the CHP air ops camera. All of our accounts matched up with the footage, including mine. I felt a lot better.

I also learned why the guy ran from us. The man was 40 years old with a preexisting mental condition. His mother had power of attorney over him. He also was high as a kite. When the CHP officer tried to pull him over for jumping a curb, he was under the delusion that his ex-girlfriend had lied to the cops, and we were out to kill him. The suspect went to a mental hospital, and the case never even made it to court.

I don't remember having any emotional side effects related to the shooting. It was exciting, and it ended the way it was supposed to—with all officers and civilians okay. Even the suspect recovered.

Looking back now, I realize this incident gave Liz and I preliminary training, knowledge, and expectations for the call that would soon change our lives.

Getting ready to assist with the warrant, October 24, 2014.

Photograph was taken by a ride-along who was with us that morning. I don't know his name.

Booking photo in the jail—the last photo of Danny alive.

Photograph is from the jail surveillance tape.

2

COLLISION COURSE

"They had an evil purpose. God had a good purpose. God didn't start cleaning up halfway through this sinful affair. He had a purpose, a meaning, from the beginning. From the start, He meant it for good."
—Pastor John Piper

Vacaville
Wednesday, October 22, 2014

Monroy's bloodcurdling screams pierced the car as the semi's horn blared. Bracamontes's car barely missed it.

The two were headed for San Francisco from Carson City, Nevada, via the I-80. They stopped in Vacaville, about an hour west of Sacramento. Vacaville offers several options for food, gas, and lodging just off the freeway.

Bracamontes's orders to quiet down were ignored. Instead, Monroy was hyperventilating, whimpering, and waving her arms. He pulled his blue Grand Marquis into a Union 76 gas station and parked. He tried to calm her down, but she was out of it. He yelled to a man dumping trash, "Call an ambulance!"

He held her as she continued gasping for breath, but as soon as the fire department showed up, she seemed to calm down. They took her vitals and confirmed she was not having a heart attack, but recommended she be checked out at the hospital.

Bracamontes stood back, worried. When they said it was a panic attack, he grew frustrated quickly, and wanted the medics to leave.

"I'm not going to the hospital," Monroy argued. "I'm fine, now."

The paramedics saw Monroy's episode as a ploy for attention and felt uncomfortable with the way Bracamontes looked at them. Sensing something off, both felt the hair on the backs of their necks stand up. They accepted the denial of assistance and left. The police, already on their way, were called off.

Bracamontes drove to a motel across the highway, splurging for the honeymoon suite with a hot tub. While Monroy rested, he headed to a store and bought two burner phones. They were almost out of meth, so he would need to find more soon.

****

Sacramento

I've always had a strong desire to help others. I have a need to protect victims and see that justice is done. This drive has been inside me since I was a kid. I was raised this way.

Our family went to church, so we heard sermons from the Bible, which we consider God's letter to man. The Bible is very clear about right versus wrong. Don't kill, steal, cheat, lie, or treat others badly. If you do any of those things, you should be held accountable and ask for forgiveness. My parents taught me to tell the truth, take responsibility for my actions, and work hard. My dad instilled in me the importance of looking at people when I talk to them, shaking hands when introducing myself, and opening doors for women.

I was never to start fights, but was allowed to finish them. As a kid, the only fight I ever took part in (other than those with my twin brother, Tim) was to defend a kid who was being picked on. Despite his size, he was being bullied, so one day, I called the bully out after school. We met in the park, and I whooped his butt. That was the end of it.

My purpose and motivation for what I do as an officer has changed in light of my marriage and family. If the world didn't need police officers, I would rejoice for my kids and gladly find something else to do.

But that is not the world we live in.

Ours is broken … full of evil deeds, and in some cases, evil people. I don't believe that most people are evil, even those who commit crimes. Most people I've dealt with over the years are God's children, just like me. They might be in a bad way—addicted to drugs or alcohol, scared, broke, and/or desperate—but they are still people with souls. If they commit a crime, it's my job to call them on it and make them face the consequences of their actions.

I try not to judge or condemn. I am a sinner and have no right to judge anyone. I hope those I arrest learn from their mistakes and don't repeat them. Being a cop is one of the only jobs in which saying, "I hope I never see you again" is a good thing!

When I became a deputy, I was single. I didn't have kids. Working late and on holidays, or odd shifts only affected me—I was the only one who sacrificed. I worked to make Sacramento a safer place. I went into houses, kicked in doors, and stopped vehicles without worrying if something might go wrong.

Now that I have family who depends on me, I go to work to make the world a better place for them. For Liz and the boys, I want to make it as safe as I can, but honestly, I feel as if we're losing the battle.

I also know someone has to keep up the good fight, regardless.

Now, when I miss a holiday, I miss moments with my family. That is time I will never get back. When work causes me to be late, and I can't call Liz, she worries. So does Connor. What 10-year-old asks his dad when he will retire, so he won't have to worry about him getting killed? My son's question floored me.

Now, every time I kick in a door or stop a car, I know it could be the last thing I do. My faith in God gives me comfort when I think of dying. But the thought of leaving the boys without a dad and leaving Liz alone to raise them really scares me. So, on the job, I use caution when charging ahead.

As a cop, I protect the weak. I stand in the gap between good and evil, and I do it with all the integrity and faith I can muster.

****

Vacaville
Thursday, October 23, 2014

Drugs and sleep calmed Monroy down, but the meth was gone. Sacramento was closer than San Francisco, so Bracamontes and Monroy headed back that way. The couple asked around for a place to purchase drugs and ended up at Motel 6 in the Arden area. They quickly found what they were looking for and stayed the night in Room 150.

****

Roseville
Thursday, October 23, 2014

After a time as a Field Training Officer, Deputy Danny Oliver urged me to join the North Patrol Problem Oriented Policing (POP) team in May 2014 as his partner. The POP team is made up of six deputies and a sergeant and is considered the "Swiss army knife" of the department. The purpose is to identify community and quality-of-life issues and develop long-term solutions. We addressed everything from transients and drug houses to prostitution and massage parlors. We conducted undercover john stings, operations to shut down massage parlors, high impact sweeps, search warrants, community events, public relations events, community meetings, meetings with business owners, and specific tasks for the sheriff. When we had time, we assisted other units like SWAT and detectives with search warrants. I loved the work! To this day, my time at POP with Danny constitutes the most fun and fulfilling assignment I've had as a cop.

Thursday evening, October 23, a probation officer called asking the POP team for assistance. One of his officers had gone to a house on Renick Drive. The parolee and her boyfriend had attempted to intimidate the officer, refusing to allow the deputy to do her job. We were to assist with the search, our large presence to counteract their attempted intimidation.

Danny's wife, Susan, was in San Diego for a business trip at the time, and since she had told him he'd be bored if he went with her, he stayed home. Deputies Smith and Patton[6] were off duty. That left Deputies McCabe and Pratt[7] to help with the search, along with some trainees. That wasn't enough. So, Danny and I decided we'd join them early the next morning.

I wish we had decided differently.

****

[6] These are pseudonyms.

[7] These are pseudonyms.

Greater Sacramento Region
Friday, October 24, 2014, 5:00 a.m.

I arose early Friday morning, trying to be quiet so I wouldn't wake my family. After getting dressed, I kissed Liz goodbye as she slept, "just in case," as we joked. Little did I know that it could've actually been my last time kissing her.

I checked on the boys, who were sound asleep and looked as precious as always, and crept out the door.

My drive to work took about 20 minutes, and like most days, I was excited about going.

Danny was already at his desk and greeted me when I arrived, which was normal. Right away, I learned that my temporary status on POP had become permanent. It was a great way to start the day, because I loved the team, the job, and especially working with Danny.

Earlier in the week, I was told I might go back to patrol. Danny pitched a fit and fought for me, marching into the sergeant's office, yelling that I deserved to be on the team. If it meant he had to give up his own spot so I could stay, he would. Sarge told him he was being ridiculous—he had already decided to keep me.

We gathered up the team and drove to meet the probation officer in front of the probation office near Roseville Road and Myrtle Avenue. It was Danny, Deputies Pratt and McCabe, me, and two recently finalized trainees on a two-week temporary tour with POP. The morning was cold and foggy, so I wore my normal BDU's, POP shirt and TAC vest, but also had on my black beanie to keep my bald head warm.

We stood in the parking lot going over who we were going to contact and why. A ride-along from probation took pictures of our team as we prepared. Once the plan was briefed, we convoyed to the address, which was close by. Renick is not exactly a cop-friendly street, so everyone knew within minutes that we had arrived. We gained entry into the house and detained our subject and her boyfriend. We also located five to six "ghetto sheep" (pit bulls) in the backyard, and they looked horrible. Danny and I helped with the house search before volunteering to take the female to jail for a violation of her parole.

We loaded up the suspect and drove downtown to our main jail. She talked the whole way about random stuff. Once we arrived, we ran her through the medical screening process, and the jail deputies took custody of her. Danny and I stuck around and chatted with the booking crews, who we knew well since we were there two to three times a day. The booking area of the jail has a camera system, which filmed the interaction.

These captured images would be the last of Danny alive.

Our next destination was the District Attorney's office, which is located two blocks from the jail in downtown Sacramento. I dropped off a warrant for a guy I caught with a decent amount of methamphetamine earlier in the week but did not arrest due to a medical emergency. The clerk asked if I wanted to walk it through myself, which typically takes a few hours, or to drop it off, in which case, she'd call me when it was ready. Danny and I decided we didn't want to wait that long—we wanted to do something productive.

That decision became my first regret of the day.

Officers on scene at Motel 6.

Photograph was taken by Randall Benton of the Sacramento Bee.

3

MOTEL 6

"If the same person that wants to defund me and tell me I'm a piece of shit is taking rounds ... I would take a bullet and I would die for him."
—Placer County Deputy Joe Roseli

Motel 6, Sacramento
Friday, October 24, 2014, 10:22 a.m.

After departing the jail, Danny and I drove east on Highway 160 toward the Arden area. As we were each silently considering our next move, we looked at each other and said, "Motel 6!" almost simultaneously. This was our common practice, to check out the motel parking lot—it was easy to find hookers, pimps, and drug dealers loitering around, especially in the far south lot.

A few weeks prior, Danny and POP Deputy John Ilaga caught a guy there with a MAC-45 and a 30-round mag slung around his neck with a shoelace. Danny chased him briefly, caught him, and hauled him off to jail.

We pulled into the parking lot from Arden Way near the main entrance and drove our white, unmarked Crown Victoria south along the first building. Even though lights were only mounted near the rearview mirror and along the bottom of the back window, everyone recognized it as a cop car.

The parking lot was fairly full, and there were a few people wandering around. As we made a right-hand turn to head west along the north side of the south building, we noticed a car possibly related to a burglary we dealt with earlier in the week. Danny stopped and got out while I ran the plate. He got the VIN off a dirty van parked next to it. Danny stopped to talk to a guy on a bike, then looked up and said something I couldn't make out to a guy on the roof. It didn't sound like a very exciting conversation, and Danny didn't say anything when he got back in the car. He gave me the VIN, and I ran it while he resumed driving around the building.

From our first patrol until the last, Danny drove. This was for several reasons. First, he was the senior deputy, so he had first choice. Second, I came from the night shift and was not used to daytime traffic; frankly, I hated driving in it. Third, Danny was previously a driving instructor and drove like a maniac that never crashed. He said I drove like his mother. Lastly, Danny was built like his English bulldog, Smalls, so I was a little faster on the run. (I'm sure he would argue that!)

The south building ran east to west with the south and west side as the parking lot. The north side was an interior grass area, and the east was a walkway opening from the parking lot. The two-story building had a second story walkway with a metal railing running the length and stairwells at either end. The parking spots were against the south side of the bottom floor with the spaces facing north-south. On the south side of the parking lot was an eight-foot cinderblock wall. On the other side of the wall was a large movie theater.

Danny drove around to the south parking lot and pulled the car to a stop. As he got out, he said, "There are two in the car." Having worked with Danny long enough at that point, I knew that meant *stop what you're doing, and let's deal with these two together.* I looked up and saw a male in the driver's seat. The trunk was open, which prevented a clear view of the passenger side. I could not yet see if there was a passenger in the rear seat.

The suspect vehicle was the far most west car. There were multiple cars continuing east from it, and a large delivery truck was parked along the cinder block wall. We parked facing east, about 15 feet or so off of the suspect vehicle's driver's side rear bumper, but did not block it in. We didn't run the lights or siren, either, because at that point, we were simply making consensual contact.

The car was a greyish-blue Mercury Marquis with standard wheels and dark, tinted windows, which made it almost impossible to see inside.

As Danny walked up to the driver's side, he called out, "Hey, how ya' doin'?"

At the same time, I looped out toward the passenger side. As I cut the angle, I saw a large, white female with blonde hair standing in the open car door. Her attention was toward Danny, so she startled when I spoke.

"Sit down on the back seat, and keep your hands where I can see them," I ordered.

She looked at me with panicked eyes as she put her hands on the trunk and shut it.

Something's up. Gotta get into that trunk—it's either guns or dope. Searchable probation?

She just stood there with a weird look on her face, not following my directions.

Something isn't right ...

"Sit the fuck down!" I repeated.

This time, it seemed to sink in that I wasn't playing. She slowly sat down, and as her butt hit the seat—

Pop! Pop-pop-pop-pop-pop!

Six gunshots rang out from the driver's side of the car. I heard only the first few, and not a thing after.

My senses were altered ... sort of like in the *Matrix* scene, when Neo dodges bullets as they fly slowly by. Time truly slows in life-threatening situations.

Those who study use-of-force scenarios describe auditory exclusion as a phenomenon where, under life-threatening stress, the body limits what is heard.

I looked up and did not see Danny. He's short, but not that short ... he was down. My adrenaline shot up, and survival mode kicked in.

I never gave the female another thought. If she had pulled the handgun I later learned she had in her purse and shot me, I would not have seen it coming. Instead, she just laid down in the backseat to avoid the exchange of fire she must have assumed was about to take place.

I backed away from the car at a 45-degree angle while drawing my gun. I am not sure if I got it out of my holster by the time the suspect came up from the driver's side of the car. He leveled his handgun at me and began shooting. I didn't know if it was a revolver or a semi-auto, but I knew I had no cover in the middle of the parking lot.

The suspect shot at me six to eight times. I saw the flash of the gun from the end of the barrel, but didn't actually hear a single shot. If my perceptions were just based off of sound, the entire world went quiet, except for the screaming in my head.

I felt several shots fly by my head, narrowly missing. At least one whizzed by my ear ...

I'm 6'2" and 240 pounds ... keep moving!

Time slowed to a crawl.

It seemed the suspect was hunkered down just outside the driver's side door, so I returned fire, aiming through the back window at an angle that would travel through to that area. I watched the glass shatter with the impact of each bullet in slow motion, a tight grouping in the left rear window.

The silence continued.

I grabbed my shoulder mic and shouted, "Shots fired! Shots fired! Motel 6, Arden Way!"

Although it seemed I was planted firmly in one spot as I returned fire, I began to slice the pie[8] and shuffle-step to my left to reacquire the suspect, hoping he was down and that Danny was okay. (Bracamontes later said it seemed like I was doing cartwheels around the bullets … that I moved so much, he couldn't hit me. It is crazy what the body and mind do during high-stress situations. Later, in my statement to detectives, it bothered me that I could not remember more detail around the sounds and my movement. I am okay with it now, as I've heard enough stories to know it was my body's way of keeping me alive.)

Before I could get a view of either the man or the woman, I recognized the barrel and front site of an assault rifle coming up from the car. The barrel had a flash suppressor on it, and the front site was an A-frame post site.

Shit! This guy has an assault rifle … I only have my Glock 17 and no cover here …

I turned, sprinted to the east, and took cover behind the rear tire of a car approximately five cars down the row. I knew rounds could fly through a car trunk, but a solid metal wheel might offer me some protection. Danny's rifle was in the trunk of the car, but based on how we parked and the position of the suspect, there was no way to make it there.

I don't know if the suspect fired the rifle at me or not, but if he did, he missed.

I heard the dispatcher on my radio, "Motel 6, Arden Way. Which unit is there?" I didn't answer.

Dispatch again, "I believe I heard shots fired at the Motel 6, Arden Way."

---

[8] Slicing the pie is a basic tactical move when approaching an area of concern in a potentially dangerous situation. The objective is to move diagonally through to the other side, which in my case was to get a better look at the other side of the car, giving the shooter as little a target as possible.

This is when I heard a single shot come from the car, and I knew in that moment the shooter had just executed Danny. I flashed back to my training … dash and body cam video of shootings that showed suspects returning to the officer, standing over him, and shooting point blank to make sure he or she is dead.[9]

I had no idea where the suspect was, but I was not going to let him come around on me. Staying low, I worked my way to the gap between the south building and the building to the east. My plan was to run to the gap, reacquire the suspect, and re-engage him. As I began to pass between the gap, I kept my eyes focused on the direction of the suspect vehicle and saw it back up.

I immediately started in that direction, intent on firing more rounds once I could identify a target other than the car. I couldn't say for sure if there were others in it.

Before I could get any shots off, the car jumped up and rolled, like it had just run over something. I yelled, knowing that animal had run over Danny. I can't even begin to describe the horror in witnessing this. Based on his injuries, Danny was most likely already dead at that point. But it doesn't change the pure evil it takes to do something like that. And it doesn't relieve the horrible, continuous replaying of the video of it in my head to this day.

My plan of pumping more rounds at the car was thrown out the window. By the time I regained my train of thought, the blue Mercury rounded the corner and was gone.

Sacramento County had lost several deputies in the line of duty since I had come on. On October 27, 2006, Deputy Jeff Mitchell had been shot and killed on a farm road with no witnesses. That was before cameras had been installed in patrol cars. To this day, his killer is still at large.

As soon as that car rounded the corner, I worried we were never going to catch Danny's killer, either. I thought Danny's murder would then go unsolved, too.

I finally responded[10] , "Officer down …"

"Copy. Officer down. Units start 2030 Arden Way."

"Officer down. Blue car …" Hyperventilating … "Male Hispanic

---

[9] This was my perception only. There is no evidence to show Bracamontes did this.

[10] Because time slowed, it seemed like it took forever to answer. In reality, the time between my first and second radio communications was about 30 seconds.

passenger ..."

As I rounded the last car, I got my first look at Danny. He was lying on his back, his gun still in his holster and his eyes wide open. I ran up to him and began checking for a pulse and breathing. I couldn't find any sign of life.

As I quickly looked him over for injuries, I found a bullet wound to the front of his head. It wasn't bleeding as much as I thought it should, although blood was starting to pool around his body and head area underneath him.

"Oh my god," I cried into the mic.

I heard dispatch, "Officer down. Motel 6. Arden Way. Unit, identify."

"Pop 14! Officer down! Officer down ..."

His eyes—the window to the soul—were open and fixed. I had seen the same look on other victims before. I knew he was gone ... his soul was no longer there. I wanted to close them, but I was so afraid of tampering with the crime scene, I didn't.

"Pop 14, 10-4," dispatch replied. "Any available units just go. We'll get you there. Pop 14, if you have a description of the vehicle, go one more time."

I could barely breathe. "It's a blue ... four-door ... looks like a Mercury ... um ... um ... a Hispanic, male driver ... um, black, black, white, black shirt, white female, large, blond hair ... in the back ... passenger seat."

"10-4, and give me direction of travel ..."

Danny was gone.

"Code 3 Fire! Code 3 Fire," was all I could say. The tears were coming now.

"Yep, Code 3 Fire is en route. Pop 14, do you have a direction of travel on the car?"

I couldn't answer. These and more were the images I could not get out of my head for months to follow, even when awake.

I dropped to my knees beside Danny. Looking up, I saw people standing on the balcony just above us, staring. A woman was screaming with her hand over her mouth.

"Get back in your rooms," I yelled. "And don't go anywhere!"

Evidently, one of those people caught that and more on a cell phone camera.

I don't remember hearing the sirens from the incoming units, or seeing anyone pull into the parking lot where I was. I do remember someone pulling me away from Danny, which I learned later was Deputy Bob French. He resumed taking care of Danny after I stood and began to pace, covering my face. Sergeant Dean Bowen pulled me to his car, and he drove around the building. I found out later that I told them there were bullet holes in the back of the Mercury, and that the guy had an assault rifle. I don't recall saying that.

Sergeant Bowen pulled in front of the Applebee's that shared the parking lot with Motel 6.

"No, no, no! I can't stay here! Get me away!"

Sergeant Bowen complied.

On the way to our Centralized Investigation Division, I called Liz. She didn't answer her phone, but I left a tearful message, "I'm okay." That's all I could get out, then hung up. I then sent her a text, "I'm okay."

At least she would know I was alive if she heard it from someone else, social media, or the news.

****

Friday, October 24, 2014, 10:30 a.m.

Deputy French kneeled over Danny as McCabe and Pratt approached. He checked Danny's pulse, and there was nothing. Deputy Pratt sat down and grabbed Danny's hand while French and McCabe removed his vest and gun belt and started compressions.

Once fire arrived and was admitted to the scene, Pratt jumped in the ambulance to accompany Danny while chest compressions continued.

Deputies on scene where Danny was murdered.

Photograph taken by Randall Benton, Sacramento Bee.

4

DEVASTATION

"We're not here to make excuses or justifications for Luis' actions, we can't do that ...Even his family and his friends found what he did unfathomable."
—Norm Dawson, Bracamontes's Public Defender

Sacramento
Friday, October 24, 2014, 10:28 a.m.

As I attended to Danny, Bracamontes tore out of the Motel 6 parking lot via Arden Way. I didn't know it then, but one of my bullets had hit his left hand.

He accelerated, then braked for traffic at Arden and Howe. Temporarily blocked, he pulled the car around the traffic aggressively, and blew the red light heading up Howe. Monroy handed him a towel from the back seat. Bracamontes wrapped his hand in it, then blew the second red light at Howe and Hurley.

****

Granite Bay

In stark contrast, during this same period of time, Liz sat on the floor in her pajama pants and T-shirt, playing with Brandon, who was three, and Tyler, 15 months. Connor, our six-year-old, was at school.

From the corner of her eye, she saw movement and realized her phone was blinking. She picked it up and noticed it was still on Do Not Disturb status. She quickly scrolled through and saw I had tried to call three times.

"Oh, no," she thought. "I missed his call again! He already teases me that I screen his calls ..."

She then read, "I'm okay."

Her heart sank. She knew what that meant—I might be okay, but the situation is not.

Rather than listen to my voicemail, she called back. The seconds ticked by … something was wrong.

I answered the phone in a breathless panic. "Liz … I-I'm …" I hyperventilated between the words. "Okay …

"I-I'm … okay …"

"What happened, Scott? Where's Danny?"

My words were intelligible. Sergeant Bowen took the phone from me to speak on my behalf.

"Liz, Scott is okay physically. But mentally, he is not," he said. "Scott needs you here. We're coming to get you."

"What happened?!" she blurted.

"We'll give you all the information once you get here," he replied. "Just be ready to go."

Liz hung up the phone and immediately dialed her mother. My mother-in-law, Catherine, was usually at work by then, but Liz's sister had been released from the hospital the night before and was recuperating at Catherine's home, so she was there.

"Mom, I need you to come here immediately. Scott's okay, but something happened!"

"What happened?"

"I don't know, but it's something bad. They're coming to get me. Please come now!"

****

Spanos Court, Sacramento
Friday, October 24, 2014, 10:35 a.m.

Adam Holst[11] was early for his doctor's appointment, so he sat in his car listening to music as he waited. A thick, tough man of 280 pounds, he was wearing his favorite Dallas Cowboys cap.

Suddenly, a blue sedan came to an abrupt stop right behind his car.

Thinking it was police, Holst turned the ignition off and started to exit his car. Bracamontes appeared, pointing a gun at his head.

---

[11] This is a pseudonym.

"Give me your car," Bracamontes demanded.

"Fuck off, man, I don't even know you," Adam retorted, turning to restart the car.

Bracamontes smiled, leveled his pistol at Holst's face, and pulled the trigger.

Yelling out, Holst attempted to shield his head with his arms, but not before a round traveled through his ear and into his mouth just above his chin.

Bracamontes pulled the trigger four more times.

Bullets ripped through Adam's flesh—two in the arms, one in the elbow, and the other in his back. He slumped over, trying not to close his eyes.

Monroy, who was standing at the shot-up Mercury with her hands on her hips, uttered half-heartedly, "Stop."

At that moment, a voice called out from the eye doctor's office… "We're calling 911!" The shooting had been witnessed through the window by employees.

Bracamontes turned and ran back to the Mercury, and Monroy jumped in.

****

Sacramento
Friday, October 24, 2014, 10:37 a.m.

Paramedics continued performing CPR on Danny as they rushed to UC Davis Medical Center. Pratt remained by his side, speaking words of comfort. Despite having no pulse and being unresponsive, the paramedics continued their work all the way to the hospital.

Other deputies were beginning to hear that it was Danny who was down. Although they bravely and professionally worked the scene and pursued the suspect, grief, anger, and even desperation began to creep in.

At one point, someone accidentally leaned in on his mic, and a deep and guttural weeping was heard over the radio. Dispatch said nothing. Everybody felt it, including me.

****

Auburn
Friday, October 24, 2014, 10:40 a.m.

Sergeant Randy Winn, the team leader for the Sacramento Sheriff's Special Enforcement Detail (SED), has always responded to calls with expertise and professionalism. I've considered him the "G.I. Joe" of our department.

He answered his phone and listened to the voice on the other end provide a quick synopsis of what was known.

Within minutes, he initiated a call out, and deputies were responding to the Command Post (CP) located at the Century Theaters at Ethan and Arden Way.

As word spread, hundreds of deputies all over the Sacramento region suited up and headed into work ... most of whom were not scheduled to do so. Good thing, because it turned out they were needed—along with hundreds of other law enforcement officers, as crime scenes started to stack up.

****

Spanos Court, Sacramento
Friday, October 24, 2014, 10:43 a.m.

Bracamontes was bloodied, in a frenzy, and searching for a different car.

The two were making a U-turn to head out of the court when Cheryl Robbins[12] returned from the gym driving her white Ford Mustang with the window down. Bracamontes came to a stop near her and blurted out, "Excuse me!"

Cheryl stopped her car and acknowledged him. "Yes?"

Suddenly, Bracamontes leaped out of the car toward her window with gun drawn. He was bleeding, holding his left arm close to his chest. "Get out of the car," he ordered.

---

[12] This is a pseudonym.

Cheryl immediately exited her vehicle, walking away quickly toward her apartment. She looked back, seeing Bracamontes enter her vehicle. She then noticed Monroy, whom she hadn't seen before. Monroy transferred the rifle and ammunition to Cheryl's Mustang. She jumped in, and they screeched out of the court.

Cheryl hurriedly walked to the manager's office and called the police. She didn't have any idea about the exchange Bracamontes had with Danny and I earlier, nor what happened to Adam Holst. Recounting what had happened, she mentioned that the pair had left behind a blue car. Dispatch asked her to get the license plate, which she did. Cheryl then returned to the manager's office to wait for police.

That's when she noticed drops of blood on her leg. The manager handed her a tissue. She couldn't wipe them off fast enough.

****

Sacramento Sheriff CID, Sacramento
Friday, October 24, 2014, 10:48 a.m.

Bowen and I arrived at our Centralized Investigation Division (CID), and I was escorted into his office.

"Are you okay?" he asked.

Not really.

"Are you injured?"

At first, it seemed like a strange question. I didn't know. I was shot at several times at very close range, but when the adrenaline flows, you don't always feel it.

I removed my tactical vest and gun belt, and we checked my body for bullet holes. I patted myself down, then held out my hands—no blood. Thank God. I used to joke that I wanted to leave the world with the same holes I was born with. I don't joke about that anymore.

Bowen took my phone, which he later gave to Liz. I wouldn't see it for the next month, as she screened calls and social media posts I didn't need to see.

I heard crying and saw a few people walk by, but no one came into the office.

"Do you need anything?"

"I need to break something," I admitted.

"Go ahead and break anything in this office you need to, Scott."

I didn't break anything there, but God, it would've felt really good.

"How about a county chaplain?" Dean asked.

I didn't have much contact with our law enforcement chaplaincy at the time, so I requested someone from Bayside Church, where Liz and I attended. I told them to ask for our senior pastors, Ray Johnston or Curt Harlow. I was sure they'd be busy, but would send someone to represent.

****

Granite Bay
Friday, October 24, 2014, 10:50 a.m.

Liz turned on the TV as Catherine and her sister burst through the door. The headlines read, "Officer Shot at Motel 6."

Liz was shaking. It's Danny, she thought. Danny was shot.

Catherine kicked into business-mode. "We've got the boys. You need to focus on getting ready. Go put a bra on," she ordered.

Sister joined in. "Wear tennis shoes, Liz. You're gonna be on your feet all day. Don't forget your charger, because you'll be on the phone. And it's cold in the hospital, so put on more clothes!"

Liz went to her bedroom. She checked her Facebook account quickly, and saw that people were already posting on her wall. How did they know so fast?!

The phone buzzed. It was another deputy's wife.

****

Arden Park, Sacramento
Friday, October 24, 2014, 10:52 a.m.

Bracamontes and Monroy decided they should change cars again, as there had been several witnesses to their carjacking of the Mustang.

They wandered into a neighborhood, where they came up on a maintenance crew working at one of the houses. They had a truck, so Monroy backed their car up to the house.

Bracamontes grabbed the gun and walked up the driveway to the workers. Monroy stayed in the car.

One of the men, Jose, noticed Bracamontes was injured and called out, "Quien te hizo esto?" (Who did this to you?)

Bracamontes didn't answer. Instead, he showed the men his gun and barked, "I need the keys! I need a favor. I need the keys—now!"

Jose patted his pockets and replied, "No tengo las llaves." (I don't have the keys.)

Bracamontes backed away. "Well ... okay ... no llames a la policia!" (Don't call the police!)

Bracamontes got back into the Mustang. Monroy drove a couple blocks until they found a group of landscapers. There was a maroon 2002 Ford F-150 with a trailer hooked up to it parked on Coronado Boulevard.

Bracamontes approached the owner who was blowing leaves. "Para quien estas trabajanado?" (Who are you working for?)

"Trabajo para mi mismo," (I work for myself) he replied.

"Necesito un favor," he began. "Necesito las llaves la camioneta porque viene la policia." (I need the keys to the truck because the cops are coming.)

The owner didn't refuse the truck, but he did ask Bracamontes to leave the trailer, because it contained his tools.

Bracamontes pointed the gun at him, ordering him to detach the trailer. "Andele!" (Hurry up!)

The owner tried to lift the trailer off of his truck, but struggled with the weight.

"Baby! Park the car across the street!" Bracamontes called out to Monroy. She complied.

Bracamontes then helped the landscaper take the trailer off of the truck, dropping his phone in the process. Monroy appeared and picked it up before transferring some belongings from the Mustang to the truck, including the rifle and extra magazines.

Bracamontes slid into the driver's seat, and Monroy climbed into the back seat and hunkered down to hide.

"Gracias," Bracamontes called out to the owner. "No llames a la policia de inmediato!" (Don't call the police right away.)

Bracamontes and Monroy drove away, and once they were out of sight, the landscape business owner called 911.

****

Granite Bay
Friday, October 24, 2014, 10:53 a.m.

As Liz finished getting ready, she answered her phone.

"Hey, where you at?" asked the deputy's wife.

"I'm at home," Liz replied.

"Have you heard from Scott?"

"Yes. I'm packing a bag now to go and be with him."

"How much do you know?"

"Not much. He couldn't talk. Why?" Liz responded, grabbing a sweatshirt.

"Do you want to know what I know?"

"Yeah, tell me."

She told Liz that Danny had been shot and deputies were doing CPR at the scene and in the ambulance. He was headed to the hospital.

After they hung up, Liz grabbed her bag and related the news to her mom and sister.

Liz thought, *He's going to be okay. If he's on his way to the hospital, he's gonna be fine.*

About that time, a patrol unit showed up outside. Liz didn't recognize the driver but climbed in anyway.

He introduced himself as Sergeant Dean Bowen. He had been with me since he picked me up at the scene. As they drove, they talked a bit, but Bowen did not give any details about the shooting. Liz had no idea that Danny was already dead.

Because Liz knew Susan, Danny's wife, she asked Bowen if they had contacted her.

"They must've told her by now."

If they have me, they must have Sue as well, Liz thought. So, assuming Susan was also on her way to Danny, she shot a text to her saying, "Hey Sue, I'm on my way to Scott. Thinking of you and Danny. Love you."

The phone rang right away.

"Hey! What's going on?" asked Susan.

Liz' heart fell. "Sue, where are you?"

"I'm in San Diego at a work conference. What are you talking about?"

"Sue ... Danny's been shot."

Liz braced herself as Susan let out a hollow, piercing scream ... the kind you hear in movies.

Susan's coworker took the phone and asked, "What the hell is going on?"

"Danny's been shot," Liz explained. "And in my heart, I feel like it's going to get worse before it gets better. You need to keep her phone and answer it. They're going to need to find her. Get her home."

"Okay, we got it here. We'll get her home."

****

Sacramento
Friday, October 24, 2014, 10:57 a.m.

Sergeant Winn drove fast to the Command Post via Highway 50. At Watt Avenue, the radio broadcast a report of a carjacking at Coronado Boulevard. The new vehicle they were looking for was a red Ford-150.

Minutes later, CHP Air-21 (a fixed wing aircraft) advised they spotted a red extra cab pickup at Watt and Fair Oaks Boulevard. Sergeant Winn turned onto Fair Oaks, pulled into a gas station, and moved in behind the suspected vehicle. It was not a Ford-150, and the driver's appearance was inconsistent with the description of the suspect. He backed off.

Information was coming in fast and furious. Sergeant Winn listened intently while he searched the area for the truck for about a half hour.

****

CID, Sacramento
Friday, October 24, 2014, 11:15 a.m.

When Liz walked into CID, I crumbled. I burst into tears, and she held me for a long time.

"He's gone," I said over and over.

Liz didn't believe me. She had heard they were administering CPR on the way to the hospital, and still had hope it would work. She didn't have the image I had of Danny in my head.

She didn't know the full truth.

****

UC Davis Medical Center, Sacramento
Friday, October 24, 2014, 11:01 a.m.

Deputy Pratt followed Danny into the emergency room, compressions continuing. She handed him off to the hospital's medical staff, hoping against hope that they could revive him.

Several minutes went by, and she came to the same knowledge as everyone else … that Danny was gone. They pronounced him deceased.

Pratt slowly dialed Sergeant Chris Guerrero on the emergency room phone but couldn't reach him. She exited the emergency room and used her cell phone—that was successful. Deputy Lance Parker, at the hospital for another case, notified the communications center and then took custody of Danny's body until the coroner arrived.

****

Chevron Gas Station, Rocklin
Friday, October 24, 2014, 11:15 a.m.

On his day off, Deputy Darrell Amos volunteered at his son's school and then stopped to buy Rockstars at his regular stop and grab. As he approached the store, his brother, Deputy Brian Amos, called.

"Hey." Darrell instantly knew something was wrong by the sound of Brian's voice.

"What's up?"

"It's not good. Dude, Danny's been shot," he replied.

"What?! What are you talking about?"

"Darrell, they don't think he's gonna make it."

Suddenly, everything went into slow motion as the world spun and confusion set in.

"They're transporting him to UC Davis," Brian said. "Go to Mom's house, and I'll meet you there. We'll figure it out from there."

Darrell hung up and dialed his wife, Becky. As he relayed the news of his former partner's condition, he started hyperventilating.

Shocked by the news, Becky went into task mode. "Go home. I'll meet you there, and I'll drive, Darrell."

****

Roseville
Friday, October 24, 2014, 11:20 a.m.

The call to Bayside Church went to the Care Team, with sketchy information about a shooting and death of a deputy whose partner was a Baysider. Because it was a powerful assignment, long-time Pastor Mark Godshall was deployed.

As Mark drove to the station, he prayed. It was his experience that God orchestrates the details of our lives, so Mark knew that even though he didn't understand what it entails to be an officer, God would lead and guide his words and actions. He was honored to bring God's grace and peace to such a traumatic situation.

When Mark arrived, he hugged Liz and I, even though we'd never met him before. That's what happens when you're a part of God's church—you're instantly family. The three of us were escorted to a small conference room for privacy.

I told my story for the first time while Mark and Liz listened silently. When I finished, Mark opened his Bible. He read Scriptures that he said God brought to his mind.

"Even though I walk through the valley of the shadow of death, I will fear no evil, for You are with me; Your rod and Your staff, they comfort me. You prepare a table before me in the presence of my enemies …

"That is Psalm 23:4-5, Scott. The first thing you need to know is that there is power in God's presence … you don't need to be afraid."

He then turned to Psalm 91, and read the following: "He who dwells in the shelter of the Most High will abide in the shadow of the Almighty … For it is He who delivers you from the snare of the trapper and from the deadly pestilence … under His wings, you may seek refuge; His faithfulness is a shield and a bulwark …"

I started to calm down.

"You will not be afraid of the terror by night or of the arrow that flies by day; of the pestilence that stalks in darkness, or of the destruction that lays waste at noon … You will only look on with your eyes and see the recompense of the wicked. For you have made the Lord, my refuge, even the Most High, your dwelling place. No evil will befall you … For He will give His angels charge concerning you, to guard you in all your ways. They will bear you up in their hands, that you do not strike your foot against a stone."

Liz commented, "Oh my gosh, Scott. That's what happened."

I admitted that I felt it was my fault that Danny was dead. I'd looked death in the face—it could've been me lying there. I was thankful that it wasn't, but devastated that it was Danny. I should've done something …

Mark responded, "We never know why things happen the way they do. Right now, you have to remember your faith in God. He is the all-powerful One. Satan is powerful, too, but not equal. What happened this morning was of Satan, not of God.

"But where do you fit in here? There is a tug of war for men between two heavenly superpowers. It appears as though the enemy won today. But the reality is, Satan is a defeated foe. The battle is already over—Jesus died and then rose again to secure our freedom from sin and death. He was not a helpless victim—He is seated in heavenly places at the right hand of God the Father.

"This is the truth, Scott. This is the reality. Now you should know who you are in Christ, because Satan will try to tell you all kinds of lies. But we use Truth to counteract a lie."

"I'm not sure I can do that right now," I acknowledged.

"*I can't* is an all-out lie, Scott," Mark directed. "Philippians 4:13 says, 'I can do all things through Christ who strengthens me.'"

We talked more, and Mark read more Scripture. By the time he left, both Liz and I were comforted. Peaceful, even though the day was chaotic, painful, messy.

I cannot think of a time in my life when I needed God's presence more than that day. I know now that He surrounded me with comfort and protection, but at the time, I felt very much alone. Still, Mark read me several poignant verses that did a good job of grounding my thoughts. They reminded me that God is with me in the good times, but even more so in the bad.

In times like these, people either turn toward or away from God. Some get mad, blaming Him for the horrible things that happen. For reasons I can't explain, this horrible day eventually drew me closer to God than ever. I grew up believing in God and in Jesus Christ, and went to church, but really, my faith hadn't been a top priority.

I regret that I never talked to Danny about God and have no idea where he stood. I invited him to church a few times, and he said he was interested, but never came. I always felt like I would have more time to talk with him about it. I was wrong. It bothers me that I wasn't more persistent. I was willing to cover his back and run headlong into danger with him, but I was afraid to talk with him about God.

I can guarantee that won't happen again.

Placer County deputies share a hug after Detective Davis was shot and killed.

Photograph was taken by media who were present that day—we were not able to track down the photographer.

5

MICHAEL DAVIS, JR.

"They engaged evil for your peace. For your tranquility. That's who Michael Davis was. That's who Danny Oliver was. That is who all these people are ... peace officers."

—Placer County Sheriff Ed Bonner at Michael's Funeral

Placer County
Friday, October 24, 2014, 11:39 a.m.

As soon as the carjacking of the red Ford-150 pickup was reported, the Sacramento Sheriff's office requested the California Highway Patrol activate the Blue Alert. This system notifies all law enforcement agencies of a suspect involved in the serious injury or death of a peace officer. A vehicle description and license plate number were disseminated, and the information was posted on changeable message signs along the I-80 freeway.

Bracamontes and Monroy raced eastbound along the I-80 corridor, eager to watch Sacramento disappear in the rearview mirror. As they neared the small town of Newcastle, Monroy peered out from behind the front seat. She caught sight of a message sign on the freeway and called out, "They've got this truck on that sign!"

Bracamontes took the next off-ramp, not knowing where the hell they were. They needed to get the plates off and disappear.

****

Sacramento
Friday, October 24, 2014, 11:45 a.m.

After arriving at Motel 6, Sergeant Winn and the SED team cleared the suspects' room. Not much was found, as they had already checked out when Danny and I encountered them. Dispatch received yet another sighting of a red pickup nearby, so they saturated the area looking for the suspects. It was determined the sighting was not who they were looking for.

Just then, it was reported that two subjects matching the description of the suspects were observed on Van Alstine Avenue, east of Fair Oaks Boulevard in Sacramento. The SED team responded, setting up a containment perimeter in the area.

****

Placer County Sheriff's Office, Auburn
Friday, October 24, 2014

Within the Placer County Sheriff's Office were two homicide detectives named Mike. Both Michael Davis and Mike "Moose" Simmons were seasoned cops—there wasn't much they hadn't seen. Michael was pushing two decades of police work. Moose had three decades of experience with time at nearby Rocklin Police Department. The two worked well together and considered each other partners. Every Friday, if both were on call, it was a sure thing the night would be busy—that's just how it went, more often than not.

Detective Michael Davis had been unusually quiet that morning.

Moose didn't clue into the fact that it was October 24th, the anniversary of the line-of-duty death of Michael's father. It had been 26 years, after all, since it happened in southern California.

That Friday was supposed to be a "catch-up" day, and they both had a ton of tasks to complete. The television was on while they worked, so they could monitor the developing situation in Sacramento complete with carjackings and shootings. Not only that, but the whole mess seemed to be moving east, toward Placer County.

Michael, who was on an Atkins-type diet, made himself a bacon sandwich, filling the investigations section with the aroma. Moose was pissed. The whole place stunk, and it made him hungry. Knowing it was Friday, Moose knew he and "Mikey" would be part of whatever was about to go down, so he left to get something to eat while there was still time.

Moose was in his car when, just moments later, the radio picked up something about the suspect they'd seen on tv being in the Rancheria area—a residential neighborhood in the small city of Auburn. He cursed, having missed his window to eat—the suspects were already there.

****

Roseville
Friday October 24, 2014, 11:46 a.m.

Darrell, Becky, and Brian Amos were driving to UC Davis Medical Center when Mike Hernandez[13] from SSO Employee Relations called. He alluded to the fact that Danny had passed, and then mentioned that Darrell was designated to notify Susan. Darrell panicked. "Pull over!" he ordered. They did so, and Darrell's chest went tight.

"I'm supposed to tell Susan about Danny," he admitted. "I want to fulfill that obligation, but she's out of town, and I don't know how to reach her."

"Look at me, Darrell. Call that guy back and tell him you'll do it," Becky asserted. "We'll figure it out."

Darrell called Hernandez and told him to keep him in the loop, and that they were headed to UC Davis.

"I'll do it," he said.

****

Mesa Vista Way, Auburn
Friday, October 24, 2014, 11:59 a.m.

Retired California Highway Patrol officer Jerry Keller[14] lived in Auburn, not far from the I-80 freeway. He was tinkering in his garage, enjoying a cup of coffee as he worked. As was his practice, he listened to KFBK, Sacramento's premier news talk radio station where Rush Limbaugh and Tom Sullivan got their early start. He had heard a little bit about

[13] This is a pseudonym.
[14] This is a pseudonym.

the drama that had developed in Sacramento throughout the morning. Glancing toward the street, a maroon mass caught his eye.

Jerry turned his attention to it as his former law enforcement "spidey senses" went on alert. A man and a woman who matched the description of the suspects involved in shootings earlier that day were taking the license plates off a red Ford F-150.

He grabbed the phone and called 911.

****

PCSO SWAT Member Jason Davis' Home, Rocklin
Friday, October 24, 2014, Noon

Placer County Sheriff's SWAT team member Jason Davis was sleeping soundly after working the night shift at the jail. His wife, Traci, entered the bedroom and woke him up.

"There's an active shooter reported on tv, Jason. Sounds like a Sacramento deputy was shot. You're probably gonna be called out."

Groggy, Jason checked his phone. Nothing yet.

Nonetheless, he pulled himself out of bed and started getting his gear together.

****

Maidu and Riverview, Auburn
Friday, October 24, 2014, 12:15 p.m.

Placer County Deputies Chuck Bardo and Joe Roseli were looking for the cop killers in the maroon truck with no plates. The suspects had been spotted in the Rancheria area. The two deputies had searched the area three to four times, but had found nothing.

Bardo and Roseli met up on Maidu just past the fire station. Roseli suggested they investigate a nearby desolate area where people often go horseback riding. At the next intersection, Roseli saw a vehicle that matched the description they had, but at that moment, dispatch provided updated information. The vehicle was not the one they were looking for.

Roseli arrived at the intersection of Maidu and Riverview and waited for Bardo to join him. He took his rifle out of the rack and laid it across his lap—if anything should happen, he wanted to be ready. As Bardo pulled up, dispatch reported that the suspects had been spotted in the Riverview/Skyridge area.

"The intersection is right here," Roseli said to Bardo. "You know, this isn't a good spot. He's got the high ground if he comes this way."

At that exact moment, Bracamontes pulled up to the stop sign about 10 yards away. Roseli looked straight at the driver. There was no mistake—it was him.

The truck reversed, backed up at a high rate of speed, then stopped right next to a BMW parked on Riverview, the driver of which was exiting. Bracamontes reached across the seat for his pistol, exited his vehicle, and instantly began shooting in the deputies' direction. The BMW owner took off running, slipping inside his house.

Bardo flipped on the overhead patrol lights and rounded the corner onto Riverview. As Bardo was barraged with bullets, he opened the door and slid out, running behind his car and around toward the maroon truck. Roseli pulled in behind Bardo's car and stepped out behind his driver's door.

Bracamontes, Bardo, and Roseli exchanged gunfire, and then, Bracamontes reached into the truck and grabbed the rifle.[15]

Bardo ran back toward the back of his vehicle, then directly in front of Roseli's car. Roseli's thoughts went to fear for Bardo—*He's gonna fucking get killed*! He stopped firing, so as not to shoot him on accident.

"Go left, Bardo, go left!" yelled Roseli, but Bardo didn't hear him.

Bardo ran right past Roseli to the back of Roseli's car, falling briefly and tearing his uniform pants.

At that point, Bracamontes reached back into the truck as Roseli laid fire. When Bracamontes came back out, he fired at Roseli. Realizing that Bardo was no longer in the line of fire, a calm settled over Roseli. Then, he felt close rounds near his head. The only sounds Roseli heard were of Bardo's boots on the ground, despite the crack of his own rifle.

By the time Bardo reached cover, his gun was empty. He did a mag

[15] Bracamontes's pistol stovepiped, or jammed, we learned later.

exchange, pocketing the empty one.

Roseli ran to the rear and quickly checked Bardo over for injury. Seeing no blood, he looked out to find Bracamontes, who was climbing into Bardo's patrol car that had rolled down Riverview and hit the BMW.

Bracamontes hit the gas, quickly glancing Roseli's way. Roseli stepped out and cranked out four rounds, aiming for the headrest in the patrol unit. The rounds hit the trunk instead.

Bracamontes drove down Riverview, not knowing he was headed straight for a dead end.

Bardo broadcast on the radio, "Multiple shots fired! Suspect is in patrol unit, marked unit, has access to my shotgun and bandolero.[16] Unit 368!"

The problem was that others were talking into the radio at the same time, which garbled the radio traffic. Other deputies in the area heard that shots were fired, but no one caught the fact that the patrol car was stolen by the suspect.

Bardo and Roseli started toward the car to pursue. About that time, another PCSO patrol unit came barreling their way. "He's coming back!" Roseli yelled. They moved to the right side of the road and dipped down into a ravine. They raised their guns to ready for a second fight when Bardo called out, "Placer County green behind the wheel!"

****

UC Davis Medical Center
Friday, October 24, 2014, 12:20 p.m.

The Amos's arrived at UC Davis Medical Center and parked around back. A family member who worked for the UC Davis Police Department met them at the door. "Can you show me where everyone's at?" Darrell asked.

The officer led them through the entrance, to the right, and into a private room. The three stopped in their tracks. There was Danny, lying on a gurney, deceased. Two homicide detectives looked up.

---

[16] A sash that holds bullets

"I don't think we're supposed to be in here," Darrell stammered. "I'm sorry." The four did an about-face and left the room.

The Amos's found Lieutenant Santos Ramos and shared with him his unfulfilled responsibility. "We'll get this done, Darrell," Ramos offered.

Meanwhile, Becky was on the phone, relaying and receiving information. Eventually, Darrell was told that everyone had been notified.

****

Van Alstine Avenue, Sacramento
Friday, October 24, 2014, 12:20 p.m.

As the SED team prepared to search the containment perimeter, the Sac Sheriff helicopter advised that Placer County deputies had just exchanged gunfire with suspects that matched the description of those they were looking for. The shooting was in Auburn, miles from where the SED team was at that moment. The helicopter diverted to the Auburn call.

Sergeant Winn notified his lieutenant, who authorized the SED team members to respond to the Auburn Command Post. The Placer County command post had been established at Maidu Market, less than a mile from where Bardo and Roseli were engaged with Bracamontes.

They also called in the K-9s.

****

Rancheria Area of Auburn
Friday, October 24, 2014, 12:18 p.m.

Moose diverted from his home and headed for Rancheria via I-80. As he drove, a convoy of Placer County vehicles passed him in the fast lane. He accelerated and pulled in behind them.

Michael Davis called him on his cell, "Where are you at, Moose?"

"I'm headed for Auburn-Folsom and Indian Hill. That's where everyone is meeting up, putting on their gear."

"Don't do anything until I get there!" Michael hung up.

At the meeting point, several officers gathered. Quickly, Moose put on the gear he carried in the back of his car for just such an occasion. He then spotted PCSO Deputy Ryan Zender and told him to jump in with him. Zender's wife just had a baby, so Moose wanted to get him off target.

There were several sightings, so Moose was doing area searches when Michael pulled up behind him on Auburn Ravine and flashed his lights. They pulled over, Moose bringing Michael up to speed. They decided to make a U-turn and head north, with Michael in the lead since he knew the area.

Suddenly, the radio traffic went nuts—a shootout at Maidu and Riverview. Moose and Zender had trouble figuring out who was where, because people were speaking over each other on the radio.

Moose was irritated. He thought he heard the words, "in pursuit."

Michael went CODE 3 with Moose on his bumper. Deputies Jeff Davis (no relation to Michael) and Jack Hickey joined in and followed just behind. They all passed the Maidu command post, turned right on Sacramento Street, and then took another right at Skyridge, because that would put them above the shootout.

Out of nowhere, a patrol car went whizzing by, right to left, ahead of them on Riverview heading towards the dead-end cul-de-sac. Michael, Moose, and Jeff turned left after it, thinking they were joining the pursuit.

As Moose came down the cul-de-sac, he saw the patrol car door open, and assumed the pursuit had gone to a foot bail.

Bullets began raining down on the car. Michael took off to the left of a large oak tree that stood in the middle of the dead-end street. Moose peeled off to the right of the tree, but grew concerned that he was in the crossfire. He saw the muzzle flash of an AR-15 at the patrol car, but assumed it was a deputy.

Time slowed down and instincts took over.

Duh, duh, duh, duh, duh … duh, duh, duh, duh, duh …

It was a controlled deploy, not sporadic. Moose couldn't see who was shooting, but he had a bead[17] on somebody.

****

---

[17] Was taking aim at.

Riverview Court, Auburn
Friday, October 24, 2014, 12:20 p.m.

Placer County Deputy Jeff Davis followed Michael and Moose into the cul-de-sac, swung left of Michael's car, and stopped. He rapidly exited his patrol car, gun drawn, and peered over at Michael. Michael's head was swiveling as he too searched for the suspect. He then saw Michael jerk slightly, and at that, Jeff turned and crouched just inside the driver's door. Gunfire seemed to be coming from everywhere. As he watched and listened, he realized the shots were coming from the direction of the patrol car.

****

Riverview Court, Auburn
Friday, October 24, 2014, 12:21 p.m.

Zender bailed out, and Moose came around the driver's door and over the engine block for cover. "Crossfire! Crossfire!" he yelled.

Duh, duh, duh, duh, duh … the shots from Bracamontes's rifle echoed through the cul-de-sac.

Moose was confused—where was the shooting coming from? Because none of the officers knew Bracamontes stole the patrol car, their minds did not compute that it was him shooting at them from the unit. Moose had his gun drawn, but he didn't know where the target was.

Then, off to the right, Moose saw hands appear from out of some bushes. He assumed it was the suspect, so he duckwalked[18] right toward the arms, pistol in hand, ready to fire if the suspect did not comply.

But something was off. The arms were white, not Hispanic. They were old arms. Moose realized this was not the suspect.

"He r-ran around the s-side of the house!" the man stammered.

****

[18] Also referred to as the "Groucho," duckwalking is a way of moving forward ducking low and level rather than bobbing up and down, which lends horizontal stability to the sight picture. Moose is keeping his eye and weapon trained on the possible suspect as he stays low and quickly walks forward.

Riverview Court, Auburn
Friday, October 24, 2014, 12:21 p.m.

Crouched low with one hand on the car, Jeff Davis ran around the back of his unit to the front right of his vehicle. He spotted a pair of feet sticking out of a door of the parked patrol car as the suspect rooted between the seats for something.

As the suspect stood with two guns slung around his neck, they locked eyes for a second.

Jeff fired. Pop, pop … nothing. His gun wouldn't fire!

Bracamontes emptied the clip, hitting Jeff in the holster and through his pant leg, before turning and disappearing into the canyon behind the houses.

As Jeff looked down at his gun, he realized his arm was covered in blood. His hand wouldn't move. He went to his knees and called out, "I'm hit! I'm hit!"

****

Riverview Drive, Auburn
Friday, October 24, 2014, 12:21 p.m.

PCSO Deputy Jack Hickey had already responded to the sighting of the suspects taking the plates off the truck. After interviewing the witness and relaying the information, he cleared Mesa Vista and headed to the Maidu/Riverview area. As he approached the intersection of Skyridge and Riverview behind Michael, Moose and Jeff Davis, he saw them turn left, unaware they were following the patrol car. Maidu was the other way, so he made a right turn. Looking up the hill, he saw the maroon truck in the street, and Deputies Bardo and Roseli beyond it. They drew their guns, and he heard gunfire.[19] He got low and gunned the patrol car past the truck to where the deputies stood.

[19] The gunfire Hickey heard was from Bracamontes in the cul-de-sac behind him. Sounds echoed in this area because of the nearby canyon—he assumed the gunfire was coming from Bardo and Roseli. No one but Bardo and Roseli knew Bracamontes was in the patrol car.

He briefly checked himself, thinking perhaps those bullets were meant for him.

"Is he in the truck?" he asked.

"No," Bardo replied. "He took off that way." He then joined Roseli in the patrol car and drove away.

But Hickey saw a hand waving inside the maroon truck.

Oh, shit, he thought. *There's someone in there.*

****

Riverview Court, Auburn
Friday, October 24, 2014, 12:21 p.m.

PCSO Deputy Ken Addison crested the hill and pulled into the long cul-de-sac. He heard the gunshots and saw Michael's Charger below, so he attempted to park as close as he could to offer cover. Addison scanned the small area, unable to discern where the shots were coming from. He saw Michael in his periphery standing near his car. Suddenly, Michael spun around in slow motion, then moved to the back of his car and lay down slowly, watching Addison through his glasses. At that moment, Addison didn't realize that Michael had been shot.

Still looking for the shooter, Addison heard desperation in Jeff's voice as he called out, "I'm hit! I'm hit!" He saw Jeff at the front passenger wheel, so he took off running, arriving beside Jeff.

"I've been shot," Jeff panted.

"Can you walk or run?" Addison asked.

"I think so."

"Well, get your ass to my truck!"

They both took off running to Addison's truck, jumped in, and reversed out of there. Addison drove Jeff to a firehouse a few blocks away and left him in their care.

****

Riverview Court, Auburn
Friday, October 24, 2014, 12:24 p.m.

After firing all his rounds at deputies, Bracamontes jogged through the carport and around the house with his AR-15 and the shotgun he had retrieved from the patrol car.

There were men working in the cul-de-sac who were hiding in the backyard because of the bullets. When Bracamontes appeared fully armed, they froze. He yelled out something unintelligible as he raced by and out a gate that led into the canyon. He dropped the rifle just outside the gate, and then slid down through the brush and into the canyon.

****

Riverview Court, Auburn
Friday, October 24, 2014, 12:22 p.m.

As Moose returned to the car, he noticed Michael on his knees. More deputies were entering the cul-de-sac, but Moose didn't notice.

"Michael! You're gonna catch a skip! What are you doing?!" he called out.

Then he grabbed the radio and screamed, "He's around the back of the house!"

But nobody heard him.

Moose looked over at Michael, who had moved onto his belly. His toes were down.

Suddenly, PCSO Detective Richard Gray appeared by the trunk of Michael's car. "Moose! Michael's been hit!"

Moose ran across the crossfire zone to join Detective Gray. Michael was lying on his stomach, arms tucked under his chest. His pistol was still in the holster.

Moose grabbed Michael and rolled him over. There was blood coming from his nose and mouth, and his eyes were at half-mast. They had an ashy look, the sparkle gone.

"No, no, no, no, noooo! We gotta go to work! Get up!" he pled.

Gray snapped Moose out of it. "Get him outta here!"

Moose and Zender grabbed Michael by the legs and chest and shoved him into Michael's Charger. The back seat was full of stuff, so his body folded like rubber. Moose pushed him in as far as he could, then dove into the driver's seat. He stopped to push the seat back, then jammed on the gas. Nothing.

Moose then remembered to put the car in drive. The car moved up the hill, and Moose yelled to several deputies, "Where's the LZ (landing zone)? Where's the ambulance?!"

No one answered. Desperate anger filled Moose. "Why don't they answer me?!" he grumbled.

Then he realized … the window was up. They couldn't hear a word he said.

After Moose rolled down the window, he yelled out, "Where's the LZ? I got Mike in the fucking car!" Bardo and Roseli pointed him toward Maidu. Moose drove a few yards up the road and met Auburn Police Department Sergeant Dale Hutchins, also Michael's first FTO. He stepped up to the car.

"Dale! Mike's been shot!" called Moose.

"Get him out of the car, Simmons."

Sergeant Hutchins helped Moose pull Michael out of the car, laid him on the road, and then started cutting off his gear and clothes with Hutchins' knife. Hutchins didn't see any blood on his body and his vest was intact.

"Where is the wound?" he thought. Finally, he saw a small puncture wound under Michael's left arm, but it was not bleeding. He rolled Michael to his side, and it was then Dale noticed the blood. Not from the wound, but from his mouth.

"I can't find a pulse, Dale," stammered Moose.

"Bullshit! I've got one!" Hutchins argued.

The men tried to clear his airway, and while doing that, lost his pulse.

Moose knew Michael was gone, but he wasn't going to give up. He started chest compressions, and Hutchins blew air into Michael's mouth and lungs. What they could not have known is the bullet had essentially cut him in half internally.

Just then, Hutchins got a call on the radio, directing him to head to a location where the suspect was spotted. "We're doing CPR—I need an ambulance! Right NOW!" was his reply.

Having just guided in the helicopter and watched it land, PCSO Sergeant Bill Walton pulled up, exited his vehicle and directed, "Let's get him up on the car; get him to the helicopter! CHP's H-20 just landed!"

The men lifted Michael onto the hood of the patrol car, Hutchins on one side still blowing air into Michael's mouth and Deputy Hickey on the other. Walton hopped onto the hood and held Michael there. Moose hit the gas, and Hickey and Hutchins had to peel off, because Moose drove too fast.

Hutchins watched them go…hoping they'd revive his friend…that Michael would be okay. He remembered he'd been with Michael on his first day as an officer…and prayed it wouldn't be his last.

Sergeant Walton obstructed Moose's view of the road because he was facing Moose on the other side of the windshield and holding onto Michael. He had the presence of mind to shout opposite directions, guiding Moose the short distance to the helicopter, which was waiting at an offsite landing zone at Canyon View Community Center on Maidu Drive. Moose jumped the curb, coming to a stop about 20 yards from the bird.

Officer Eric Eastman of Roseville PD, who had been patrolling in the area, joined Walton at the hood of the car. Walton jumped off and the two carried Michael to the helicopter.

Jimmy Hendrix, a California Highway Patrol paramedic flight officer and former Navy Corpsman, had been watching from the air until the helicopter landed. He saw the officers doing CPR on the hood of the car and suspected Michael was gone. But there was no giving up. He instantly set to work on Michael, assessing first, then clearing his airway and intubating him with the assistance of Eastman and Walton. He informed the panicked officers that H-20 wasn't an option. "There's no room to do high-quality CPR—so let's get him ready. As soon as the ambulance gets here, we're going."

The 10-minute wait was excruciating[20] . Hendrix, Eastman, and Walton continued to work while Moose hovered closely, doing what he could as well. They also looked over Michael's body for entrance wounds.

[20]The ambulance was not far away, but EMS and fire are required to stay out of the "hot zone" for their safety until the threat has been neutralized by police.

They found a stupid little acorn-shaped hole near his shoulder blade.

The ambulance rolled up and in went Hendrix, Michael, a young, brand-new firefighter, the other ambulance medic, and Moose. The doors were shut, and they were on their way to Sutter Roseville Medical Center, 16 miles away.

****

Maidu and Riverview, Auburn
Friday, October 24, 2014, 12:43 p.m.

Deputy Hickey kept an eye and a gun trained on the maroon truck. He continued to see a hand waving, but Michael's CPR stopped everything else. Once Moose took Michael in the direction of the helicopter, PCSO Deputy Curtis Jones[21] and Hickey got out the PA to call out the female in the truck.

Janelle Monroy came out of the truck cooperatively. They guided her down to the ground, handcuffed her, patted her down, and put her in the back of the patrol car.

"Where is he?" Hickey asked Monroy.

"He took off that way," she replied.

"What's his name?"

"Luis."

After they made sure no one else was in the truck, they found a gun on the front seat, a round jammed in the chamber.

****

Ambulance to Sutter Roseville Medical Center
Friday, October 24, 2014, 12:48 p.m.

They were CODE 3, racing Michael to the hospital. The back of the ambulance was crowded, and the CPR continued. Moose wanted to help, but was flashing back to his friend, Rocklin Police Officer Matt Redding's last moments, after being struck and killed by a drunk driver in October

---

[21] This is a pseudonym.

2005.

"Talk to him!" Moose yelled to Hendrix.

"Mike, *you* talk to him! He can hear your voice—he knows your voice!" Hendrix coaxed. Then to the young firefighter he coached, "High-quality CPR … do high-quality CPR!"

"Do something!" Moose begged.

The ambulance medic took over CPR.

"Mike, hold the IV bag," commanded Hendrix.

"What? Oh, got it." Moose grabbed the IV bag, but he was in a dual reality. He saw Redding lying there, instead of Michael, the CPR continuing.

"Mike! Squeeze the bag …" Hendrix ordered.

When Moose was a sergeant at Rocklin Police Department, he was only two miles away when Redding was hit. He drove his patrol car on the right side of the ambulance all the way to the hospital, shielding the transport from potential accidents. He then watched helplessly while the doctors tried to revive Redding in the ER.

"Hendrix! I'm not a kid, let me help!" Moose pleaded as he jolted back into reality.

Hendrix obliged him, and Moose took position. He began compressing Michael's chest.

"Good depth, Mike," coaxed Hendrix. "Keep it going."

"OK, Mike, next!" The young firefighter took over compressions.

Moose felt like he'd done something, at least. As he watched the others work on Michael, he heard the lonely siren and flashed back again to Redding. It was all too familiar, so he prayed to God that it wouldn't end the same way.

Suddenly, Moose asked, "Hendrix, are his pupils fixed?" Hendrix looked down at Michael. "Mike, his pupils are fixed, but I have other things going here that say he still has a chance. He's not dying here!"

"Fuck," Moose cursed. "I gotta tell his wife."

At that moment, something shifted in Hendrix's mind. Michael went from a brother in arms to a husband, father, and son. The human connection that Hendrix always tried to set aside when he worked on someone descended on him like a flood. It became personal.

When they arrived at the hospital, the doors burst open, and they clamored out. Moose followed them in but was stopped at the door to the trauma room. He stood there in his tack vest, Michael's blood all over him.

****

Sacramento Sheriff CID, Sacramento
Friday, October 24, 2014, 12:30 p.m.

Pastor Mark, Liz, and I emerged from the conference room. We thanked him as he left, as I felt so much better. This feeling wouldn't last for long. We drifted into the area where a few deputies were watching the events as they unfolded.

"Oh my god," said one. "They just shot a PCSO deputy!" The others sucked in his breath in shock, realizing I was there.

"Oh, Scott—" I heard Liz gasp.

I completely lost my shit. Liz stood by helplessly as I screamed, yelled, and paced back and forth.

And although it seemed I had no more tears to cry, they just … kept … coming.

****

Sutter Roseville Medical Center, Roseville
Friday, October 24, 2014, 1:01 p.m.

After leaving the fire station via ambulance, Deputy Jeff Davis was taken to Sutter Roseville Medical Center. He was surrounded by doctors and nurses pulling shrapnel out of his arm.

Suddenly, a gurney burst into the trauma bay, and Hendrix, flight helmet still on, sat atop the patient, administering CPR.

Jeff recognized Michael Davis and watched in horror as several medical personnel rushed to the bed, taking over compressions, doing everything possible to get Michael's heart started again.

Hendrix climbed off the gurney and called out, "Downtime approximately 20-25 minutes! Shot left rear shoulder … teardrop shape … had to extubate to put a King Tube in … capnography in the 20s …"

The doctor replied, "Hold CPR!" Hendrix finished the report in detail.

"Fight, Davis!" Jeff called out. The seconds ticked by with no response.

And then, everything stopped. The doctor called it. Time of death, 1:12 p.m.

The trauma team silently walked out. No one even covered him up.

Several moments went by as Jeff stared at Michael.

When Jeff finally moved to get up, he saw Hendrix, who had continued Michael's CPR the entire way in. He stood there, helmet on, silent in the corner of the room.

A nurse came back in, telling Hendrix he should go. But Hendrix didn't move.[22]

****

Sutter Roseville Medical Center, Roseville
Friday, October 24, 2014, 1:15 p.m.

When the news came that Michael had passed, Moose thought it was too soon to stop CPR. It had seemed as if it were only a couple of minutes since they went in. His mind went to losing Redding.

"How the fuck can you stop?!" Moose roared at the hospital personnel.

He felt a tug from the back and wheeled around, ready to strike. It was Undersheriff Devon Bell.

Moose calmed slightly as Bell tried to talk some sense to him.

****

A bit later, Hendrix washed his hands as Moose stood nearby. "I'm sorry I couldn't do anything more," he offered.

"If I ever get shot, I want you to be the one working on me," Moose answered.

Moose stepped forward and wrapped his arms around Hendrix.

---

[22] As was his practice since his military days, Hendrix was saying a prayer of blessing for Michael and his family. He told Michael he wished he could've done more for him. That his family would be okay. And that he'd see him soon. Although Jeff didn't see it, Hendrix had his hand on Michael's forehead as he prayed.

They embraced for a time, and then Hendrix stepped back, grabbed the litter[23] that they brought Michael in on, and headed back to work.

****

Jason Davis's Home, Rocklin
Friday, October 14, 2014, 12:45 p.m.

While all of this was going on, Jason had been waiting. When the call finally came in for PCSO SWAT, he was ready. Word on the news was that another deputy, this one from his own agency, had been shot. He wondered who it might be.

He kissed Traci goodbye and jumped in the truck.

As he drove eastbound on I-80, he remembered what day it was. It was October 24, the day his father died. He wondered if there would be irony—that perhaps this day would be his last. He pushed the idea aside, without even a thought about his brother, Michael.

When he arrived at the SWAT staging area, he began putting on his heavy vest. He heard some commotion off to the side, and thought he heard his name.

About that time, the captain approached and looked him in the eye. "You need to report to the Command Center right away, Jason."

He'd seen that look before.

It was Michael.

---

[23] A helicopter stretcher

Sheriff Scott Jones gives a press conference, announcing the death of Danny Oliver.

Photograph was taken by the press—we do not know which one.

6

CONSEQUENCES AND CARNAGE

"I wish someone would've told me that you can do everything right tactically, and still not have a good outcome."
—Deputy Scott Brown

Greater Sacramento Region
Friday, October 24, 2014, Early afternoon

As the day wore on, people all over the region were affected by the carnage and violence the two thugs had caused. Sacramento and Placer County deputies, police officers, and highway patrolmen, reeling from the loss of brothers in blue, searched the region for the fugitives. Dispatchers took numerous calls from a concerned public, relayed information to officers, and were careful to communicate effectively and quickly.

Crime scene investigators photographed and logged evidence at four separate crime scenes in Sacramento County and three locations in Placer County. Bracamontes's DNA, thanks to one of my bullets, was left at each and every scene. There were ample witnesses. Still, throughout the entire ordeal, detectives felt as if they were a step behind "Bonnie and Clyde," racing to stop them before anyone else was hurt.

Two deaths, two injured. Several others feeling grateful they were alive.

Danny's body was taken to the Sacramento Coroner's Office. Allied agencies in San Diego scrambled to get Susan on a flight back to Sacramento and were successful through Southwest Airlines.

Adam Holst spent hours in surgery, his condition listed as "grave."

Civilians who'd gone face-to-face with Bracamontes were shaken to the core.

Schools went on lockdown all over the region, because Bracamontes was still at large.

Helicopters dotted the sky, warning folks through the PA system of a "dangerous person in the area."

Every news channel followed the spectacle.

It'd been a long, painful, and arduous day. And I felt like it was all my fault.

****

American River Canyon, Auburn
Friday, October 24, 2014, 12:43 p.m.

Bracamontes wound down into the canyon, coming to a canal. He was thirsty, so climbing into it, he reached down for a drink and came up with muddy water. He consumed it anyway.

About the time he crawled out, a woman, her son, and her dog approached on the trail.

The woman was startled and froze. She grabbed her dog's collar.

Bracamontes stood up, grabbed the gun from the ground, and said, "I'm not going to hurt you."

He began to leave, and she let out her breath. "Don't tell anyone you saw me," he called after her.

The woman flagged down a deputy soon thereafter and reported the sighting.

****

Sutter Roseville Medical Center, Roseville

A Roseville Police officer drove Jason Davis to the hospital after he notified Traci of Michael's shooting.

Although it wasn't confirmed, Jason knew Michael was gone. He thought of his mother—how was he supposed to share this news? Another loss, on the same day she had lost her husband.

His thoughts then went to when he had to tell her that his younger brother had taken his own life 17 years ago.

Today, he would break her heart again.

****

Sacramento Sheriff CID, Sacramento
Friday, October 24, 1:45 p.m.

"Hey, Scott, think you're ready to go back? We need you to walk through the scene with us."

I didn't want to be anywhere near that place.

"Not really, but if it'll help …"

"Yes, it will."

In the meantime, Sergeant Dan Cabral, who was also the Vice President of our union, was assigned to me. He didn't leave my side then and took care of us for months afterward. He was comforting, reassuring, and very helpful.

Liz had been on the phone all day with Becky Amos, who was involved with getting Susan home from San Diego and notifying family members. Becky also went to the hospital to wait for family to arrive.

Susan was due to arrive around 3:00. Liz was still under the hopeful impression that Danny had survived at that point … until Becky mentioned they were on their way to the Coroner's Office.

It was then that Liz realized what I had been saying was indeed true. Danny was gone.

Liz wasn't allowed to come with me to the scene. I also had to give my statement, and a lot of other details the investigators needed from me.

Liz spoke up. "Scott, I think while you're busy, I'll go to Sue. I can take care of you later."

"That's a great idea. You need to be with her … because I can't right now."

It was agreed, and logistics were put into place. A sergeant guided Liz and the other deputy's wife who had shadowed Liz, to a car that was part of a full motorcade, to meet Susan at the Sacramento airport.

****

Sutter Roseville Medical Center, Roseville

Jason Davis walked into the waiting room. Everyone stood about, in shock.

It was confirmed that Michael was indeed dead.

He stepped aside until his mother arrived. They walked together to the quiet room.

"Mom, Michael was shot and killed," he stammered. And at those words, she crumbled.

He held her for a long time. They were eventually allowed to see Michael. It was five days before his birthday.

****

Sutter Roseville Medical Center, Roseville

"I'm so glad Mike is your partner, Moose. You always gotta take care of him, because I don't know what I'd do if I lost him …"

Jessica Davis, Michael's wife, had said those words to him just two weeks earlier. Moose was not looking forward to seeing her.

When Jessica walked into the room, she was visibly shaken. Moose went to her, and the first thing out of his mouth was, "I'm sorry, Jessica. I let you down."

"What the hell are you talking about, Moose?" she asked.

"It was my responsibility to watch out for him. Mikey's gone."

Jessica's face showed surprise, then went four shades of red, and she started in. "How dare you take on the guilt! It's not your fault, Moose! It's the fault of that asshole who shot my husband!"

She went on and on.

But Moose couldn't accept her words. His mind was fixed on one thought: he had failed Michael.

****

Command Post, Auburn

Once Monroy was in custody, deputies tried to ask her questions that would shed some light on the murderous crime spree she and her husband had gone on that day. She spoke freely, but unfortunately, she was lying through her teeth.

She provided a false name for Luis, said he forced her to take drugs and held her against her will, and claimed they were headed elsewhere than they really were. She told police that she had no knowledge about the guns, and then claimed she had taken them and ammunition away from her husband along the trip. Basically, she professed to be a complete victim in all of it. She cried on cue and said she was terrified and abused. Deputies did find bruises around her neck, but evidence collected later showed that the couple regularly engaged in choking during sex.

While she was in the back of the patrol car, she described symptoms that sounded like a heart attack and then pretended like she'd stopped breathing. When they pulled her out of the car to render medical aid, she suddenly caught her breath.

The investigation would eventually reveal a woman who may not have pulled the trigger that day, but she was no victim, as she claimed. Her actions before and during that day showed she was a willing, manipulative partner in the scheme.

****

Motel 6, Sacramento
Friday, October 24, 2014, 1:56 p.m.

The detectives drove me back to Motel 6. Judie Odbert, a representative from Mastagni Law Firm retained by our union, was also present. Anxiety wrapped around me tightly, and I started sweating. My breathing became shallow; I could barely pull air into my lungs.

The crime scene was busy, despite the taped off area being as deserted as an abandoned ghost town. There were patrol cars, unmarked cars, media, and all kinds of people milling about.

I don't know if I walked on my own or if they pushed me forward, but I somehow made it to a large vehicle parked on the edge of the scene. I paused, catching my breath, then willed one foot in front of the other until it came into view.

Pop! Pop! Pop … darting to and fro … shooting back …

It was as if it were happening all over again.

There was a puddle of blood on the ground where Danny had been. Our car was still parked where we had left it. There was crime scene tape and evidence markers everywhere.

I began to shake but forced myself to keep walking. I indicated where the Mercury was parked, where I stood when the suspect shot at me, and where I returned fire. They listened intently and didn't ask many questions.

After 40 minutes or so, we returned to the car. I tried not to look around, because I felt like everyone was staring. I would not let them see me cry.

****

Placerville
Friday, October 24, 2014, Afternoon

My twin brother, Tim, was in his class at Union Mine High School when he got a panicked email from our mother. It sounded as if I were the one who was shot, not Danny.

Panic set in. Tim's heartrate soared. He quickly ran into a neighboring teacher's office and told him I had been shot. "Watch my class—I'm heading to the hospital!"

He jumped in his car and drove like a bat out of hell to his home about 30 miles away. His wife, Jenn, was waiting for him, having already received the news. She knew he was on his way down the hill, thinking it was me who'd been shot.

My brother is horrible with technology and even worse at keeping his cell phone with him and on. That day was no different, so his wife was unable to let him know I was okay.

Tim skidded up the driveway, threw his bag at the front door and yelled that he was going to the hospital.

Jenn luckily caught him. "Tim! It wasn't Scott who was shot! He's okay!" Tim collapsed in the front yard, crying tears of relief.

Afterward, we had the talk—if anything should ever happen to me, he will not get a call or email. He'd get a visit.

****

Sacramento International Airport
Friday, October 24, 2014, 2:55 p.m.

Liz arrived at Sacramento International Airport. They were escorted through the back channels of the airport, through security, then settled into the security office. There were several people there, although Liz didn't really know anyone. Chaplain Frank Russell approached, and they talked awhile. As the logistical plan was drafted while they waited for Susan Oliver's flight, it became clear that no one there knew her personally. They weren't even sure what she looked like.

Chaplain Frank said to Liz, "You're going to be our eyes and ears today, Liz. None of us know who Susan is." Liz felt that was kind of sad, but she agreed.

The flight landed around 3:30, and the plane taxied to the gate. Liz was taken to the door of the plane. It opened, and there stood Susan. The two women hugged, and then were whisked down the stairs outside to the tarmac. Liz held onto Susan's hand, as she was wearing tiny-heeled shoes and feared she'd take a tumble on the steep, metal stairs.

The patrol unit was waiting on the tarmac. They all slid in, Liz and Susan in the back seat and the other deputy's wife up front with the sergeant, who was driving. The motorcade slowly made its way out of the airport.

"How is Scott, Liz?" asked Susan.

"He's good physically; mentally, not good," she answered.

"You're taking me home, right?"

The sergeant answered that one. "No, Susan, we're going to the Coroner's Office. That's where Danny is. That's where your family will meet you."

Tears.

Liz decided she would match Susan's emotions. If Susan was pissed, Liz was pissed. If she cried, Liz cried. It was all about Susan.

Then, Susan and Liz became mesmerized by motor officers as they held back traffic. It was like a dance, circling back and forth as they escorted the patrol car and two others to the Coroner's Office 15 miles away.

****

Sacramento Sheriff's Office Headquarters
Friday, October 24, 2014, 3:00 p.m.

Sheriff Scott Jones stepped through the clear doors and took his place at the podium. Several cameras snapped pictures.

"Good afternoon, and thank you for being here.

"Before I start, I'm going to tell you a few things we do know. And I will caution you that because this investigation is still ongoing, there are a number of things that we do not know. I will make my remarks, and then we will leave it open for any questions you may have.

"At 10:22 this morning, Sheriff's Deputy Danny Oliver, who was a POP officer and working with a partner, engaged with a suspicious vehicle that was parked in the Motel 6 parking lot near Arden and Ethan Way. As the officers approached the vehicle, the person inside the vehicle fired several rounds at Deputy Danny Oliver. At least one of those rounds struck Danny Oliver in the forehead, which caused his death. The other officer was able to return fire as the suspect fled the scene.

"The suspect went to a nearby neighborhood and attempted to carjack a vehicle. The owner of that vehicle fought back to prevent the carjacking and was himself shot in the head. I don't know the state of that civilian; he was alive and conscious when he was transported to the UC Davis Medical Center. I don't know the current state of that citizen.

"The suspect then drove to another nearby neighborhood and carjacked another vehicle, the red Ford F-150 that was announced to the media. At one point, we got a credible tip that the two suspects, a male and a female, were changing clothes and continuing on their way. We set up on a scene in Carmichael, which turned out to be a scene they were not at.

"About that time, we got information about the incident that continued up in Placer County. Unfortunately, I don't have a lot

of information about that incident.

"I would like to say to other law enforcement agencies that have reached out, thank you very much. It's a difficult time, and we appreciate your sympathy and offer of resources as we work through this.

"To the community we serve, we thank you, as always, for your support and sympathy. And I want to assure you the entire Sacramento Sheriff's Department stands ready and able to continue to provide the excellent service to which you've become accustomed.

"And to the men and women of the Sheriff's Department, we stand as a family. Today, we grieve as a family. Tomorrow, we will start healing as a family. I pray for each and every one of you, that you will have the courage that I know you have."

****

Sacramento Sheriff CID
Friday, October 24, 2014, 3:05 p.m.

Once Judie and I returned to CID, she waited with me for hours. She was a little pissed at how long it took to get my interview, because I'd already been there the whole day. I just wanted to get it over with and leave.

Detectives were evidently gleaning information from other scenes before they spoke to me. They wanted to question me only once. The department lawyer was acting in my best interest, as well. I was still in a state of shock, but so grateful people were looking out for me.

CSI showed up and needed to take photographs. They needed me dressed as I was at the scene, so I put my gear back on, which sucked. The two girls who were taking my picture had these terrified and stunned looks on their faces. They didn't say much, and I didn't blame them.

I was probably the least horrifying thing they saw that day!

Sacramento Sheriff SED Team on the hunt for the fugitives.

Photograph by Randall Benton of the Sacramento Bee.

7

SURRENDER

"No one is compelled to choose the profession of a police officer; but having chosen it, everyone is obligated to perform its duties and live up to the high standards of its requirements."
—President Calvin Coolidge

Belmont Avenue, Auburn
Friday, October 24, 2104, 1:09 p.m.

Bracamontes struggled up the canyon, leaning on the shotgun at times, pushed on only by pure adrenaline. He was scratched up by the blackberry bushes he'd tried to eat from. In the sky, he saw and heard the helicopters across the canyon. He heard dogs barking not too far away.

He needed to hide.

A yellow house came into view. It looked harmless enough, so he climbed the steps, shotgun in hand, and tried the sliding glass door. It was unlocked!

Listening, he entered through the door, looking to see if anyone was home. No one was.

He first went to the kitchen, looking for something to drink. The refrigerator had food, but no beer. In the door, he found a bottle of Limoncello.

Twisting the cap, he put the bottle to his lips and took a swig before downing it all. Still thirsty, he found a liter of apple juice in the cupboard. He drank almost the entire bottle of that, as well.

He sat down, looking over the shotgun, trying to get it to unlock.

****

Belmont Avenue, Auburn
Friday, October 24, 2014, 1:09 p.m.

Joshua[24] lived in a yellow house on Belmont Avenue in the foothill town of Auburn. From the street, it looked like a small, one-story home, but in the back, there was a downstairs area that overlooked a beautiful, steep, forested canyon. His sister and brother-in-law lived upstairs; Joshua resided in the basement.

Earlier, he'd gone to the store and heard gunfire just after returning home. Stopping to listen, he noticed three different tones of the shots.

About 15 minutes later, he heard a loudspeaker announcement: "There is a dangerous person in the area. Stay inside for your safety."

Seated in a chair and peering out into the canyon, Joshua saw a Hispanic male run up the back steps of his home.

Then he heard the sliding glass door open, and someone walking around in the kitchen, rummaging through the cupboards.

Joshua quietly slipped out the back door, circled around the side of the house, and hid in the woods. At that time, a Roseville[25] police cruiser came down the street, so Joshua flagged him down, and told him he thought the man they were looking for was hiding in his house.

****

Command Post, Auburn
Friday, October 24, 2014, 1:11 p.m.

Sergeant Winn arrived at Riverview and Maidu with Placer County's Bearcat[26] and picked up Joe Roseli, who was also a SWAT team member. PCSO Deputy Jack Hickey handed him a radio.

At that moment, the radio announced that a resident had reported an unknown Hispanic male hiding in his house.

Got him!

****

---

[24] This is a pseudonym.

[25] Several departments were in the area looking for the suspect, including Roseville Police Department.

[26] This is an armored vehicle.

Yellow House on Belmont Avenue, Auburn
Friday, October 24, 2014, 1:20 p.m.

Bracamontes had taken the shotgun apart to try to get it to work, but he could not figure it out. Frustrated, he opened closets and drawers, looking for another weapon. After a short search, he found what he was looking for in the master bedroom ... a .380 handgun.

He was soaked with sweat. His hand was still bleeding. His belly began to rumble. He sat on the bed and thought of Monroy. She didn't follow him into the patrol car. She didn't even get out of the truck. He suspected she had been injured or killed in the shootout.

His stomach lurched. He stood, dropped his pants, and crapped on the carpet. He then laid back on the bed and fell asleep.

****

PCSO Bearcat, Auburn

Joe Roseli's phone rang. Roseli checked the incoming call—it was a 333 number, which turned out to be his daughter's school. The school was on lockdown, because it was in the vicinity of the shootout area. After questioning whether or not to answer, he took the call. It was his 14-year-old daughter, who was very upset. She had not been able to get much information, and just needed to know if her dad was okay.

****

Belmont Avenue, Auburn
Friday, October 24, 2014, 1:20 p.m.

Sergeant Winn and his team drove the Placer County Bearcat down the narrow lane of Belmont Avenue. Several resident and first-responder vehicles were parked along the street. If they were in the way, the Bearcat "moved" them to clear the path for the SED team. The SED Bearcat was also on its way from the Auburn Overlook.

Auburn and Roseville Police Departments had already surrounded the yellow house. This was it.

The SED team exited the vehicle, armored up and rifles in hand. The first point of contact was the house next door—to make sure the suspect hadn't moved as was mistakenly reported via 911.

Once that house was cleared and residents evacuated, the team moved to the yellow house, where the owner had reported an intruder. Police helicopter pilots confirmed the suspect was inside as they could see him from their vantage point. Plus, the SED team had cleared the yard, as well. It was empty.

****

Inside the Yellow House on Belmont, Auburn
Friday, October 24, 2014, 2:15 p.m.

Bracamontes jolted awake as he heard something outside. He looked through the window, seeing police everywhere. He flew to the kitchen and turned on all of the knobs on the stove, as well as the oven.

****

Outside the Yellow House on Belmont, Auburn
Friday, October 24, 2014, 2:23 p.m.

Sergeant Winn was given authorization to deploy chemical agents, so he and his team put together a plan. First, they used several direct impact rounds to break the living room picture window. Then, they threw gas canisters through the window and front door, in addition to several more through windows on both levels. They then threw a flash bang[27] right on the front porch.

They waited. No response.

****

[27] A non-lethal explosive device that emits an extremely loud bang and bright lights to disorient people.

Inside the Yellow House on Belmont, Auburn
Friday, October 24, 2014, 2:40 p.m.

Bracamontes covered his head as windows shattered and pink gas began to fill the house. His face was on fire, pain shooting throughout his body as the powder attached itself to his sweat.

Every five minutes, more gas came in through different windows in the house. There was nowhere to go. Then, he heard someone calling out to him.

"Mr. Marquez, give yourself up! We don't want you to end up like your wife …"

His worst fear was true—his wife was dead. He stumbled to the kitchen and grabbed a pen and a yellow, lined notepad. He wrote:

"Forgive me God
Take me whit u
Love u Forever
Ja Baby"

He sat, exhausted. It was hard to breathe with the gas, and his face hurt. He was alone.

****

Outside the Yellow House on Belmont
Friday, October 24, 2014, 3:30 p.m.

It was a standoff. He was surrounded. And they had all the time in the world. He would not get away this time.

"Mr. Marquez! Come out with your hands up! You don't want to have the same fate as your wife! You're all alone," Sergeant Winn announced through the PA.

As they waited for him to come out, Winn continued to order Bracamontes to surrender. Every three minutes came a renewed command.

They would not allow him to kill anyone else.

****

Inside the Yellow House on Belmont
Friday, October 24, 2014, 3:45 p.m.

Bracamontes peered out the window. There were armed cops everywhere, aiming their weapons at the house. He didn't want to die.

He moved toward the front door and opened it. He laid down on his back with his hands behind his neck.

The cops told him to move outside the door on his back. He did.

Deputies were on him in an instant. They grabbed his hands, rolled him over, and quickly put the cuffs on him. It was over.

****

Front Porch of Yellow House on Belmont, Auburn
Friday, October 24, 2014, 3:48 p.m.

Sergeant Winn stood over the man who terrorized two counties and took the lives of two of their own. He reached for his mic and declared, "He's cuffed."

Winn stood over evil while the others cleared the house. They turned off the stove and the oven, found the weapons in the bedroom, and avoided the human waste and blood. The house was absolutely trashed.

Bracamontes stunk like feces. His hand was bloody and open, which Winn expected. Bracamontes had left blood at each and every scene and in every car he stole.

He wouldn't escape justice.

There was relief that he was caught. There was frustration that he came out on his back like a coward. There was anger that he was still alive, yet our deputies were not.

Sometimes, it really sucks to be the good guys.

****

Sacramento
Friday, October 24, 2014, 4:05 p.m.

Inside the patrol unit that carried Susan and Liz in the middle of the motorcade, the air hung heavy with grief. There were silent tears and sniffles as they watched the motorcycles clearing the roads. If the day weren't so horrific, it would've been beautiful.

In the front seat, a phone buzzed with a text. "Oh my God! The fucking dirtbag surrendered!" the deputy's wife blurted out.

"*What* did you say?!" Susan countered.

"Oh, I'm sorry—" she backpeddled.

Susan lost it.

"Why didn't they KILL him?! He killed my husband!" she screamed.

****

Coroner's Office, Sacramento
Friday, October 24, 2014, 4:10 p.m.

Liz arrived at the Coroner's Office with Susan, who was in shock and visibly shaking. Susan's sister, who looks exactly like her, greeted them, and Liz handed Susan over. Not knowing what to do next, Liz took a seat in the back corner, silently watching the family in their grief.

Darrell, Becky, and Brian Amos were already there. Deputies McCabe and Pratt arrived. Liz noticed that Pratt's vest was bloody.

Danny's parents were there. His oldest daughter, Melissa, was there. Someone brought in an ice chest of food and water.

Sheriff Jones arrived and gave his condolences to Susan and her family. Liz listened to the interaction.

Then, people started mentioning me, asking how I was and if I was okay. Sheriff Jones quietly moved to another corner and blended in.

The deputy's wife with Liz nudged her, "You should go introduce yourself to the sheriff. Tell him you're Scott's wife." Liz silently shook her head. "This is not my moment. It's not about me. I'm here for Sue."

As Liz sat quietly, taking all of it in, it hit Liz how the scene unfolding in front of her could've easily been very different. If I had been driving that morning, she would've been the grieving widow, and it would've been our families there. It had been a 50/50 chance for the two of us—because whoever approached that blue Mercury Marquis first was the one who was going to die.

****

Coroner's Office, Sacramento
Friday, October 24, 2014, 4:35 p.m.

Danny's mom, Jeri, went back to view his body. They had cleaned him up and dressed the wound.

"It looks like he's sleeping," she said when she came out.

After seeing Danny, everyone left. Susan caught a ride with her sister, so Liz' responsibilities shifted back to me.

"Are you ready to leave?" Sergeant Bowen asked.

"Yes, please take me to Scott. And maybe we could stop for a bit of food on the way? I haven't eaten all day." That's exactly what they did.

Looking back, Liz regrets not viewing Danny while at the Coroner's Office. Nobody offered, so she didn't really think about it. But she didn't get to say goodbye.

Her last image of Danny is vastly different than mine. I see him on the pavement in the Motel 6 parking lot. She sees him standing in our living room.

****

Sutter Roseville Medical Center, Roseville
Friday, October 24, 2014, Late afternoon

Moose was raw, flayed open. He hurt all over. Everything was surreal.

He had served in law enforcement for 28 years. He'd seen murders, liars, shootings, hate, dead kids, dead friends. The pain … the bullshit … piled on top of one another in chaotic layers strewn across his soul.

He had to get away. He had to get out of there.

He left the hospital, a chill in the air. As he waited in the parking area for a ride home, Placer County Sheriff Ed Bonner approached.

"Simmons," he said softly, and wrapped his fatherly arms around Moose.

"I'm done, Sheriff. I'm done with this fuckin' job! I just can't do it anymore. What'd I miss? I don't miss shit! I've never had a call, or a decision go wrong. Until today. I just can't get past it."

Sheriff Bonner listened. He knew. He hurt for Simmons. He said some comforting things like he usually did; said it was "okay."

But Moose knew it wouldn't be okay. Not this time.

****

Sacramento Sheriff CID
Friday, October 24, 2014, 5:30 p.m.

I entered the interview room with Detectives Scott Swisher and Angie Kirby, Union Vice President Dan Cabral, and my lawyer. They listened while I told my story.

At one point, they had a photo line-up for Bracamontes and Monroy. They showed me six color photographs—one of the suspects and five others who had nothing to do with the shooting.

They were the same sex, race, hair color, and build, so that the suspect didn't stand out any more than the others.

When I tried to picture the guy's face, though, I either saw the flash of his gun or Danny lying on the ground.

I don't think I ever saw his face.

I felt like shit—a horrible cop. I felt I let Danny down by not identifying his killer.

This is typical. In scenarios where a gun is present, victims are often able to describe the gun, but not the suspect. This is because they were so distracted by gunfire or other details, and it happens so quickly. I knew all of this, but it did not calm the guilt.

I did have a picture in my mind of the woman suspect and pointed her out. I learned later that I pointed to the wrong person, but that gal actually looked more like the current Monroy than the booking photo they used in the lineup.

It is horrible what damage meth does to a face.

****

Dean and Liz arrived at CID with a bag from Burger King. They entered the conference room, where my POP teammates were eating pizza, waiting for me to finish my statement.

Pratt approached Liz. "You were at the Coroner's Office," she said. "Are you Liz?"

Liz nodded.

My wife then spent the next hour sitting with the POP team, talking about the events of the day.

After the interview, they escorted me back to the room I'd been waiting in. We walked past the main hall of the building where the interrogation rooms were. I noticed two deputies standing by the doors. I was later told that Bracamontes was being held there. If I had known he was there, they would've needed more than two deputies to stop me from killing him.

I am a Christian man and have made peace with many things surrounding that day. I also know that man's death or eternal destination is not up to me. At the time, I was not in a good frame of mind—my emotions were high. Rage consumed me. He'd taken my partner violently—and I wanted revenge.

Liz joined me and we waited together with Dan Cabral. They turned off my Facebook account. Then, she and Cabral talked about living arrangements for the weekend and our plan.

"Our kids are with babysitters, because we were supposed to go out of town tonight," Liz explained. "It'd be good to let him decompress some before having to think about being a dad."

"What if we put you and Scott up in a hotel, Liz?" Cabral asked. What he didn't say is that they had no idea who the suspect was or if he had gang affiliations. There were whisperings that he may be connected to the drug cartel in Sinaloa. It wasn't a good idea to have Liz and I at home until we had a better idea of who the guy was. They also wanted to keep me away from the media.

"Oh, okay, that works," she responded.

"What else do you need?" asked Cabral.

Although Liz had never been in this situation before, she thought for a moment and said, "We need a suite—there's nothing more awkward when people come to visit in a hotel room than sitting together on the bed. We'll need some room."

"Okay, you've got it."

Next, Liz started thinking about how to calm me down.

"How about a jacuzzi tub?"

****

Placer County Sheriff's Office, Auburn
Friday, October 24, 2014, 6:53 p.m.

Sheriff Ed Bonner of Placer County Sheriff's Office held an emotional press conference just before 7:00 that night. He started off by thanking those who'd come alongside him personally and professionally, and then gave a report of the day's events.

> *"Today, Detective Michael David Davis Jr., veteran officer and detective of the Placer County Sheriff's Department, was killed in the line of duty in Auburn.*
>
> *"Michael was 42 years old. He'd have been 43 next Wednesday.*
>
> *"He first came to the sheriff's department as a reserve deputy sheriff in 1996. He then became a police officer with the city of Auburn in 1996, and he came to the sheriff's department in 1999—15 years ago. He served his last ten years as a homicide investigator.*
>
> *"He leaves behind a wife and four children. Amazingly, Michael's father, Michael David Davis Sr., was a Riverside County deputy sheriff, and he was killed in the line of duty on Oct. 24, 1988—exactly 26 years ago today.*
>
> *"Deputy Sheriff Jeff Davis was also shot in the arm during this assault. He has been treated and released from the hospital, and he is expected to recover. Jeff has been with the sheriff's department 17 years.*
>
> *"I thank you again for your patience, your kindness. This is a very difficult day for all local law enforcement, and we spent a lot of time with the families before I came here to confirm what you already know and to give you more details.*
>
> *"I don't have a lot of details on the events that led up to this. They are currently under investigation, and all that I can assure you is the scene was incredibly chaotic. And working with*

Sacramento County and Placer County Sheriff's Office, as well as our allied agencies, we will piece this together over the coming days and weeks and keep you appraised of what we've learned.

"The suspect is in custody, as you know. I think there are those people who would say, 'You know what, I wished you'd killed him.' No. That's not who we are. We are not him. We did our job.

"I'm incredibly proud of the men and women who go out there every day and put their lives on the line. And today this organization—this family—has suffered a horrific loss. I give my heartfelt thanks to all those who have reached out to us, and again, the media, who are respectfully allowing us to work with our families in this time of sadness and madness."

People from all over the country sent condolence messages—this one from Anne Arundel County Police Department in Maryland.

Social media graphic created by Anne Arundel County Police Department.

8

AFTERSHOCKS

"There are now no small tasks. No going on 'as usual ...' Not to mention the toll that grief and loss take on your emotional, physical, mental, and spiritual health, which has the power to alter every relationship you hold."
—Vanessa Shepherd, *The Good in the Awful*

Sacramento Sheriff CID
Friday, October 24, 2014, 8:30 p.m.

When I returned to the conference room after my interview, my POP team was waiting for me. There was a lot of hugging and crying. I apologized over and over for what I felt I should've or could've done. They said it wasn't my fault. Didn't help much, but it was good to know they didn't blame me. I, on the other hand, blamed myself.

"Where are you staying tonight?" they asked.

"Lake Natoma Inn. In Folsom," I replied.

Liz and I were originally scheduled to head to Humboldt, about three hours north, for the weekend. A student I helped coach as a place kicker was in his last season of football. His father, who had faithfully attended most of his games, died suddenly of cancer. We were going to show support, so we arranged for the kids to stay with Grandma for the weekend. Looking back, we saw this as God looking out for us ahead of time.

We met my mother in-law at our house, and I saw the boys for a bit as Liz packed bags. It was so hard not to cry in front of them, but it did my heart good to see their innocent, smiling little faces. We strapped them in the car and sent them on their way without sharing what had happened. They had no idea that they'd come very close to losing me that day.

We drove to the Lake Natoma Inn where Sergeant Cabral had booked the suite and then joined us. Before going up to the room, we decided I needed a drink at the bar. Truth is, I could've had a hundred drinks, and it wouldn't have helped. I ordered, then looked to my right and saw Danny's face on the television above the bar.

"TURN THAT OFF!" I screamed at the bartender.

He looked at me and froze for a few seconds before reaching for the remote. Liz grabbed me, and we headed for the room. I later asked Sergeant Cabral to apologize for me. He already had and left a very nice tip. It would be the first of many anger incidents.

Once in the room, we barely settled in when the POP team arrived. We all kind of sat around and avoided talking about Danny. I have no idea what we talked about. Time passed slowly.

At some point, my parents and brother arrived. From the bedroom, I heard my mom and dad saying "hello" to everyone. On the surface, everything seemed fine, but the moment I walked around the corner, my mother lost it. She cried loudly and held me very, very tight while I repeated several times that I was okay. She had heard the words, but I think she needed to see for herself whether her baby was okay or not. Even though I was a late 30-something, I was still her boy.

This gave me a small glimpse into how Danny's folks felt … without the relief.

My dad did not cry out loud, but I did see a tear or two running down his face. He handed me a giant bottle of Jack Daniels and said he didn't expect to get it back. I assured him that he wouldn't. Neither my dad nor I are big drinkers.

I have since seen my dad mist up a few times when I share my testimony. He's not a big hugger, and we don't share our feelings much, but I know he loves me. Now, we make more of an effort to give that hug, to say we love each other, and to spend more time together.

My dad and I attended a men's Bible study group at Bayside Church in Granite Bay before Danny's death. Afterward, the group took on a whole new meaning. Prior to this study, I never heard my dad talk about God or his faith. After Danny was killed, he began to talk openly about his feelings about God, his faith, and some things he wished he had done differently. I have grown to cherish the time after the meetings when Dad and I stood in the parking lot just to talk. It became our chance to catch up every week. It is one of the many ways God has surrounded me with people who have made me stronger.

Sometime after midnight, Liz and I kicked everyone out. She kept asking what I needed and if she could do anything for me. We decided maybe a bath would help calm me down enough for some sleep. Our suite did indeed have a jacuzzi bathtub, so we both got into it, sat in the water, and tried to relax. We didn't do much talking ... just drinking and soaking.

Once we got out, we dried off, moved to the bed, and made love. A near-death experience made me realize I almost missed the chance to touch and hold my wife again, so we had what I felt was great and much-needed sex. (Later, Liz referred to this as "survivor sex"—the intense need for sexual intercourse after trauma. Instead of being embarrassed about it, she openly talks about it when speaking to other wives.)

In the moment, Liz thought it strange—she thought I needed to talk about what happened. Why would I think about sex at a time like that? I told her I just needed to be as close to her as possible.

Unfortunately, sleep did not come easy or for long. I slept for short periods—no more than 30 minutes at a time—and had horrible nightmares. I woke up terrified, heart racing and mind spinning. It went on all night.

Being awake didn't help, because I couldn't get the last images of Danny out of my head. When awake, I saw him lying on the ground with open, lifeless eyes. It was like having the worst thing you've ever seen permeate your vision continuously—whether asleep or awake.

It doesn't take long for that to get to you, no matter how strong you are.

****

Rocklin
Friday, October 24, 2014, evening

Darrell and Becky Amos left for home when it seemed appropriate. He was dehydrated. No tears left. Exhausted. Drained.

It had been a rollercoaster day. With each new person, there were tears and hugs, and then they'd find a happy median inside and level off. Then, the next set of people showed up, and they'd experience it all over again. Plus, throughout the day, they'd heard updates about the suspect.

Darrell was angry, sad, and everything in between.

Once home, he completely let go and found more tears.

****

Lake Natoma Inn, Folsom
Saturday, October 25, 2014

The following morning, we got up, showered, and walked to a café just around the corner from the hotel. It felt good to get outside after being stuck indoors the day before. As we waited in line to order our food, I looked down at a guy reading the newspaper. The headline read, "MANHUNT," and had a picture of the SSO Bearcat with several officers riding on it on the front page. I looked at Liz with tears in my eyes, and said, "I'll wait for you outside."

I ducked out the door and quietly cried, pacing back and forth until Liz came out with our food. I wasn't ready to see anything else, so we returned to our room. It was the first indicator that there would be no escaping what happened the day before.

Around lunchtime, I sat in a courtyard area forcing down a sandwich with Deputy Tim Mullin and Sergeant Cabral when it was suggested we visit Susan. I knew I had to see her at some point, but I wasn't ready. I felt like she must blame me for Danny's death. I was his partner, after all, and my job was to watch his back and protect him. I had failed her. The request implied that Susan had asked for me, so I of course did not refuse.

****

Folsom
Saturday, October 25, 2014

Senior Pastor Curt Harlow of Bayside Church had been keeping in touch with Pastor Mark Godshall since the first call was made. Curt couldn't get there right away because of his responsibilities, but by the next afternoon, he stopped by the hotel.

He entered our suite, noting the several people there—cops and family—who were grieving together. The mood was somber, intense. I was in the bedroom, because I was absolutely spent and couldn't handle a lot at a time. Liz, on the other hand, was in full Mama Bear mode. She and Curt joined me in the bedroom, where it was quiet.

Curt asked the important questions—what happened, who is

taking care of us, and what can Bayside do? Liz shared with him all of that and more, because I was exhausted by repeating the story. She shared what happened from the shooting to the hotel, the strategy for the next couple days, and how attentive the department had been to our needs.

Curt let us talk, and we did. It was good to have him listen, and when we had shared much, he asked if we needed prayer. We of course said, "Yes!"

He prayed for us, starting with "Lord, there are no words," and asking for help, strength, and comfort. We were all crying.

Curt and other pastors have continued to check on us over the years. There are two things he has observed. First, he commends us for how we continue to ask for help. This is not necessarily my doing. It's Liz. When things get a little dark on my end, she puts bugs in key people's ears, suggesting they "give my husband a call." And they have. And it really helps.

Curt has also observed over the years how things have happened that take me right back to Day One. Trauma attaches itself to trauma. As I share more of our story, you'll understand how and why.

****

Garden Valley, California
Saturday, October 25, 2014

We started the long drive up to Susan's house.

The Olivers had moved from El Dorado Hills to Garden Valley maybe a month or so prior to Danny's death. I helped move some of their stuff from their old house into storage.

I was silent as we drove. I tried to think of something profound to say to Susan. Someone asked what I would say.

"I can't think of anything else than to fall at her feet and beg for forgiveness for letting Danny die," I replied.

They told me I didn't need to do that and probably shouldn't. But no matter how hard I thought of alternatives, that was all that came to me. I prayed quietly for God to give me the right words and the strength to say them.

The closer we got to Susan's home, the more nervous I became. The anxiety built up so much, I thought I would have a heart attack. We parked the car and started for the house. It was already getting dark, and the porch light was on. A female exited the front door. For a few seconds, I thought it was Susan, and I started bawling.

"That's Sharon, Scott," Liz comforted. "That's Sue's sister!"

I had not met Sharon and didn't know they looked so much alike.

As we entered the house, I heard voices coming from the living room, including Susan's. They were talking and laughing, but I walked slower and slower until I felt like I was being pushed from behind. When I cleared the hallway and found myself standing in the kitchen, the conversations stopped. Everyone stared.

As Susan approached, I did exactly what I had told myself I was going to do. I fell at her feet and cried like a baby asking for her forgiveness.

Susan pulled me to my feet and said, "Let's go for a walk." Her face showed pity, not anger.

****

Susan and I walked around the five-acre property with her doing the comforting. She said there was no one she would've rather had with Danny at the end than me. She didn't blame me at all. She was glad I was okay.

I still can't get over Susan's strength. She may never know how much I needed to hear her exact words. Despite my doubts and "what ifs" around October 24th, I never doubted that Susan meant every word she said to me that night. Honestly, I don't know how my life would've gone had she screamed, blamed, and kicked me out of her house. That is what I expected to happen.

God didn't give me the right words for Susan, but He sure gave her the right words for me.

I told the family I would never hold back from them. If they had any questions, no matter how hard, I'd answer. Later that evening, Danny's brother Chris came to me. I'd never met him before. Much to my horror, he wanted to know what happened to his brother. Although I was not ready to share, I did not deny him.

We walked to the horse barn, away from everyone else, and I told him the entire story, minus a few of the gory details. We had a good cry together, and he thanked me for sharing.

Susan never asked for details.

By the time we left Susan's, I was emotionally drained and exhausted. I did not sleep again that night, and it was starting to get to me.

In addition to sleep deprivation and fatigue, I was showing other signs of emotional trauma. I wasn't eating much, as my stomach was in a constant state of either heartburn or nausea. My muscles were constantly tense—especially around people—which was causing headaches. I was startled by loud noises, felt anxious in crowds, and wanted to hide in a hole and never come out. If I'd seen a list of physical responses to emotional trauma, I'd have probably checked them all.

****

Auburn
Saturday, October 25, 2014

Moose awoke with a start. Groggy, he leaned over and checked the time—two in the morning. He had gone to bed not an hour before.

He turned over, wide awake. Staring at the ceiling, he could smell the iron from the blood he thought he'd showered away.

Nothing made sense. Before he even knew what happened, Michael was down. He didn't even know where the bullets came from. Never even saw the suspect. He kept asking himself what he missed out there.

He missed Mikey so much it hurt. Michael was opinionated, but fair. He didn't care what people thought of him, and when he disagreed with something, he let you know. But Michael never judged others.

He was the Good Samaritan—the first one to lend a hand. He once helped put together a funeral for a baby he'd learned about through work, and he was the one who showed up at the hospital for Moose's son's surgery. When others needed help, Michael was there without fail.

Moose remembered the early confusion when some of his co-workers thought it was actually him who was killed, not Mikey. He wished it would've been.

Three o'clock. Staring at the ceiling.

Four o'clock. Still wide awake.

This would become the new normal … for the next two years.

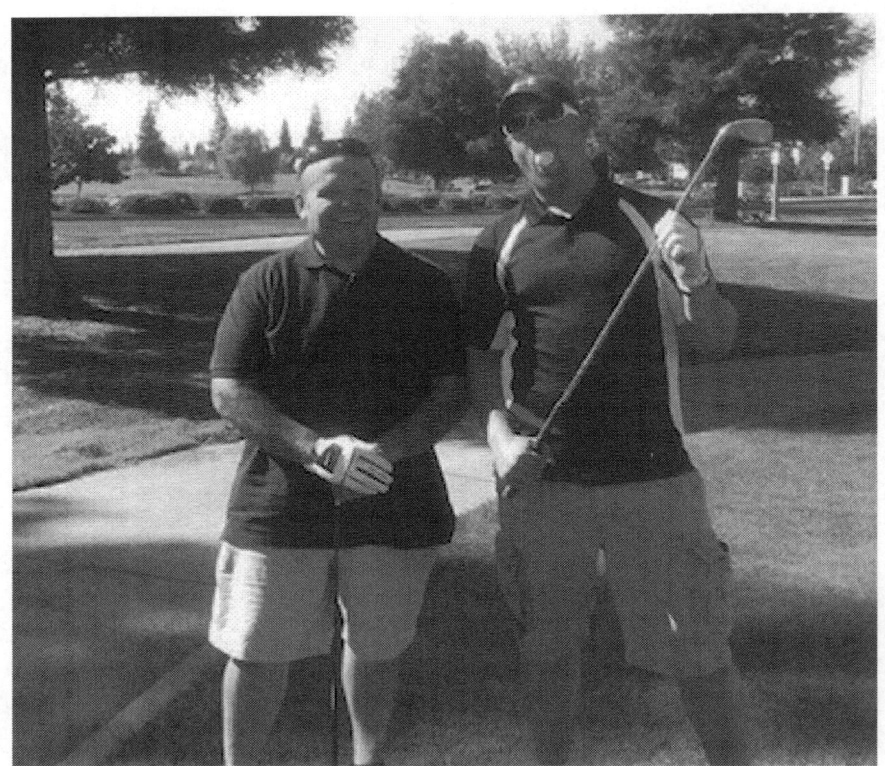

Danny and I playing golf and being silly—my favorite pic of us together.

Photo from the Brown album.

9

DANNY

"As a daughter, you know, your Dad is invincible. He's my Superman."
—Melissa Oliver

My identical twin brother Tim and I were born in San Luis Obispo, a small coastal town in California. We moved to Fair Oaks with my parents and older sister when we were seven years old. Fair Oaks is a suburb of Sacramento that is somewhat rural with many oak trees. Chickens roam the streets freely.

I had a standard childhood in a nice neighborhood. I went to school, played sports, had jobs, and pretty much kept my nose clean. I got a football scholarship to California State University, Sacramento, and eventually got my degree in psychology with a minor in criminal justice.

I was lucky enough to meet Liz while in college, after she went on a date with Tim. But that's a story for a different time.

I then went through the academy, finishing in the top ten academically and nabbing our top gun award. I was hired right out of the academy and completed my patrol training. Like many sheriff's departments, deputies serve several years of jail duty. I was no exception. After three-and-a-half years, I returned to the street and worked the graveyard shift in the north area of Sacramento County.

The city of Citrus Heights had contracted with Sacramento County Sheriff for police services for several years. Danny was assigned to Citrus Heights Police Department but elected to return to the sheriff's department when the city established their own police department. This is when I first met Danny.

For the next few years, I had the best time working with the best crew. At one point, the team was comprised of Danny, Darrell Amos, Darren Benato, Matt Burton, and several others, including Sergeant Chris Guerrero. We grew close in those years and were greatly impacted by the events that transpired years later.

Fast forward a few years to when Danny joined the POP team with

Sergeant Guerrero. I was still working graveyard with Darrell. Burton had become a helicopter pilot for the department, and Benato was Danny's POP partner until he left to be a gang detective.

Danny started harassing me to come to the POP team, but I was reluctant. I loved the graveyard schedule and all the crazy things that happened late at night. He eventually broke me down, and I joined the team. We were paired up, which made us both happy.

Danny was adamant that I be his partner and swore I would be his last before he retired in a few years. He made me promise not to put in for any other jobs or positions until then. After that, I could do whatever I wanted, he said. I loved my job and the team, so it was an easy call.

Danny had a different upbringing and path to the department. He was the only mutual child of a blended family with a firefighter/Marine father, mom, and two brothers and sisters. He was the youngest, growing up in Del Paso Heights, a rough part of the Sacramento region. He attended Grant High School, which is not in a nice area.

After graduation, Danny worked with his brother in the trucking industry. After Susan and Danny were married and Melissa (Missy) was born, Danny decided he needed something new. He went through the Sheriff's Academy, came on as an on-call,[28] and eventually was hired full-time. Jenny was born several years later, after they had given up on the idea of having more children, because they had tried and were unsuccessful conceiving. Danny used to say the 12 years between the girls made it seem like he had two only-child daughters.

Danny was very proud of his girls. He used to brag about Missy's humanitarian trip to Costa Rica to help save turtles, laughing about how she had to wade across a river with her rolling luggage. He also told me how smart Jenny was, and would shake his head when explaining how she'd do her homework but forget to turn it in.

Danny worked his way through the jail, then patrol, training officer, and driving instructor. Eventually, he joined the POP team, establishing a reputation as a no-nonsense guy who gave his opinion whether asked or not. People either liked him or they didn't, but they always knew where he was coming from—which garnered him respect.

---

[28] A part-time deputy .

He was a great cop with an eye for finding criminals, and I knew without any doubt or hesitation that he had my back. Danny loved the POP team so much, he even turned down a promotion to sergeant in order to stay on.

Danny, the guys, and I not only worked together; we did life together. Danny was at the center of much of it. We went on guys' trips to Tahoe and Reno, had drinks, told stories, and always had a great time. He constantly had get-togethers at his house, and most of the time, Liz and I were there.

One of my best memories with Danny occurred at a golf tournament. Susan's company entered a foursome, which meant she needed three more employees to play. Danny was officially the vice president of the company, so he was one. Another employee had played golf in college, so he was their second pick. I was designated as an employee for the day, so I could round out the foursome. All four of us had a beautiful-but-goofballish day—the drinks handed out at each hole didn't help. We didn't win any prizes, but we sure had a great time. One of my favorite pictures of Danny and I was taken that day.

About a month before he died, my parents, Liz, the boys, and the Oliver Family went camping at Olema Campground, located on the northern California coast. Danny, Susan, and Jenny stayed in their RV, which was super nice and looked like a rock star's tour bus. My parents had their fifth-wheel trailer. Liz and I were "living large" in a tent. One or two of the little ones stayed in the trailer with my parents to keep things from getting too crowded in the tent.

We set up near dinner time, and the kids hung out in the RV while the adults sat around the campfire. Tyler, our youngest, was still a baby, so he was with us around the fire most of the evening. Suddenly, the RV revved to life! It scared the hell out of us, so Danny jumped up and scurried into it to see what happened. Turns out our three-year-old, Brandon, had started it up and was apparently very proud of himself! Cop kids …

Shortly after Liz put Tyler down for the night, Danny and Susan packed it in. Susan wasn't feeling well, so the rest of us hung out. It was a good night, but to be honest, I was a little bummed, because I wanted to hang with Danny. I wanted Liz to get to know my partner better. We had a few drinks, talked, planned a few things for the next day, and went to bed.

In the morning, we took a trip to see a nearby lighthouse. While getting lost looking for a specific place to eat lunch with Danny and Susan, we saw some elk, which the boys loved. Overall, the camping trip was nothing spectacular, but it was a good memory.

Danny was great with kids, and mine were no exception. By the end of the trip, they were calling him "Uncle Danny" and wanted to know when they could play in the RV again.

Shortly before his death, I helped Danny move from his house in El Dorado Hills to a new ranch-style home further east. He was so excited. He referred to it as his "retirement home." The house was beautiful, and the property was amazing. There was an area for his huge RV and a detached garage/workshop where he could enjoy his hobby—fixing up classic cars. There were horse stables and an arena he planned to use as a mini go-cart racetrack. Unfortunately, those plans were cut short.

****

El Dorado Hills
Saturday, October 25, 2014

Danny's daughter, Jenny, attended school in El Dorado Hills even after they moved to Garden Valley. Along the road is a large boulder that, over the years, people have painted various things on, like "Happy Birthday," "Congrats," and graduation greetings. The day after Jenny lost her father, her friends painted the rock in his honor.

The rock, which measures approximately six feet by six feet, was entirely painted black. Large yellow words read, "Danny Oliver Our Hero," and there were two large stars on either side. Jenny's friends took a picture of themselves holding signs that read, "We Love You, Oliver Family." Jenny loved it. So did I.

That same rock has turned into a constant show of support when we've lost local officers, having been painted again for the deputies we've lost since. I hope those kids keep the love in their hearts for the Oliver Family, and our law enforcement community as a whole.

****

East Lawn Mortuary, Sacramento

Sunday, October 26, 2014

The time had come to transport Danny's body from the Coroner's Office to East Lawn Mortuary, where he was eventually laid to rest. I was invited to attend and readily accepted.

The night before, Liz asked if I was going to view Danny before they moved him. I told her I wasn't sure. The last image in my mind was horrible. I thought a viewing might help in that respect, but I also didn't know what to expect, which scared me. We talked about the pros and cons. When it was time to go, Liz stayed at the hotel while I left with Sergeant Cabral.

Cabral prepared me as we drove to the Coroner's Office. I was in the lead car, escorted by several motor units. He warned me that nothing official had been announced, but to expect to see units on the overpasses.

As we pulled into the back of the Coroner's Office, there were already several patrol cars and a host of motor units present.

We parked, and Cabral exited, walking toward the crowd of deputies that had gathered. I got out but stayed by the car. I couldn't bring myself to look at anyone or let anyone see me cry. I don't think anyone on the POP team would've judged me for crying, but like most cops, I wanted to keep a tough image. Only problem was, I wasn't feeling tough.

Cabral walked back my way. He was on the phone with Liz, and as he approached, the tears came immediately. I knew what he was coming to ask me, and I wasn't sure I had an answer.

"Do you want to see him before we go? It's okay if you don't, Scott. It'd be understandable why you wouldn't ..."

I shook my head side to side, but replied, "Yes."

We headed for the building. As we walked past everyone, they stopped what they were doing and stared. Well, at least that's how it felt.

An immediate rush of cold air hit me as we entered the building through the double sliding doors. We proceeded directly to a room where Danny's body lay on a gurney. They positioned a cloth on his head in a way that concealed much of the damage. I was so relieved that his eyes were closed, so I wouldn't see them the way they looked at the scene.

I stood there for less than a minute before asking to leave. The tears came on then with a force, and I found myself bawling like a baby in front of my co-workers. I gradually composed myself as we waited, longer than expected, for the hearse to arrive.

I joined the rest of the POP team to roll the casket out and loaded Danny into the vehicle. Cabral and I followed directly behind the hearse, motor units surrounding us at all times.

It was amazing to see the motors work. They cleared intersections and parted traffic like Moses at the Red Sea. As we drove, we passed several units at each intersection, men and women standing outside their vehicles, saluting as we drove by. Once we hit the freeway, we saw patrol cars and fire engines with lights on at almost every overpass, officers and firemen alike saluting a fallen hero.

I had seen videos of this before, but to live it was both amazing and awful at the same time.

We exited the freeway, and very shortly thereafter arrived at East Lawn Mortuary.

Exiting Cabral's car, I heard a female wailing uncontrollably. It was Danny's mom, Jeri, and his father, Bill, and a few of his siblings stood nearby. My heart almost stopped. I was not prepared to see them. My mind raced with several of the same thoughts that occurred when I saw Susan. They had to blame me for Danny's death. I was sure they wondered why I didn't protect him.

And why the hell am I still alive?!

We rolled Danny into the viewing room where several honor guard deputies were waiting to receive him. A slain deputy is never without an armed guard until he's laid to rest. After a few ceremonial moments, we were dismissed. It was then that I approached Danny's mom and dad.

I wept, apologizing for not saving him. They responded much like Susan—it wasn't my fault; they're glad I was with him, and thankful I was okay.

I wondered how I had any tears left, but they kept coming. The exhaustion from so much emotion was beginning to set in, even though I wasn't doing much.

The pain of losing Danny was all-consuming. Perhaps a part of me died with him, in the parking lot of Motel 6 on October 24th. It certainly felt that way.

Our oldest son, Connor.

Photo taken by Liz Brown.

10

THE DAYS AFTER

"I don't want these incidents to happen to put my life into perspective. We try to do the right thing regardless. I don't like these events making me feel like I need to change my life. But they do."
—Deputy Darrell Amos

Granite Bay
Monday, October 27, 2014

After a long weekend at the hotel, it was time to go home and try to figure out how to live again. I was not expected back at work anytime soon.

Before everything happened, I argued with Liz on a regular basis about how messy and cluttered our house was. It wasn't a direct criticism of her, although I am sure she felt differently. I was voicing a general frustration. I am the minimalist and cleaner in the family, and Liz is a bit of … well, let's call her a collector. We also have three boys. As you can imagine, these dynamics come to a head from time to time.

Knowing the house was a stressor, the Union hired a company to clean it for us as a surprise. When I walked in the front door and saw everything clean and organized, I burst into tears. It was the dumbest thing to cry over, but I was overwhelmed by the gesture.

This wasn't the last time someone's generosity caused me to get all choked up. God has blessed us in so many ways.

Like when one of our friends drove our kids somewhere in our van and noticed the maintenance light on. She took it to a mechanic who just so happened to be the one we went to, as well. While our friend planned to pay for the service, once the mechanic learned of the circumstances, he took care of it free of charge.

Others wanted to help as well, so a meal train was organized. Over the next few months, people dropped off food for us. Dishes ranged from home-cooked meals to pizza and gift cards—and we appreciated all of it. We had so much food, we had to utilize our freezer. When all was said and done, we didn't have to think about dinner for over three months.

For stress relief, I regularly play poker with a combination of guys from the department, old friends, family, and my brother Tim's friends. Tim knew I needed distractions. He also knew I loved to play video games. My old console broke, and I didn't have the money to replace it. Tim and the poker guys gathered enough to get me a new gaming console, along with a few games and controllers. They presented it to me at poker night. As usual, I leaked a little from the eyes. My brother gave a speech, which didn't help. I still attend poker nights, and I love those guys. Not because of the gaming console, but the love behind it.

****

Sacramento Sheriff North Central Division
Monday, October 27, 2014

It is the practice of many law enforcement agencies to conduct a voluntary critical incident debrief after violent exchanges. These debriefs are usually held at the department in a private area and are led by a culturally competent therapist (a therapist who understands the ways and culture of police). They typically include all those involved in the incident.

The first critical incident debrief for the POP team and their wives was scheduled by the department and held at our old North Central Division building on Marconi Avenue. I had yet to tell the team what happened, and suspected they blamed me for Danny's death. I was sure they thought I ran and hid instead of fighting back. I assumed they thought I could've prevented it. I went to speak my peace, so they would at least have the facts and could decide their feelings from there.

Liz, Sergeant Cabral, and I arrived and made our way to the conference room where most of the team was already waiting. I was nervous, scared, and sad, which were all new feelings around that group. Only a week earlier, they were the most comfortable people in the world to be with.

Walking in, I saw a longtime co-worker and casual friend, Deputy Bobby French, sitting at the end of the table. Although he was a former POP team member, he left before I joined, so I had no idea why he was there.

We sat down, and the therapist explained how the debrief would go. The first trip around the table would allow each of us to talk about how we were involved.

Before anyone spoke, I looked up and said, "No offense, Bobby, but what are you doing here?" It was then that I learned he was first on scene. Bobby was the one who pulled me to my feet, away from Danny, before placing me into Sergeant Bowen's car. He then administered first aid to Danny until the medics arrived. Bobby removed Danny's gun belt and secured his weapon before he was transported to the hospital. I had no recollection of any of it—no memory of him there at all. In fact, I would've bet you a month's pay that he wasn't.

Then Susan arrived with Union President Kevin Mickelson, who walked alongside her like Cabral did with me. WTF? Whose bright idea was it to bring in Susan to listen to us talk about Danny's death?

The willingness to share anything about what happened immediately dissipated from the room.

Patton said, "This is the first time I've seen Susan. I just want to stop this and give her a hug." We realized that several of the team members had not seen her since the incident, so we took a break.

There were hugs and condolences for Susan, and then, she decided to leave. By this point, the debrief was over, and everyone decided to reconvene later.

I panicked. "Wait," I said. "If you want to try again later, that's fine. But I gotta say something right now."

They stopped talking, and I began to tell my story. I started to shake. I kept apologizing in embarrassment, but couldn't control it. I told the story quickly, and then walked out of the room. I paced the halls, shaking my hands out to get rid of the tremors. Cabral and Liz followed me out, and we left.

I don't think anyone else spoke. The debrief was over, which was a shame. To my knowledge, none of them ever talked about what happened in a group setting thereafter.

****

Granite Bay
Tuesday, October 28, 2014

Our boys were young when Danny died. The younger two had no idea what was going on at all, and for the most part, they still don't. They know Daddy lost a good friend, and we occasionally go to events for him, but they don't have any details. Someday, I will tell them about it. Maybe they'll even read this book, but not until they are much older.

Connor, on the other hand, knew something was off. We felt like we had to tell him something. The problem was, we had no idea what was appropriate to share. How do you tell a six-year-old about something so brutal? How do you destroy that innocence? He knew mom and dad were sad and that we were gone a lot. He had been told that someone had died, but that was about it. Or so we thought.

Liz contacted one of her mentors, Annette Spangler, Director of Parenting Ministries at our church. Apparently, she was Bayside's go-to person for giving little kids bad news. She came to the house and first sat down with me. We talked about what happened and what my goal was with Connor. I explained how I didn't want to lie to him, or give him too much information. We knew he would hear something soon, and wanted the information to come from me.

She told me to talk to him, hug him, and give him a chance to ask any questions he might have. She warned that he might not ask anything right away, but bring it up again after he processed it. After working out a plan, we brought Connor into the living room and sat him on the couch. It was awkward. He knew something was up just from the way we were acting. Annette stood in the kitchen where she could see and hear us.

"Do you know why Daddy has been sad, Connor?"

"Yes."

"Why do you think Daddy is sad?"

Connor leaned in, put his arm around my neck, and said, "Because your partner died?"

"That's right, Connor. Do you know how he died?"

Connor looked me straight in the eyes and said, "He was shot in the head by a bad guy."

Oh shit.

I almost lost it, but managed to keep myself together for his sake.

He told me he heard it from one of his friends at school. He didn't have many other questions. I did my best to assure him I was going to be okay.

I looked at Annette, and she motioned for me to hug him, so I did. At that point, he went outside and walked around by himself. We could tell he was thinking about it. As we watched from the window, Annette said, "You're learning about your son today. Watch how he processes it."

She was right—Connor did come back with questions about the bad guy. He asked if he'd been caught. I told him "yes,"—that he was going to jail for a very long time.

We later learned Connor's friend at school had heard all the details from his dad reading him an entire news article. It was more information than I wanted to give my son and way more than I think his little friend should've had, but I have no judgment toward that parent. It's just that, while we wanted to give Connor the "Disney version," he instead got the PG-13 version.

****

Sacramento County Courthouse
Tuesday, October 28, 2014

Bracamontes and Monroy entered the courtroom and were led to individual cages. They were shackled at the wrists and ankles and wore matching orange suits. Bracamontes's left hand and arm were bandaged.

Our only consolation was that the murderers were in custody, and would likely remain so for the rest of their lives.

Those present said Bracamontes was trembling. I'd like to think he was sorry for what he'd done, but soon enough, we would learn that was not the case. More likely, he was experiencing withdrawal symptoms from methamphetamine.

Bracamontes and Monroy were charged with 14 felony counts, including murder, attempted murder, carjacking, and possession of weapons by a felon. Five of the counts were considered "special circumstances," which could make them eligible for the death penalty.

Because Bracamontes had several aliases, the judge first asked if he was being charged under the correct identity. It was then we actually learned his real name: Luis Enrique Monroy Bracamontes.

After the arraignment, he was escorted back to the jail. It is policy for prisoners to be strip-searched after they've been in public. He refused to cooperate.

"No! Fuck you! I'm not your bitch!" he snarled at the deputy. "You guys can't force me to do anything here. Do you know why I shot the first cop? Because he tried to search my car!"

****

Auburn Police Department
Tuesday, October 28, 2014

Moose attended a critical incident debrief held by Auburn Police Department. Afterward, a detective approached him.

"Hey, Mike, we need to do your interview. Any chance we can get that done tonight?"

"Well, I haven't reviewed anything. I haven't slept since. But okay."

They retreated to the office, and Moose recounted the day Michael died in full detail. It was like he was there all over again, and it took everything he had to finish.

By the time he walked out of the interview, he was spent. He couldn't catch his breath, so he took a moment before walking down the stairs.

Krista Wood[29] , an investigator with the DA's office, greeted him.

"Hey, Krista, didn't you go to Mikey's autopsy?"

"Yeah, just came from there."

"What'd you learn?"

"You don't want to know, Simmons."

"Krista, that's not an option for me. I *have* to know."

She gave some detail, then added, "He was dead in a minute and a half, Mike."

Moose felt slightly better—it didn't matter that it had taken so long to get Michael to the hospital. He was already gone. There was nothing he could've done.

---

[29] This is a pseudonym.

But then the questions came in relentless waves—*what the hell did I miss out there? How did this happen?*

****

Bayside Church, Granite Bay
Wednesday, October 29, 2014

Liz and I are very close to our families. In fact, every Sunday evening, we have dinner at Liz's mother's house. Liz is the oldest child of seven, so you can imagine the love and chaos that comes with a large group of adults and children coming together each week. We rarely miss it. So of course, when the shooting happened, the family was very concerned and eager to hear about it.

The Law Enforcement Chaplaincy of Sacramento was very connected with our department, but we had only met Master Chaplain Mindi Russell briefly. In the wake of this trauma that had affected so many, she held a critical incident debrief at Bayside Church. Everyone was welcome, including family members.

Because Catherine, Liz's mom, lived around the corner from the church, we decided to meet together as a family first, so Liz and I could share what happened. Our families listened, but we ran out of time for each to respond.

We all trekked over to the debrief together. There were about 50 people there, and we went around the room allowing each participant to talk about their involvement or how they felt about what happened when they heard about it.

This time, I elected not to speak. I felt it'd be too much for those who were there, and I had just shared with my family. Chaplain Mindi then explained the potential reactions each of us might experience in the days to come. Afterward, people milled about drinking coffee and eating cookies.

I was still in a fog. Still amped and sleep-deprived. And although I talked with people that day, I have no idea what I said.

****

Greater Sacramento Region
Wednesday, October 29, 2014

The greater Sacramento community was mourning alongside our departments. Dutch Bros, a coffee franchise whose locations are stand-alone drive-up coffee shops, held a fundraiser, proceeds of which went to the Davis and Oliver families. Nine shop owners participated, using the hashtag #MakeLove to mark the event. Together, they raised $96,597 in one day! Since then, they have been overwhelmingly supportive of law enforcement, and have raised over $320,000 for the families of fallen officers in our area.

Danny was a huge Sacramento Kings fan and held season tickets. The basketball team honored Danny and Michael at their season opener by observing a moment of silence before the game. Danny's seat was empty, draped in his dress uniform and accompanied by a single white rose.

Cabral told me it was Michael Davis's birthday, and that his wife, Jessica, and PCSO had planned a block party for him despite his being gone. They treated it as a celebration of life. I had mentioned to Cabral that I wanted to meet Jessica and offer my condolences at some point. So when Cabral brought up the party, he reminded me of my request, adding that Jessica wanted to meet me, as well. Just as it was with Susan, I was not about to refuse Jessica anything. As much as I wasn't ready to meet her, I decided to go.

Liz and I met Cabral at Jessica's house in Rocklin. Due to the number of cars, we had to park pretty far away. As we walked toward the cul-de-sac, I saw a crowd had gathered and noticed a lot of PCSO cars. The BBQ in the street had taken over the entire court.

My anxiety grew. I had major guilt issues—surely every single deputy with PCSO blamed me for Michael's death and hated me for it. If I had taken care of business in Sac, Michael would still be alive. I felt like I was walking the gauntlet—at any moment, someone was going to yell at me or try to kick my ass.

Cabral told me about Michael Davis' partner, Mike "Moose" Simmons. He said Moose wanted to meet me, too, and reassured me that there was no blame for what happened to Michael. When we reached the end of the court, a very large guy walked over, grabbed me, and led me to a secluded side area of a neighboring house. It had to be Moose, and I was pretty sure we were going to throw down right then and there.

Reality couldn't have been further from the truth. Moose hugged me, and I hugged him back, both of us crying without a word.

We shared our stories. For most cops, a lack of information is horrible. Once Moose told me what happened from his standpoint, as horrible as it was, a weight lifted off my shoulders. Just knowing what took place gave me clarity.

"I'm sorry, Moose. Michael wouldn't be dead if I would've killed that guy."

Moose grabbed the back of my neck and locked his forehead with mine. "Now you listen, Scott. It's nobody's fucking fault, except that fucker who killed our partners. Nobody here is thinking what you're thinking. You can be 100% tactically correct, 100% in an OIS[30] , and people still die. I don't know why … it's your fucking time, errant rounds … even if you do everything tactically right, it could still turn out the way it turned out. Now knock it off!"

At another point, Moose also said, "If it started in Placer County, you would've fought your ass off to try and catch the guy, because we're all brothers no matter what patch we wear. There is no other place Mikey would've rather been. Don't take that away from him—that would be an insult."

I admitted I was nervous about meeting Jessica, and described what I had done with Susan. He warned me against it—he had done the same, and Jessica was very irritated with him. We talked for a little while more, and I introduced him to Liz. We eventually made our way inside to Jessica.

It turns out that Liz went to high school with Jessica's sister-in-law, Traci, who is married to Michael's brother Jason. We didn't know it then, but Jason and Traci would become close friends in the months to come.

When I approached Jessica, she gave me a hug and asked, "How are you doing?" She paused, and before I could answer, she said, "Never mind, dumb question!" We had a funny conversation about how many times people had said the same thing to her, and then she turned around and did it to me.

---

[30] Officer Involved Shooting.

Jessica was strong, but looked tired, as one might expect. We didn't stay long.

Meeting Jessica was a weight off my shoulders. Meeting Moose enabled me to fill in parts of the story I'd been missing, and I also made a lifelong friend. Moose and I became brothers for life—cops who lost our partners and will never be the same. Very few will ever truly understand how we feel, but all I have to do is give him a look or a nod, and he knows. He knows with all his heart.

****

Ancil Hoffman Golf Course, Sacramento
Thursday, October 30, 2014

The POP team needed a day of rest, so they decided to play a round of golf at Ancil Hoffman Golf Course. The folks at the golf course allowed us to play with a larger group, which was much appreciated. My friend Ralph also joined us to round out the numbers.

I suck at golf. A good day is if I end with the same ball I started with. I have never broken 100; half the time, I don't even keep score. I just like being outside on a nice day with my friends, smoking a cigar and having a beer or two. This round was exactly that.

At one point, Pratt tried to pet a squirrel on the green. It just sat there, so she got on all fours and crawled toward him making what she felt were squirrel noises. She got pretty close, and I believe someone snapped a picture, but he didn't let her touch him.

The day was relaxed and fun. We laughed a lot, and made fun of each other. We didn't talk about the shooting once. It was a short break from the hell we'd been enduring.

****

Granite Bay
Thursday, October 30, 2014

While I played golf, Liz decided to open our home to the spouses. Earlier that year, she had joined a LEOW[31] group led by Victoria Newman, author of A CHiP on my Shoulder. The group members were married to cops from all over the Sacramento region, and after the first meeting, Liz realized the need to get together with other cop wives. Because of the shooting, she thought it'd be a good idea to bring the wives together to hang out and talk.

About 30 women showed up over the course of the day, including some from the book club. Friends brought pastries and sandwiches for those who stopped by. Liz made some new friends, and those who came were encouraged. They also learned some things about being cop wives.

Crystal Mitchell, SSO Deputy Jeff Mitchell's widow, stopped by with Starbucks cold brew and wine. She told her story to those who were there and gave Liz some tips on how to help Susan. What an incredible help she was!

Placer County spouses had the same idea. Their spouse group was in its early stages, so they opened a home to their department spouses. Sixty women showed up!

****

Heredia Park, Roseville
Thursday, October 30, 2014

Danny's workout partner and daughter, Missy, were among the dozens of people who paid tribute to Danny by doing a workout together at Heredia Park. They wore dark blue shirts that read, "Do It For Dan." The workout included 714 exercise repetitions, as Danny's badge number was 714.

Afterward, each person took a candle and the group paused for a moment of silence. Missy finished the evening with these words:

---

[31] Law Enforcement Officer Wife.

"This meant so much to my dad. He loved to work out with each and every one of you. I just want you to know that, and thank you."

****

Granite Bay
Friday, October 31, 2014

Halloween was tough. It was exactly one week after the shooting, and I was still in a state of total guilt, sorrow, depression, and misery. My kids, on the other hand, just wanted to get in their costumes and go get candy.

Usually, we get pizza, invite family and friends over, and trick or treat in the neighborhood. This year, we limited the number of guests. I couldn't bring myself to wear a costume like I had in years past.

The kids were very excited as they ran from house to house. It did my heart some good to see them so happy and loving life. Mixed in with that joy was the guilt of being happy. I kept picturing Susan and the girls without Danny.

Near the end of the night, it started pouring rain, so we hightailed it back to the house. I was exhausted. I'd been trying to hide my feelings, faking it around others—and it completely drained me.

But I couldn't stop being a dad—I had to go on for our family.

******

Sacramento
Early November 2014

A second critical incident debrief was held a few weeks after the incident. I was told going in that it was a tactical debriefing, so I went. I had several questions I wanted answered.

None of the other team members attended, but we planned to meet for pizza later that night. Liz did not attend this time.

Cabral drove me to the Marconi station. A large conference room was set up with a table and big circle of chairs. Thirty to 40 people were already seated when I walked in. Most of the conversations stopped, and they stared at me. I knew something was up, because I didn't recognize quite a few people, and those I did recognize didn't belong in a tactical briefing.

The format started like every other stress debriefing, and that's exactly what it was—a critical incident stress debriefing for everyone involved who wasn't on the POP team.

I tried to be a good sport and sat through a lot of sharing. When it was my turn, I passed at first, but then realized that most of them had no idea what really happened. I knew it would ease their minds to hear. So, I told the story again, shaking, but not as badly as before.

The debriefing dragged on for hours, and I just couldn't be there any longer. I was about to leave when the on-duty dispatcher started sharing. Until then, I hadn't thought about how the incident would affect him.

When he was done, I apologized to the group, explaining that I had to go. I told the dispatcher that his calm demeanor, clarifying my radio traffic, and retransmitting what I said in a clear voice was comforting in the midst of a crazy situation. He dispersed critical information necessary to keep others safe.

Until this conversation with the dispatcher, I was torn up about whether or not I had actually provided information about the car and AR-15 to dispatch. I wrestled with thoughts of Michael Davis walking right into an ambush, unaware that the suspect was armed with the AR-15. Talking with the dispatcher and having him confirm that I did give him that information turned into a piece of the puzzle I didn't know I needed until that exact moment. The details helped me understand exactly what happened that day.

After leaving, I met Liz and the team at a pizza place—and had several drinks.

I barely slept that night. What I didn't know then that I know now is while I thought alcohol would help me sleep, it actually worked against me. Alcohol prohibits REM sleep, which is the sleep cycle that helps the brain process trauma. I'd been through something horrific, and my brain needed to process what happened. Drinking just made it worse.

PART TWO

MAYHEM

"Resist him, firm in your faith, knowing that the same experiences of suffering are being accomplished by the brotherhood all over the world ..."
1 Peter 5:9, NASB

Bagpipes play at Danny's Funeral. The Honor Flag is displayed directly in front of his flag-draped casket.

Photo taken by Randy Pench of Sacramento Bee.

Moose riding Michael's Harley at the Davis Funeral.

Photo taken by Randy Pench of Sacramento Bee.

11

FUNERALS

"The [honor] flag brought this kind of weird comfort to me during the funeral. I couldn't cry. I couldn't touch anything else. It brought meaning to me. It represented patriotism. It represented respect. I was humbled and proud to carry it."
—Deputy Darrell Amos

Adventure Church, Roseville
November 3, 2014

When a police officer is killed in the line of duty, the assault is on the community as a whole, not just on those who knew him/her. Peace officers serve and protect the public—and when someone lays his or her life down for others, it is a great sacrifice. It is for this reason that law enforcement funerals are attended by officers from many miles away, some even from other states and countries. There is protocol to be followed, and ceremonial tradition is incorporated.

Since I had come on as a deputy, our department had lost six officers in the line of duty. I didn't attend those funerals, because I didn't know the deputies well. Instead, I volunteered to work shifts for the guys who did. I didn't feel right taking a seat.

Because I had never attended a law enforcement funeral, I was not ready for the magnitude and impact of Danny's.

The day began early, meeting Danny's family, the POP team, and other officers at our old, brick union building in downtown Sacramento. We had breakfast together, and then Sheriff Jones presented Susan with a large plaque. The girls were given badge pendants, which were replicas of Danny's badge. They were a gift from Syd Curtis of S Curtis Fine Jewelry.

The memorial service was scheduled for 10:00 a.m., and we needed to be at the church by 9:00 a.m. So, we all got into our cars and caravanned to Adventure Church, which was a 20-minute drive.

When we arrived at the church, it was already very crowded, and one couldn't walk ten feet without running into someone with a badge. The church, which seats about 3,000, was packed, and many, many more stood in the hallways and outside. There were thousands of people there.

I was Susan's escort officer for the ceremony. I was told to go wherever she went and sit next to her in the front row per her request. I agreed, but didn't want Liz to be alone. But Liz always works things out—she quickly hooked up with the POP team and sat with them.

While waiting for the service to start, I was in a back room filled with lots of important people: Sheriff Scott Jones and most of our brass,[32] California Highway Patrol Commissioner Joe Farrow, a few other local chiefs, senators, and congressmen, and Governor Jerry Brown. Most of us could've lived without the politicians, but since Sacramento is the capitol of California, we have to tolerate politics. I tried to stay out of the way until things got started.

Sergeant Jason Ramos hosted the event. Everyone in the room stood, and every uniform saluted as I escorted Susan and the family to the very front of the massive sanctuary. The Sacramento Fire Pipes and Drums played traditional Celtic music while we walked, and once the family was seated, they paraded throughout the aisles. There were over two dozen bagpipers and drummers dressed in tartan kilts and hats.

I sat to Susan's left—directly in front of Danny's flag-draped casket. The honor guard detail that stood at either end of the casket rotated every 10 minutes. The officers in that detail were from far and near.

After the posting of colors by the Sacramento Sheriff Color Guard, Sergeant Ramos read a passage Susan had chosen:

> *"The bonds between officers are strong, and you look out for each other on sunny mornings and in the shadows of danger. Your loyalty to one another and your service to America is a great honor to the system of justice. Thank you all, family members, who are with us today. Our nation is grateful to you. We hope that you find strength to bear the loss."*

[32] Police leadership. This refers to the stars and bars on their uniforms that represent rank.

Sheriff Scott Jones started off the speeches with well-spoken but melancholy sentiments. He thanked Danny for his service and sacrifice, then apologized to Susan and the family.

> *"I want to tell you that I'm sorry. Not just for your loss, but for not making good on the promise that I make to every family that lends me their loved one—that I'll return that person safely at the end of each shift. I failed on that promise. But I will make you a new promise ... that we will hold Danny in a place of honor and distinction ... celebrate his life ... and he will never be forgotten."*

Sheriff Jones then went on:

> *"I, like everyone else who wears a badge, ask myself, 'Is it worth it?' Is it worth putting on a badge and uniform every day, dealing with society's worst, wondering if we're appreciated by anyone? Wondering if it's worth the physical and emotional price we pay? Wondering if push came to shove, would I really be willing to lay down my life for my community? Wondering if I had the chance, would I do it all again, or would I choose a different path?*
>
> *"Well, the answer for me and everyone here, and for Danny, I'm sure, is 'yes.' I would do it all again. Yes, it's worth it. Yes, we're appreciated. Yes, this profession—this calling—of the highest honor is worth the physical and emotional sacrifice we're asked to make. And yes, without hesitation or remorse, we would lay down our lives for the community we serve."*

Captain Matt Morgan then talked about how Danny knew what it meant to improve the community. He told of a community meeting a few weeks before his death during which a community member asked how he could contact Danny. "I always check my emails," Danny answered. Two other community members confirmed, saying how he indeed answered their emails and solved their issues. The room broke out in spontaneous applause for validating their concerns. Danny made them feel safe. Captain Morgan then said that 70 people from that meeting showed up at a candlelight vigil for Danny the previous week.

POP team Sergeant Chris Guerrero gave a speech while our team stood behind him. He thanked Susan, and said Danny was "irreplaceable." His voice broke as he told the Teddy Bear story. He talked about how Danny modeled the balance between work and family. Then he said he was proud of me—said that Danny and I were two peas in a pod. He mentioned that he was glad that I was there, because they could've lost me that day, too. He then read the Warrior Poem included at the beginning of this book.

Undersheriff James Lewis spoke after placing a Grant High School Pacers uniform over the podium. He and Danny had been childhood friends who attended Grant High.

The last speaker was Captain Dave Torgerson. He offered encouragement to all—first to Susan, and then to the POP team. Next, he said these words:

> *"To Danny's partner, Scott Brown. Brother, you're a hero. I'm 100% confident as I stand here saying that Danny wouldn't want any other partner covering his six. You did everything humanly possible to help your fallen brother as you forced a suspect in a position of advantage as a violent predator into a frightened prey trying to scramble and trying to escape. Your heroic efforts at the scene were instrumental in the apprehension and ultimate arrest of the suspect.*
>
> *"There is a short excerpt of a poem I want to share with you:*
> *"'To my Partner,*
> *You did all you could.*
> *I fell, you stood.*
> *You know, sadness was never my style.*
> *Those were the cards that we drew,*
> *Nothing else more to do*
> *Except remember me, Friend, with a smile.'"*

I tried to hold it together. They presented a slideshow celebrating Danny's life, which made me laugh and cry at the same time. I was a mess when "Amazing Grace" played on the bagpipes—to this day, I can't hear it without leaking a tear or two. It still amazes me that Chris Tomlin's version can inspire me to praise God, while the bagpipe version makes me sick to my stomach and full of sorrow.

At the end of the service, a parade of officers from every department filed by Susan to pay respects. Many friends were there, too, along with officers from NYPD, the Canadian Mounties, and a few Bobbies from England. Numerous officers from all over California attended, as well—too many to count. It was an example of the strength of the brotherhood cops have and a demonstration of the far-reaching impact Danny's death had on others. In what was one of the saddest moments of my life, I was deeply honored to be a member of the thin blue line.

The motor procession from the church to the cemetery tore my heart out. Following the Darren Wilson/Michael Brown incident in Ferguson, Missouri on August 9, 2014, law enforcement as a whole had been undergoing protests and accusations. But on this day, citizens lined the streets holding signs of support and many blue line flags. As we drove down Interstate 80, they joined the lighted patrol cars and fire engines on the overpasses, waving and standing at attention, saluting Danny. It was both a proud and sorrowful moment not to be forgotten.

The low of the funeral to the high of the procession was quite an experience. We said goodbye to Danny, but felt hope and love from the community afterwards. I was emotionally exhausted and spent at the end of the day. Not sure why—all I did was sit!

Following Danny's casket throughout the day was the United States Honor Flag. This flag has traveled over seven million miles by ground, air, and even on a space shuttle mission. The flag has been flown at military funerals, law enforcement funerals, state capitols, and war zones. During the funeral, it was displayed in front of Danny's casket. It was carried by a designated officer, Deputy Darrell Amos, Danny's first partner, who Susan had chosen for the honor. The flag is never to be carried by bare hands, but by a clean pair of white gloves. The gloves Deputy Amos wore were given to Susan after the service. He had to hold the flag in a specific manner, next to his heart. He was also to have an escort, because he couldn't touch anything except the flag. He chose his brother, Brian.

After a 15-minute drive to the cemetery, we proceeded to Danny's burial location. His casket was closed. That was the first time I saw Danny's badge beautifully engraved in the wood on the top.

I sat with Susan and her family and friends. All uniformed officers stood in rows to the south of the coffin. I felt so out of place, not being with them. When the ceremony started and the honor guard folded the flag, all of the officers saluted at attention. I did the same, but being the only uniform with the family, I did so alone. It felt strange, like I was not in the right place.

The ceremony consisted of the normal tributes expected at a graveside service. There were horses with uniformed riders and the horse with the backward boot in the stirrup to represent the rider-less horse. Police helicopters flew over, and just overhead, one broke off to represent one of our own was gone. This is the so-called “missing man formation.” It was so much to take in.

Although I expected a 21-gun salute, the sound of the guns shell-shocked me. I almost jumped out of my skin when they went off. I stood alone at attention, shaking all over. It was the first time I'd heard gunshots since the incident. The casings were later collected and most of them given to me. I later had them engraved with Danny's name, badge number, and End-of-Watch (EOW) date. I collected enough to give to the family and the team.

Afterward, at Susan's request, Liz and I joined her in a limousine to accompany her to the reception that followed. There were a lot of people eating and talking, but I was done. I had no desire to be there. Liz and I stayed for about an hour and then left, so I could rest up for the next day—because we were going to do the same thing all over again for Michael Davis's funeral.

Danny's death changed my perspective. Now, I am committed to attending local LEO funerals to honor the fallen no matter which patch they wear, and whether I knew them or not.

****

Adventure Church, Roseville
November 4, 2014

Many officers and dignitaries travel to attend services, so it was better to have Danny and Michael's funerals back-to-back. This way, people could attend both. Someone asked me why I would go to both—wasn't that too much? Yes, it was. But there was no way in heaven or hell that I wasn't going. I was not missing the funeral for the detective who died trying to catch my partner's killer.

Liz and I drove to the same church, having planned to sit in the back and hide. Those plans changed when Susan asked us to sit with her in the survivor section behind the dignitaries. Unable to say "no" to her, we did as she asked.

The service was amazing and very painful at the same time. After the opening bagpipes and the pastor's remarks, they played "Home Sweet Home" by Motley Crue. Pastor Ed Grover offered some meaningful words of encouragement, mentioning Job in the Bible.

Placer County Sheriff Ed Bonner was fatherly and comforting, mentioning my attendance at Michael's birthday party. He said to me directly, "Your grace and kindness helped us all. And we thank you."

Michael's brother, Jason, gave an incredible speech with his SET partners standing behind him. I was amazed at his strength. To lose a father and two brothers and still have the strength to stand up and represent your family and God in the way he did was inspiring. He, too, spoke to me directly. "I want to thank Scott, Danny Oliver's partner. You know, you can beat yourself up in these situations, but you never know what's gonna happen, and it's not your fault. And I thank you so much for being there for him." He also said to our department, "Sorry for Danny's loss; thank you for assisting in the apprehension of the suspect."

Jason concluded with words I'll never forget:

> *"There are two ways I can respond to this. I can be angry and bitter and resentful, or I can forgive and be free from the bitterness that will consume me if I don't. With Sheriff Bonner's words in my head, I am who I am. I am not him. That's not who I want to be. So, I choose to forgive."*

The entire audience united in a standing ovation for Jason.

After the service, we followed Michael's white hearse in the motorcade to a cemetery in Newcastle. Moose, dressed in his suit to honor his partner and best friend, rode Michael's Harley Davidson. The procession wound its way through back roads and a few small towns as people stood on every street corner saluting, holding signs, and waving. We drove by Del Oro High School, where a sea of students stood waving, saluting, and holding signs that read, "We Love Mike." We learned later the students were given a break to watch the processional.

It was a sight to behold … one I prayed I'd never see again.

****

Sacramento County Jail
November 4, 2014

Deputy Justin Work[33] conducted beginning-of-shift count in Sac County Jail. As he came to cell 301, he observed the inmate reading a large book on his bunk. This total separation inmate was on discipline for facility rule violations, so Work needed to check the book for contraband.

He opened the food port to the cell. "Give me the book," he ordered.

Bracamontes smiled, then walked slowly to the door. He handed the book to the deputy through the food port.

"That doesn't look like a Bible, now, does it? You can't have this while on discipline," Work said, closing the food port.

Bracamontes leaned into the window and snarled, "Fuck you! I should've killed you, too!"

Not 45 minutes later, Deputy Work and his partner conducted pill call. At cell 301, he asked Bracamontes if he wanted his medication.

"Yes," he replied.

Work opened the food port; the nurse handed Bracamontes his medication and closed the food port. The inmate stood with the medication by his side, staring at the deputy.

"Take your medication," Work ordered.

Bracamontes dropped the cup, and repeatedly kicked at it. "Fuck you, Work! Someone is fucking your wife! When you are at work, someone is fucking your wife!"

The deputies left him to rant, so Bracamontes activated the emergency button inside of his cell.

Another deputy activated the cell intercom from the control room. "What is your emergency?" he asked.

"Fuck you, someone is going to be waiting for you in your house when you get home. Someone is going to be there to kill you. Fuck you!"

****

[33] This is a pseudonym.

Auburn
Early November 2014

Moose was a mess. The trauma of Michael's passing was taking over his mind, his body, and his soul. The anxiety attacked him, hiding behind the fog of grief and reappearing whenever it desired. He lost his shit three to four times a day.

Moose wasn't normally a crier, but he was crying a lot. Nights were bad. He smelled blood all the time.

He realized he'd better get it together, or he wouldn't be able to work.

****

Sacramento County Jail
November 5, 2014

Sheriff Jones made a decision to transfer Bracamontes to the El Dorado County Jail in Placerville.[34] He did this to spare SSO and PCSO officers from having to interact with those responsible for the death of our deputies.

For Sacramento Deputy Brian Guzman[35] , this was a relief. Bracamontes was accused of killing two of his own and attempting to kill several others. He was a foul-mouthed piece of shit, as well. Guzman wasn't sorry to see him leave.

After Bracamontes left, Guzman entered the cell and stopped. All over the cell, scratched in lead pencil, were threats and rants. One of them read, "*The Sinaloa Cartel is watching all your fucking asses. You motherfuckers going to pay for all this shit.*"

---

[34] Monroy was moved to Yolo County Jail a week later.
[35] This is a pseudonym.

My men's group praying over Liz and me.

Photo taken by Jason Hensley.

12

CHURCH, SCUBA DIVING AND GOD

"The Lord is my rock, my fortress, my deliverer, my God, my stronghold in whom I take refuge, my shield, the glory of my salvation, and my high tower."
Psalm 18:2

Bayside Church, Granite Bay
Early November

The second Sunday after Danny was killed, we went to Bayside, our regular church. There was no way I could handle being in a large room with a couple thousand people, so we were given permission to watch the service from what they call the "Green Room"—the place where the pastors and worship team gather when they're not on stage. The guest speaker that morning was a man from Northern Ireland by the name of Andrew McCourt.

Andrew's father was a police officer in Northern Ireland and was shot in the line of duty. Andrew's travel companion was a man named Paul, whose great-great-aunt was Corrie Ten Boom, a survivor of the Ravensbruck concentration camp during World War II. After the service, our extended family joined us in the production room to spend some time with Andrew and Paul. Andrew shared how he felt as the son of a police officer, making special mention of the fear they were under in Northern Ireland. They checked the underside of their cars every morning for bombs, and one time, a bomb went off on the street where they lived.

Both Andrew and Paul spoke of their faith—how God was present, protecting and loving them in very dark times.

Unbeknownst to us at the time, Andrew was considering a job offer as one of our teaching pastors. Long story short, he moved his wife, Isabelle, and their four children to the United States, where they now serve. When Andrew's parents later came for a visit, we met together. Mr. McCourt told his story—being shot in the line of duty, and also about the bomb. He shared about how he and his wife tried to raise a family in Northern Ireland as a cop during those times. When I shared my incident, it came out easily. No matter the age difference, the country, or the culture, cops have a brotherhood that spans any gap.

Liz and Mrs. McCourt had their own conversation. At one point, Mrs. McCourt leaned into Liz and warned, "The nightmares will never end." This was their experience—Mr. McCourt still had nightmares from the trauma he witnessed many years ago. It seemed daunting to Liz, as she'd been a witness to the nightmares that plagued my sleep. But it was also hopeful, in a way, because they had learned to live with them.

Over the following years, Andrew would conduct many line-of-duty-death funerals in our area. He's been an incredible comfort to many of us, as he has a personal understanding of how the job affects us and our families.

As I continued to attend church in the Green Room, we got to know our lead pastors. Founding Pastor Ray Johnston, Senior Pastor Curt Harlow, and Worship Pastor (and Christian recording artist) Lincoln Brewster, as well as Andrew helped keep me grounded in my faith. They gave me great advice during key moments in my healing. To this day, I get check-in texts reflecting genuine concern for how I'm doing.

****

Rocklin

Jason Davis was struggling. The grief was fresh. There were problems at work, and problems at home. Life just wasn't good.

He missed Michael, and really needed to talk with him. Michael was like a father—a great listener and someone who was there any time he needed him.

Jason had lost so much. His father, his brothers. In the days after Michael died, Jason even felt like he'd lost a part of his soul.

His thoughts went to God—and he wondered where He was. He felt like God had never been there before and wondered why He wasn't near now.

****

Placer County Sheriff's Office, Auburn
November 2014

Moose wanted to go back to work, but protocol required him to be cleared by a clinician before he reported. He lied his ass off in his appointment, and the therapist bought it. He was back to work within a couple weeks post-incident.

This was not particularly a good thing, however. Moose didn't lose his "shit-magnet" status, and he still wasn't sleeping. Truth be told, he was barely keeping it together.

On November 25, Placer County Homicide got a call from a woman who bought an abandoned storage unit and its contents. When she took a look inside, she found a freezer that smelled really bad. Moose responded, as he was on call.

It turned out to be a full-term fetus, and once they removed it from the freezer, they found another just underneath. Two babies … first frozen in a freezer, then thawed out and decomposing. The decomposition suggested it hadn't been long since they died.

That case will haunt Moose forever, because ultimately, there was no closure. The wait for the forensic evidence results was over two years, and time ran out. The case remains unsolved, despite the plausible theory Moose had developed.

On December 22, a man went crazy and shot rounds off in his own neighborhood. Moose was on call and responded to the scene still in progress. On arrival, the guy was shooting rounds inside his house.

Moose joined the team at the Command Post when a volley of automatic rounds went off. His lieutenant joked, "I want every round accounted for."

Moose didn't think that was funny. "Oh yeah, I'll be sure to personally count each one of the thousands of rounds that are going off."

The SWAT team eventually deployed gas inside the house to stop the shooting, but the suspect set the house on fire. In the end, the suspect was shot and killed by a deputy, and the house burned down. Moose worked to secure the scene with a fatality, a fire, thousands of rounds all over the street, and bullet holes in surrounding buildings and vehicles. 14 officers had engaged in the firefight—twelve from PCSO and two from outside agencies. The investigation was complex.

Moose worked these two investigations at the same time on very little sleep, while still fighting off the grief and effects of trauma.

****

Transport from Sacramento County Jail to El Dorado County Jail
December 9, 2014, 9:38 a.m.

On December 9th, Bracamontes appeared in court and heard for the first time that the District Attorney's Office was seeking the death penalty. His defense attorneys asked for a continuance until February to review the case.

Several deputies transported Bracamontes back to Placerville after this court appearance. The inmate sat in the back of the guarded van, wearing his orange jumpsuit.

The van passed a white California Highway Patrol unit, and suddenly, Bracamontes came alive. He stared down the CHP officer, blurting out threats and obscenities.

The deputies turned around to see the commotion. Bracamontes leaned in close to the metal screen that separated them and spewed, "Pigs … kill the pigs … pop pop pop pop pop … are you going to shoot me? I'll kill you … kill the pigs!"

****

Granite Bay
December 9, 2014

That evening, Liz watched KCRA's (one of our local news stations) coverage of Bracamontes's and Monroy's appearance in court.

"Prosecutors also announced the suspect tried to kill at least four other deputies in that crime spree six weeks ago," the reporter said. "They now say on the day the suspect shot and killed Deputy Danny Oliver outside this Motel 6, he also tried to kill Oliver's partner, Deputy Scott Brown. That brings the count of attempted murder charges to five. Four of those victims are deputies."

That was the first time my name was mentioned on the news. It was also the first time I was referred to as a "victim of attempted murder."

****

Cozumel, Mexico
January 2015

In December, I attended the Christmas Eve service at Bayside Church. Bayside's Christmas services are a huge production, complete with performers, music, message, and wonder. Our annual tradition is to bring a group of people to the service, and then afterward, to head to my mother-in-law's house for a big dinner.

One of the men who comes regularly is Tad Easterday. Tad is not only a longtime family friend, but also a retired lieutenant with my department. We saw each other regularly at family get-togethers. He is always smiling and telling good stories. I have always liked and admired him.

Since Tad retired, he's told me about amazing scuba diving trips to all sorts of cool places. He knew I loved to scuba dive, too, and always invited me to go. I politely reminded him I still worked for a living, so couldn't just up and leave. I also had a wife and three kids who spent most of my money. He laughed and said, "Maybe next time, then."

This particular Christmas Eve was no different. As Tad shared about his most recent exploit, I wished I were on a tropical island and under the water. He mentioned his group, which consisted mostly of retired first responders and some wives, was heading to Cozumel the first week in January. He asked if I'd like to join him.

Of course! I had the time, but didn't have the money. He answered by asking if money weren't an issue, could I go? I told him if pigs could fly, yes, but that money was definitely an issue, and I appreciated the offer. He dropped it at that point and the evening went on.

A few days later, with help from Liz, Tad booked me for a week at an all-inclusive resort in Cozumel. He booked my airfare and scheduled five days of diving. It was completely free for me. I just had to hightail it to San Francisco to get my passport renewed! I was completely blown away and shed some tears.

As we took off from Sacramento Airport, I watched the city shrink behind us and immediately felt better. Every person traveling with us knew about the shooting. They were conscientious not to bring it up. At that point, I didn't want to talk about it.

We landed and got a cab to the resort. No matter how hard I tried or complained, the group wouldn't let me pay for a dang thing the entire week. I was overwhelmed by their love and generosity, and frankly, I didn't know how to receive it.

Time with the group was great. They were very kind. Several times, while having a beer in the giant spa, we talked about the shooting. Not only did it feel good to talk about it, but when I shut it down or got choked up, they seemed to understand. No one judged me, and all seemed genuinely concerned for my wellbeing.

I took time by the water alone to do some reading. At that point, the images of the shooting and Danny's death continued to replay in my mind over and over again. I needed a break from those thoughts, but also allowed myself to get lost in them. I was on a tropical island with no work, no family, and no distractions. It was rest for my soul, which I desperately needed.

The diving was the best therapy. I was submerged and weightless in warm water. Everything around me was bright and beautiful. Controlled breathing of clean, pressurized air added to the weightless meditation on virtually another planet. Multi-colored fish, eels, turtles, and countless other amazing marine animals captured my attention and gave me a brief mental reprieve.

After each dive, we sat around and debriefed—what we saw, how the gear performed, and other topics that had nothing to do with the shooting. I felt normal for the first time in months, and I loved every minute.

As the trip drew to an end, I thought about how God had put Tad in my life. How, through his loving heart and shared experiences, he felt a prompting and followed through. There is no way he could've known what it would mean to us down the road. I have thanked Tad on many occasions, but I will never be able to repay him for what he did. Not just the money he spent, but the peaceful experience he provided in the midst of chaos. I will never forget it. I now pray that everyone has a Tad in their lives.

As we landed in Sacramento, the troubles and worries came right back, pressing on me with the weight of a mountain. The difference was, I now had good memories to go with the bad. That weight I carried, as heavy as it was, seemed less so than before the trip. At that time, a little lighter load made all the difference.

****

Granite Bay

As a Christian, I struggled with the concept of forgiveness, and what that really means. I kept hearing the song, "Forgiveness" by Matthew West on KLOVE radio and it would tear me up every time.

I thought if I were a true man of God, I should be able to forgive him as God has forgiven me.

But I couldn't get there.

My definition of forgiveness meant that I had to excuse him for what he did. He killed my partner and friend. He tried to kill me. He wanted me dead. There was no way that I could give him a pass for that. The more I learned of Bracamontes, the more I could not forgive him for the person he is. He spread evil easily, then laughed about it and promised to do more. He is pure evil. I cannot be okay with that. Based on that definition, I never will.

But with help from pastors, a few good friends, and God, I came to realize that I had a wrong concept of forgiveness. It was finally drilled into my head that I am not excusing his actions or even the horrible person he was and continues to be.

I am releasing my obsessive anger, my judgment, and giving myself permission to not allow him to ruin my heart and live in my soul any longer. I have to move on from him and what he did to Danny, to me, to my fellow deputies, and to my family.

Judgment isn't mine, it's God's. Bracamontes's sin is not mine to avenge. Taking my anger out on him is a great temptation, I admit. But I am to leave that in the hands of the Righteous and Almighty God who loves justice.

The rose (Liz) between two thorns (Moose and I)!

From the Brown photo album.

13

RETURNING TO WORK

"The true warrior fights not because he hates what's in front of him, but because he loves what's behind him."
G.K. Chesterton

Sacramento
February 2015

In the aftermath of the shooting, Sheriff Jones told me to take as much time off as needed. If I needed a new assignment, let him know. I took about three-and-a-half months. During that time, I focused on getting my head right and ready to go back to work.

I sought therapy—some methods worked better than others. The most helpful was journaling—writing out the images in my head. Soon after I started journaling, the nightmares grew less frequent and intense. Talk therapy—both in groups and with a therapist—was helpful. It seemed as though the incident just needed to come out, instead of being bottled up inside.

I was offered medication, but I didn't want to go that route. Because I couldn't sleep for more than 30 minutes at a time, I took an anti-anxiety sleep aid for about a week. Doing so ended the 30-minute wake-up cycle, so I stopped using it and have slept much better.

It took some time, but soon I started thinking about getting back to work. I wrote a short checklist to complete before I returned.

The first on the list was to talk with others who'd been through something similar and ask their advice. I met with Deputy Scott Padgett, Larry Canfield's partner, over dinner with our wives. Canfield was killed in the line of duty on November 11, 2008. Padgett said he made the mistake of returning to work too early at three weeks. "Take as much time as you think you need, and then add more time," he suggested.

I also met with Deputy Duke Lewis, who was shot in the line of duty by four robbery suspects who jumped out of a car and opened fire. He shared that the first time he pulled over a car after returning to work, he had anxiety. "Just keep doing it, Scott," he told me. "That anxiousness will go away eventually."

Second, I went to the range. It was crucial to make sure I could still shoot and handle gunfire without panicking. That wasn't a departmental requirement, but something I needed for confidence. With the first few magazines, my heart raced, and I couldn't hit the broad side of a barn. Normally, I had no problems qualifying. After a while, I calmed down and was hitting the paper like I should.

Third, I requested a new bulletproof vest. My old one had officially expired several years earlier. Although it may have been fine, I promised Liz I would get it replaced before returning to work.

One of the biggest challenges was adjusting to the reduced time with my wife and kids. After three months, I had gotten used to being home with them. I went to the kids' school events and games. Liz and I spent more time together than ever before, and we both loved it.

We had many conversations about the right time to return, after checking off our short list of "requirements." She was not ready for me to go back. Honestly, she wasn't sure if she would ever be. Prior to October 24th, she never worried while I was at work. That changed. I hated the idea of her at home worrying.

I also knew if I didn't go back soon, it would be difficult to go back at all. I was so happy just being a dad and husband that the thought of returning to a world that hated me didn't sound appealing. It downright scared me. On the other hand, I had to make a living and provide for my family, and I couldn't picture myself doing anything else.

I returned to the POP team in early February 2015. I had to prove to myself that I could still do it. If I couldn't go back as a POP officer, I wouldn't be good at anything. I promised Liz I would stay in the office for a week and then keep my field activity to a minimum to ease back into it.

I didn't sleep much the night before. I was supposed to be to work by 7:00 in the morning, but I took my time getting ready. I kissed Liz and said goodbye to the kids like before. Starting up my car, I heard a knock on my driver's side door window. I turned to see Connor standing there. I rolled down the window.

"Be safe!" he said, then kissed me on the cheek and walked back inside.

My son had never done that before. Thank God he didn't ask me to stay; I might not have left.

I drove down the freeway toward the office missing Danny so much, it hurt. I wasn't really ready to go back. Exiting the freeway, it took all my will not to loop around and head right back home. Somehow, I managed to get to the station, park, and enter the building.

The POP team was talking, but as soon as I rounded the corner, everyone stopped and stared. I felt out of place. After an awkward moment, they must have decided I wasn't going to blow up, because they hugged me, welcoming me back.

Since I had been off, some of the team had been promoted and moved on to our detective division. I knew the replacements, so that wasn't too bad. The hard part was that no one was willing to sit at Danny's desk. For some reason, they felt like that should be my new spot. I never told them how hard it was to sit in his chair. I would've rather sat outside by the dumpster.

When lunch came around, we decided to go out to eat. I jumped in the car with Pratt, who was assigned to babysit me for a while. En route, Deputy McCabe decided he just had to pull a car over. I was in the cover unit, but as the lights came on and they approached the car, my anxiety level went through the roof. All I could picture was the driver waiting with a gun until they got close enough to shoot them both.

That didn't happen. The driver was issued a warning and released. Problem was, I was in a full panic attack by then and had to walk around to calm down before we could leave.

After I calmed down with a little help from my partners, the stop no longer scared me. But how I reacted did. If I continued to react like that to a simple vehicle stop, I'd be done. I couldn't go through another 15 years thinking like that.

However, I didn't give up or give in to the fear. I would be lying if I said it didn't happen again, but it got easier. Eventually, the fear disappeared altogether. I drove the same car on the POP team for another six to eight months before promoting to detective.

****

Transports between El Dorado County Jail and Sacramento County Jail February 4, 2015, 7:00-10:34 a.m.

Bracamontes was placed in the back of the transport van with his body facing the rear doors and secured. Three deputies and a sergeant, one armed with an AR-15 rifle, took their positions in the van and left the Sally Port of El Dorado County Jail with a trail van behind them.

Immediately, Bracamontes turned his body, smiled at the deputies directly, then blurted out:

"They're going to be breaking me out today. Be careful you don't mess around. They're waiting for me right here!

"You better load your guns … be ready …

"The Sinaloa Cartel is coming for me today; you ever hear about it?

"You have enough people … they're right there!

"Watch it!

"Watch out for the bushes and shit … snipers!

"You better run!

"Watch out!"

The deputies were silent. But he continued:

"You guys don't trust me, or what?

"I want to offer you guys a job … Sinaloa, man.

"I'll give you some benefits … I'll get you some pensions.

"This car right here gonna kill you …

"What kind of gun is that? Do you guys feel challenged? He challenged me!

"That truck looks suspicious.

"Here's my exit … I hope you brought enough guns … you better get ready! The guys that are gonna come after me, they're serious. They won't kill you with shitty guns."

Bracamontes shifted in his seat, raising his hand to make a gun shape. The traffic grew congested, and the trail van came to a stop behind them. Bracamontes pointed his "gun" at the officers in the trail van, smiled, and sounded, "Bop … bop … bop … bop!"

And then he did it again, until they arrived at the Sacramento County Jail.

After his court appearance, our deputies escorted him through the garage receiving area. He looked directly at the sergeant and blurted, "Bop … bop … bop … bop … bop … bop … You don't like me, huh?"

Once locked in the cage in the back of the van, he continued his threats:

"The one with the rifle … he's gonna go down.

"The one with the rifle is the first one that's gonna go down. I said, 'The one with the rifle is the first one that's gonna go down!'

"You feel so brave with the rifle? You feel so powerful? Ha, ha, ha, ha … no? Yes? Ha, ha, ha, you scared? You shaking?

"What do you think about a bullet in the middle of your forehead?"

He continued to harass the officers all the way back to El Dorado County. They remained silent.

I can imagine their temptation to retaliate. I can also imagine how psychologically difficult that would've been to listen to.

The investigation was digging up evidence that Bracamontes was indeed tied to the Mexican drug cartel, so it didn't completely seem like an ambush was out of the realm of possibilities. Pure evil.

****

Placer County Sheriff's Office, Auburn
February-June 2015

On February 21, 2015, Moose was assigned yet another stabbing homicide out of Roseville. A young man brought a knife to a fistfight and cut the jugular of another young adult at a party. The victim dropped and bled out right on the sidewalk.

Moose dealt with several drunk kids as witnesses. He got lucky on surveillance and license plate readers and had the suspect in custody within 47.5 hours.

The premature return to work, coupled with difficult cases, had Moose in a bad place. By the end of that month, he couldn't even go into the office. If he made it to his desk, he couldn't stay. He was trying to just survive at that point, and no one knew how much he was suffering.

In the meantime, there were fundraising events for Michael's family, events to honor Michael, and memorial ceremonies for Placer County and California, which all take their toll emotionally.

In May, Moose went to Police Week[36] with other Placer County deputies and our deputies. He made good connections with his coworkers and spent time with family in Virginia, but he drank way too much.

His life started to unravel when he returned from Police Week. He recognized the fact that he was not doing well mentally and started to panic. He had to say something before someone at work noticed and the situation grew worse. He reached out to a supervisor and asked to see a therapist while continuing to work.

The supervisor agreed, but then the paperwork threw a glitch in the process. There was a disconnect between the therapist's office and the department, which halted the process.

A month went by without approval or referral. He never heard another word.

Moose decided that he had to just cope. It was another year and a half that Moose tried to hold it together, without sleep and without help.

---

[36] Every year, police officers from all over the country head to Police Week in Washington D.C. to honor the previous year's fallen officers. More details in the next chapter.

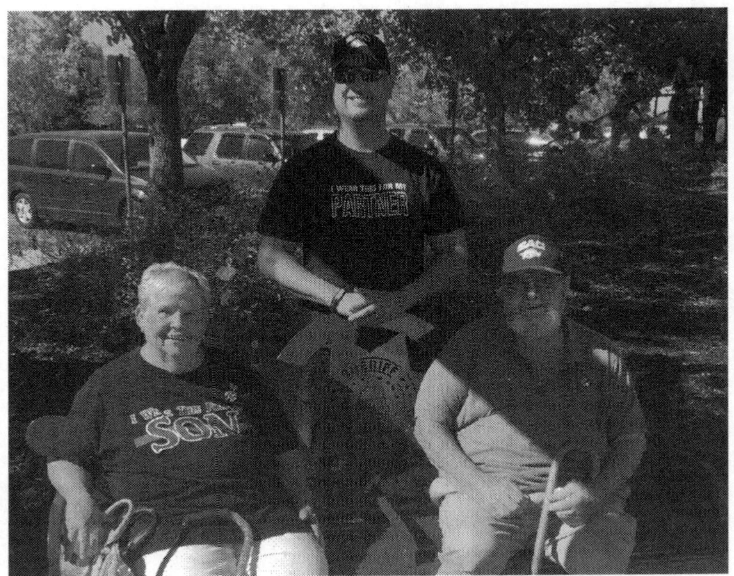

Bill and Jeri Oliver sitting on the Danny Oliver bench in Orangevale.

From the Brown album.

At the Law Enforcement Memorial Wall in Washington D.C. I am getting a wall rubbing from Danny's name.

From the Brown album.

14

MOURNING AND HONOR

"Unless someone like you cares a whole awful lot,
nothing is going to get better, it's not."
—Dr. Seuss

In the months that followed Danny's death, we attended many memorials. I felt it was my duty to represent at each and every one.

On March 13, 2015, the small community of Foothill Farms where Danny had been in charge while on the Pop team held a bench dedication. The ceremony was very nice, and the community came out to celebrate with a barbeque. On the way home, Connor told Liz that it was a nice bench they buried Danny under. Liz explained to him that it was something to honor him, not where he was buried. This was the first event we brought the boys to.

On October 11, 2015, a second memorial bench in Orangevale was dedicated to Danny. He made quite an impact in that blue-collar area of Sacramento. It is one of the most beautiful benches I have ever seen, designed with part of the Sheriff's Department emblem in the backrest and painted blue. Just in front of the bench is a plaque that had Danny's name and end-of-watch date. To go just a bit further, the bench and plaque was covered with a trellis that was created, designed, and built by a local youth as part of his Eagle Scout project.

On November 7, 2015, the Carmichael community put Danny's name at Patriot Park on what they named the "Wall of Honor." The wall contained the names of a few of our fallen deputies along with members of the military from the area who had died in the line of duty. Most of the Sheriff's Department administrative staff showed up for the ceremony.

In February 2018, a park plaza was dedicated in Danny's name at a brand-new park on Eastern Avenue. The arch with Danny's name on it is beautiful and the memorial plaque is well done. The park opening was attended by several hundred people and was a huge success.

These events show how much the community loved Danny and

what he stood for. Even though they were great events, they were very painful to attend. It was like getting a scab ripped off and kicked in the junk every time. I attended every one, to represent the department and Danny. I owed it to him, his family, and the community to have a representative from the POP team present.

These events triggered me in several ways, and the effects lasted a few days. I knew the night after an event I wasn't going to sleep much. My mind replayed memories, which caused the nightmares to return, and then headaches, stomach problems, and lack of appetite ensued. My temper was short with my family, and my motivation at work went down the toilet.

As time passed, my recovery time shortened. I have learned to live with the symptoms, and have educated myself to know they're normal. I can get through them by talking with others, counseling, and a lot of prayer.

****

Rocklin

One night, Jason Davis woke with a start. He laid back down, but his brain was fully awake.

As Traci slept beside him, he thought about his life—and how he missed Michael, his dad, and his younger brother, Chris. He thought about who he'd become as a man, how he was now his mother's only surviving son, and the mistakes he'd made throughout his life.

At that moment, a Bible verse popped into his head. "For if we go on sinning willfully after receiving the knowledge of the truth, there no longer remains a sacrifice for sins, but a terrifying expectation of judgment and the fury of a fire which will consume the adversaries." It was from Hebrews 10:26-27.

God definitely wasn't a priority—in fact, God was his insurance policy. Jason had done some research years ago into whether or not God existed and came away feeling ambiguous. He wasn't even sure if God was real or not. But just in case, he went to church here and there. If there was a place called hell after death, he certainly didn't want to go there!

So, for the first time in years, he prayed in the dark to a God he didn't know.

****

May 2015

Every May, law enforcement communities memorialize the previous year's fallen officers. Departmental memorials remember those who died in the history of their department. Surviving families attend, both from the previous year and before. State memorials pay tribute to fallen officers from the previous year. The national memorial is a week-long event surrounding the service that honors the fallen from the previous year. Thousands of police officers and survivors throughout history head for Washington D.C. to honor their fallen loved ones.

Sacramento Area Memorials

For SSO, the first ceremony was at the academy, where we have a rose garden to honor fallen deputies and K-9's killed in the line of duty. Families choose a rose, and we add that type of bush to the garden.

Susan and I sat in the front among a few rows of folded chairs. The sheriff gave a speech, talking about the rose bush planted in Danny's honor, and why Susan chose that particular rose.

The academy recruits were in attendance, and it served as a good reminder of the risks.

Later that day was the local memorial on Arden Way, where we honored both Sacramento County deputies and Sacramento Police Department officers killed in the line of duty. This service contained traditional memorial elements, including the rider-less horse, bagpipes, and a 21-gun salute.

I was once again Susan's escort. We listened to the roll call of names of fallen officers both past and present. I regretted not knowing the names and stories of the officers in my department who had lost their lives in the line of duty. I have not missed another since, trying each time to pick a new name and learn who the person was and how he or she died. Unfortunately, there are a lot of names even for a local memorial, so I haven't gotten through them all yet.

I was exhausted at the end of the day. I found it perplexing to be so tired, when all I really did was sit on my butt, hug a few people, and cry a little. It just goes to show how much effect emotions have on the body.

California State Memorial

We are blessed to have the state memorial in Sacramento. It is located to the west of the front entrance to the Capitol located in downtown Sacramento. It's a circular concrete structure with four bronze statues. One represents police departments, another for sheriff's offices, and one for highway patrolmen. The fourth is a mourning widow sitting on a bench with a child in her lap. There are metal plates along the memorial depicting the names and end-of-watch dates of fallen officers in California.

During the May memorial, there are tented chairs for the survivors, bleachers for extra family and important guests, and a stage where the ceremony is held.

The night before the memorial service, many will gather for a candlelight vigil. Survivors wear t-shirts designed to honor their fallen officer. I escorted Susan to the vigil; then, a few of us went to the hotel lounge for a drink. We called it early, as we had to be up with the sun the next day.

The next day, I dressed in my class-A (dress) uniform for breakfast. We wear these for graduation, interviews, promotions, formal events, and funerals. Before Danny's funeral, I had only worn mine at graduation. After so many years, my dad bod would not fit anymore, so I bought a new one. Deputy Tim Mullin, a friend on the honor guard, prepped my uniform for me, making sure it was ready: fabric pressed, shoes and badge shined, belt polished, and the keepers, pins, patches, and badges all in their proper location. I was so grateful to him.

The SSO uniform is creased polyester-blend black pants, black, long-sleeve button-up shirt with a collar, and black socks and shoes. There is a nameplate over the left breast pocket, and medals earned are placed above it. On the left sleeve, deputies have horizontal hash marks—one for every five years in service. There are department patches on each shoulder. Last but not least is a clip-on tie with a tie clip that is placed near the top flap of the breast pocket. On our heads, we wear a Smokey the Bear campaign hat. This is black with a metal badge in the middle, and silver rope around the brim and back to keep the hat in place.

A black leather weave belt is placed through the belt loops of the trousers, and then our black gun belt is secured by four leather keepers to hold it in place. The duty belt consists of a black leather gun holster, two leather magazine holders, and one handcuff case.

After breakfast, Susan and I walked across the street to the State Capitol building and were ushered into a large room on the first floor. Governor Jerry Brown entered with his aides and protective detail (who are CHP officers in suits) and gave a short speech.

Governor Brown had a long history of passing bills and policies that not only hurt law enforcement, but the citizens of California. Most notable is his stance on immigration and sanctuary states/cities, which is directly related to Danny's death, as Bracamontes had been deported three times. Brown also decimalized many violent crimes, making them misdemeanors, essentially taking away any consequences the suspects might have received. He has emptied our jails and prisons, putting criminals back on the streets to commit more crimes.

On a personal level, he was heard telling Danny's mom Jeri at the funeral that she should be grateful he attended, because he "should've" been out on the campaign trail.

We were paraded up to shake his hand, which I did out of respect for his position, not his person.

Afterward, we waited for what seemed like hours to make our way from the Capitol to the memorial about 100 yards away. Event coordinators told us they would call out our officer's name, and we would walk out with our group. Our group included Susan, Sheriff Jones, Missy, Jenny, Jeri, Bill, me, and Danny's brothers and sisters. Liz was seated in the stands.

When Danny's name was called, we walked out the door to a sight I will never forget. Thank God I wore sunglasses, because it choked me up. The walkway was lined with many hundreds of cops in their class-A uniforms, all standing at attention, saluting as we walked by. As we crossed the street, I saw hundreds of motorcycles, horses, and more officers, including our own department.

In 2014, California lost 13 officers in the line of duty. The memorial ceremony was long, and it was hot. Kamala Harris, who was the Attorney General at the time, read the names of the deceased as a white dove was released for each. Speakers included Captain Dave Torgerson, who had spoken at Danny's funeral, and Jason Davis. Again, I was amazed at the strength Jason had to stand up and talk so openly about losing his brother and father.

Susan stayed strong through all of it. But it had been a long week with all of the ceremonies, and it was starting to show. We needed rest, yet weren't going to get much, because we were to leave for Washington D.C. in a few days.

The D.C. trip presented another point of anxiety. Liz and I were living paycheck to paycheck and didn't have money to spare. Although my transportation and hotel were taken care of by my Union, Liz's expenses were not covered. We both agreed she needed to go. Typically, I would share a room with another guy to cut costs, but we worked it out so that she could stay with me. Still, we had to find a way to get her there. We prayed and hoped something would present itself.

On the cutoff date, we received a check from the County of Sacramento. It was for the EXACT amount, down to the penny, we needed to buy Liz a plane ticket to D.C. The letter that came with it stated the county was reimbursing me for something they had previously deducted from my check.

Now I ask you, when does a government organization admit to a mistake without you pointing it out first, and, on that note, give you money you didn't ask for? The answer is never! The Lord wanted Liz and I to go, and He made it happen! Of that, I have no doubt.

Police Week 2015

In 1962, President John F. Kennedy signed a proclamation that designated May 15 as "Peace Officers Memorial Day."

Thousands of cops and surviving families from all over the world come to Washington D.C. each year during what we call "National Police Week." It has grown to include many events surrounding the service, including a candlelight vigil, a 5/10K run, the Concerns of Police Survivors Conference, a police resource fair, special dinners, a car rally, Honor Guard and bagpipe competitions, and two 300-mile rides in which survivors ride bicycles in honor of fallen officers from other cities to Washington D.C. At the center of it all is the National Law Enforcement Officers Memorial, located in Judiciary Square in D.C.

The memorial is made up of two curved concrete walls on either side of a large court area with a reflection pool on one end and the entrance to the subway on the other. Every year, the names of the fallen are engraved into the wall. Books contain the list and locations of each name, as well as slips of paper and small pencils. The paper and pencils are for rubbings—you can place the paper against an officer's name and rub the pencil over it for a souvenir. During Police Week, survivors will place pictures, signs, notes from kids, and tributary objects near their officer's name. I've seen a few beers set beside names, as well. Many officers and survivors spend time at the wall talking with others, saying prayers, and/or spending quiet moments remembering.

Seeing Danny's name on the National Law Enforcement Officers Memorial wall (Panel 26-E:29) with so many others was heartbreaking. Liz and I visited it several times—sometimes just the two of us, and others with the team and family. Being there was a very emotional experience, not only for the memories of Danny it brought back, but in seeing all the other mourning families. Some were crying, some were laughing, and others were talking with random strangers about their officers. Several times, I found myself talking with someone I had never met about either Danny or his or her fallen. Each felt like family ... I think because we shared the same loss, the same grief.

Several people from the department came, including the POP team, Deputy Bobby French, Union President Kevin Mickelson, and Lieutenant Santos Ramos, who was Susan's appointed escort. We stayed in the same hotel, together with hundreds of other cops from everywhere. Schedules varied according to our responsibilities, but Liz and I headed for the wall first. We then took some time to visit some of the other sites, and then, we watched the Police Unity Tour bicyclists arrive at the Memorial. Hundreds of people were there, waiting for the riders, crying, laughing, and placing tributes on the wall. Many would gladly talk about their officer and then want to hear about yours. It was one big, horrible, sad, bonded family who had never before met.

The riders were escorted by motor units from all over the country. Many of them (both motor and bicycle) were crying as they rode between the walls. They looked tired, but overwhelmed by the response they received. An hour or so later, the riders came back to rest while visiting with the survivors. One of them was Detective Scott Swisher, who presented me with a metal memorial bracelet for Danny. I still wear it every day.

Kelly's Irish Times is a small bar located on F Street NW in D.C. It is tradition for cops to crowd the place in honor of their fallen officers. Picture hundreds of knuckle-dragging cops crammed shoulder to shoulder in a small bar with drinks flowing. With that many Type-A personalities in one room, there is bound to be a fight or two.

Not at Kelly's. People came together to honor friends, partners, or family members they had lost. If anyone starts to get loud, they are reminded why they are there, and it's squashed. On this day, cops talked, drank, hugged, and sung along to the DJ's music. We had a good time, which was much needed.

Kelly's walls are covered in patches from every agency, many of which are memorial. The shelves are adorned with helmets, boots, hats, and other personal effects that have been donated by those who have suffered loss to honor their fallen.

SSO and PCSO arranged a night at Kelly's to honor Danny and Michael. Both Sheriff Jones and Sheriff Bonner were there. Each gave a quick, appropriate speech for Danny and Michael, and then we raised a glass in their honor. That night, we became one department and one family … brothers and sisters in blood.

The patio outside has a short, black, iron fence that is lined with car doors from patrol vehicles that have been brought by agencies. My agency had brought a door years ago with the names and EOW dates of every fallen officer from our department written on the window. Danny's name was added at the bottom, and most of our team then signed and left messages for the fallen on the rest of the door.

The next event was the Candlelight Vigil, always held on the evening of May 13. That year, it was held at the memorial wall. Although Susan had been assigned a different escort, she decided I would be with her throughout the week. I sat with her at the vigil in the survivor's area near the front. Everyone else had to scramble to find seats where they could, including Liz and the team. The entire plaza was packed, overflowing onto side streets.

Uniformed leaders and dignitaries read the 126 names of fallen officers of 2014 as well as nearly 100 more from years past who had not been honored. Many of those names were of officers who had passed away from illnesses related to 9/11. We held candles, had a moment of silence, and were awed by a bright blue light that shone from one building to the top of the stage. Officers sang songs of tribute and gave speeches honoring law enforcement as a whole.

As Susan's official escort, I was to be at her side at the official events—the candlelight vigil and memorial service. Unofficially, I stayed with her as often as possible. I was there for emotional support and to handle anything unexpected that came up. We had our ups and downs throughout the week. We laughed, cried, and everything in between.

On May 15, the memorial ceremony and Honor Roll Call was held in front of the Capitol Building. This day was long and exhausting with several twists and turns.

The first complication was Susan's decision to name me escort instead of Santos. All those who sit in the survivor area must be cleared by the Secret Service and given a special pass. I didn't have that. Many people worked feverishly to get that done last minute.

The ceremony was long, and it was hot and humid. The names were read, and President Obama gave a supportive speech that nobody really believed. There was talk beforehand that, as he walked out, all the uniforms would turn their backs on him. Officers everywhere felt that he didn't support them, especially after the Ferguson, Missouri incident and subsequent protesting. But when it came down to it, we didn't turn our backs to him. That's not what we do.

After the speech, the survivors were invited to the front to shake Obama's hand. I asked Susan if she wanted to do so, even though I had no interest. She said she didn't want to go anywhere near him, complete with a few expletives thrown in. Good enough for me!

The last event was attending a debrief for coworkers held by Concerns of Police Survivors (C.O.P.S.) the next day. Liz attended one for coworkers' spouses. This was my first real exposure to the national organization—and we met Northern California C.O.P.S. staff at the Sacramento Memorial who soon became our new family.

****

After Danny's death, I made the same offer to Missy as I had to the rest of the family—I would answer any question about her dad's death truthfully. After some time, Missy decided to take me up on it, and asked to meet for coffee.

I dreaded the questions she might ask. There were certain things I wanted to save her from.

We met at a local Starbucks and sat outside for a private

conversation. She started out with small talk—work, family, and her relationship with Ryan. I was honored when she asked for advice and gave her the best I could. In responding, I initially tried to think of what Danny would say. I quickly realized I just needed to share my thoughts.

Then, Missy's tone changed as she lowered her head and asked about her dad in a soft voice. I reminded her of my promise to tell the truth, but I would not offer up details unless she asked. She asked a few questions about the shooting. She sought clarity about a few details she had seen on the news—nothing too bad.

The hardest question she asked was whether her dad had suffered. That seemed to be most important to her. Based on the location of the shot to his head, I believe he was dead before he hit the ground. I know it sounds straightforward and a little harsh, but it was the truth, and what she needed to hear. I understood, because I had the same questions.

This conversation sparked a friendship and trust that is still strong today.

Liz and I got to be a part of Missy's 25th birthday when we went to the End of Watch Foundation Ball on May 23, 2015. It was Missy's first birthday without her dad, and we wanted to make it special. We put a plan in motion with her cousin, Kari, and Kari's husband Kevin, Susan, and our family. Liz had a great time shopping for shoes and accessories with Missy, who also got her hair and nails done (a gift from a friend). Missy and Kari also went shopping for a dress.

Missy and her boyfriend, Ryan, arrived at our house. We surprised her with a limousine ride to the ball. The limo was late, so we had to stall a bit at first. But she loved her first ride in a limo! Susan and Jenny were waiting at our table up front. Samantha Davis (Michael's daughter) hung with us all night. Missy was acknowledged by the emcee amidst a great night of dinner, dancing, and laughs. It was a special evening that created new, happy memories … and Missy got to feel like a princess.

****

Silver Star Ceremony
July 2015

In early 2015, my department notified me that I was to be given the Silver Star for gallantry at our yearly awards ceremony. The Silver Star is awarded for outstanding performance and bravery. To qualify, the employee must demonstrate resolve despite the potential of harm. The Gold Star, which is our name for the Medal of Valor, is awarded for exceptional performance and bravery, at the risk of one's life, above and beyond the call of duty. To qualify, the employee must knowingly and willingly engage in conduct where the possibility of death or great bodily injury is imminent. This medal is the highest honor one can receive within our department.

Danny was posthumously awarded the Gold Star.

SSO has a nomination process that works its way through leadership before a deputy is actually awarded. I had not received any medals in my career, and that was okay with me. I didn't get into the job for medals, although I had been a part of several events that may have qualified me for one. The reality is, if a supervisor doesn't normally think about medals, it won't happen. My past partner used to joke that on our shift, one would have to save the Sheriff personally to get a medal … and that was a maybe.

I didn't want the Silver Star. I was feeling very guilty for what happened, and did not feel I deserved it.

The ceremony was held at the Sacramento Board of Supervisors chambers in downtown Sacramento. Sometimes, the ceremony is packed; sometimes it's just brass and a few others, and it passes without a lot of fanfare. That year, there were quite a few recipients, so they figured the room would be standing room only. I was told I would be the last recipient before they gave Susan the Gold Star for Danny.

I told Liz I didn't want to go—that I didn't deserve it, and felt guilty for being nominated. I knew in my heart I didn't deserve a damn thing, and that they had only nominated me out of pity. Why would I get a Silver Star when I did not protect my partner, nor catch the suspect who went on to shoot and kill more people? I felt it was political, and stupid. I was not going to go!

Liz softly and gently reasoned with me, reassuring me that none of that was true. She said I would regret it if I didn't go. I continued to resist. If I'm honest, I was afraid to stand in front of all those people with all that guilt still in my heart.

Sergeant Cabral told me to accept the award in honor of Danny. The Star was a way for the department to honor my actions even if I didn't feel I deserved it. He explained the work that goes into the nomination and issuing of the medal. He also said my feelings would change over time, and if I didn't accept the medal, I would regret it. Although I didn't believe most of what he said, I had tremendous respect for Cabral and his experience, so I reluctantly agreed to attend.

July 23, 2015, Liz and several members of my family arrived at the chambers. The award recipients were to be seated together. The boys were with Liz, and I was trying to stay strong for them. But the more people looked at and talked to me, the harder I found it to hold it together. I felt like a fraud and wanted to leave. My family went in to grab seats, but I waited until the last minute to go in.

I sat next to Sergeant Randy Winn, who was also getting a Silver Star to add to the chest full of medals he already had. Randy is a legend in our department. He could tell I was hurting and tried his best to calm me down. I don't remember a word he said, but I was grateful he was the guy next to me and appreciated his effort.

Sheriff Jones called me up to the front of the room, facing the audience. As he recounted the shooting and why I was getting the medal, I was overwhelmed with sadness and guilt. With tears threatening in front of so many people, I turned my back to the audience. I'm sure it looked ridiculous, but I was stuck. Sheriff Jones turned his back as well and said a few things to me that worked. I turned and accepted the award, took a picture or two, and sat down.

Next up was the Gold Star for Danny. Susan accepted the award with grace and dignity. After the ceremony, she took off pretty quickly, and I wished to do the same. In true Liz fashion, she wanted pictures, and not just one or two. It's rare that I'm in uniform with the boys, so she wanted to record it. I tried to put on half a smile for the pictures. Eventually, we departed for home.

The Silver Star pin is on my class-A uniform. The plaque and the medal that was hanging from a ribbon have been safely stowed away. Liz tells me they are in a drawer waiting for me when I'm ready to display them. I don't know if I'll ever get there.

Maybe someday, the boys will take some pride in them. That would make it all worth it.

****

Donald Trump & Immigration

Bracamontes had been officially deported to Mexico three times—twice, on drug-related charges while living in Arizona. After he changed his name, he managed to stay under the radar.

When Donald Trump was campaigning for his first term as president, he used the Oliver/Davis story as an example of the reason a wall needed to be built between the United States and Mexico.

Danny and Michael's deaths were brought to national attention when President Trump invited Susan and Jessica Davis to attend his first address in a joint session of Congress on February 28, 2017. In his speech, he made the following comments:

> *"Police and sheriffs are members of our community. They're friends and neighbors; they're mothers and fathers, sons and daughters—and they leave behind loved ones every day who worry about whether or not they'll come home safe and sound. We must support the incredible men and women of law enforcement.*
>
> *"And we must support the victims of crime. I have ordered the Department of Homeland Security to create an office to serve American victims. The office is called VOICE— Victims of Immigration Crime Engagement. We are providing a voice to those who have been ignored by our media and silenced by special interests. Joining us in the audience tonight are four very brave Americans whose government failed them. Their names are Jamiel Shaw, Susan Oliver, Jenny Oliver, and Jessica Davis.*
>
> *"Jamiel's 17-year-old son was viciously murdered by an illegal immigrant gang member who had just been released from prison. Jamiel Shaw, Jr. was an incredible young man, with unlimited potential who was getting ready to go to college where he would have excelled as a great college quarterback. But he never got the chance. His father, who is in the audience tonight, has become a very good friend of mine. Jamiel, thank you. Thank you.*

"Also with us are Susan Oliver and Jessica Davis. Their husbands, Deputy Sheriff Danny Oliver and Detective Michael Davis, were slain in the line of duty in California. They were pillars of their community. These brave men were viciously gunned down by an illegal immigrant with a criminal record and three prior deportations. Should have never been in our country.

"Sitting with Susan is her daughter, Jenny. Jenny, I want you to know that your father was a hero, and that tonight you have the love of an entire country supporting you and praying for you.

"To Jamiel, Jenny, Susan, and Jessica, I want you to know that we will never stop fighting for justice. Your loved ones will never, ever be forgotten. We will always honor their memory."

Visiting Bobby French's grave.

From the Brown album.

Danny's patch sewn into Missy's dress so he could still "walk" her down the aisle.

From the Brown album.

15

LINE OF DUTY LOSSES

"As old school as I am, I broke. There was a sense of loss and a tremendous sense of survivor guilt that destroyed me. I had to call it quits."
—Placer County Detective Mike Simmons

Greater Sacramento Region
2016-2017

Our country as a whole was drenched in anti-law enforcement sentiment after the Wilson/Brown incident in Ferguson, Missouri. The accusations were very angry and ugly, the voices loud, and our politicians quiet. It seemed as if no one knew the pain it would cause, nor the consequences.

In the meantime, our healing journey continued, through the grief process, honoring Danny through many different ways. Liz and I had no idea what lay before us as we put together our first Danny Oliver Foundation Poker Tournament with Susan in January 2016. Little did we know that we were about to descend into layer upon layer of grief as our Northern California law enforcement community experienced the deadliest three years of my career.

On March 13, 2016, California Highway Patrol (CHP) Officer Nathan Taylor was killed after being hit by an errant driver in the snow near Truckee. Officer Taylor had responded three years earlier when our extended family was caravanning to Tahoe in separate cars. One was sideswiped by another car and crashed. Our young sons were passengers in the vehicle that was hit, and we watched from the second car. He was very kind and calming in our distress.

Just three weeks later, on April 8, 2016, CHP Motor Officer Mike Ericson was intentionally run over on the I-80 Freeway, a route I take home from work. He survived his injuries but was badly hurt. He would endure two years of painful rehabilitation to be reinstated to full duty, against all odds. This was a senseless attack on law enforcement that was becoming the new norm.

Three months later, on July 7, 2016, five Dallas-area police officers were killed and seven more wounded while protecting a Black Lives Matter march in Dallas. A lone shooter ambushed them, and we watched in horror as the events unfolded on live television.

On November 13, 2016, Stanislaus County Deputy Dennis Wallace was shot and killed while investigating a suspicious vehicle, which was found to be stolen. Although he worked just outside the Sacramento area, many of us attended his funeral. His family have become our friends through shared grief and many C.O.P.S.' functions.

On February 22, 2017, CHP Motor Officer Lucas Chellew crashed while in a pursuit in South Sacramento. He was killed instantly. His widow, Christina, and children live in our neighborhood and attend the same school.

On May 20, 2017, SSO Sergeant Dan Cabral, who had been such a huge support to us on our fateful day and in the aftermath, died of pancreatic cancer.

On June 28, 2017, SSO Deputy Alex Ladwig was shot after a man he was talking with violently attacked him at the Regional Transit light rail station. The man fought him, then took Alex's gun and shot him in the face. Alex has endured many surgeries since then to repair the damage and is still on limited duty. Alex was also the one who regularly transported Bracamontes to and from the jail for court appearances.

****

Placer County Sheriff's Office, Auburn
January 2016-July 8, 2017

Moose was granted a few months reprieve from being on call so he could catch up on his caseload. He worked with a new partner, Detective Andrew Lyssand, during this time.

He was also coming apart at the seams.

There were days when he would completely fly off the handle. Lyssand asked, "What is wrong with you? Something is not right."

Even the admin in the office noticed him imploding. She told him later, "I watched you come in every day with that look on your face."

In January 2016, there was a shooting at the Placer County Sheriff Loomis Substation. Moose teamed up with Lyssand and chased the original witnesses down to Fresno. He was able to solve that case quickly, but he was emotionally raw.

On July 10, 2016, three days after the Dallas ambush, Placer County responded to a homicide at a well-known apartment complex in Auburn. Deputies chased the suspect into the cemetery in Newcastle—where Michael Davis was laid to rest. Once shots were fired, Moose was called in to investigate the OIS. He was just feet away from Michael's grave, and it messed with him.

This case was added to the burden of work already on Moose.

Around October, Moose and Detective Scott Alford worked on a case involving a son who beat up his mother, putting her in a coma for months. She eventually passed away, and a warrant was needed to search the son's home. "Go home to your wife and kids, Scott; I'll write up the warrant," offered Moose. "We'll hit it in the morning." Alford took him up on the offer.

When Alford returned to work at 6:00 the next morning, he found Moose puking into the garbage cans downstairs. He hadn't written but three lines of the search warrant. He'd sat for 12 hours unable to write the report. He didn't even know where he was. Something had exploded inside him, and he had no idea what to do.

Alford wrote the warrant, and they kept the incident a secret.

Later, during the 2016 national hysteria about clowns luring people into the woods, Moose and Alford were called out on an investigation where a 17-year-old threw a bottle at a patrol car while "clown hunting." This kid and his buddies were searching for clowns on a rural road in Roseville, and when they didn't find any, they threw bottles at cars.

From there, Alford and Moose went to the hospital to interview a rape victim, which is not a pleasant call.

Later that night, Lyssand and Alford decided it was over—Moose had to get help. They cornered Moose about his emotional state, not letting up this time.

Moose approached a leader he trusted in the department and asked for help. He began counseling with a therapist shortly thereafter, but not before taking flak for not going through the proper channels with his request.

****

Roseville, California
January 21, 2016

Jason sat next to Traci in church, half-listening to the sermon. God was prodding him, moving him, bringing him to a point of being tired of what his life had become.

"God, I'm done," he prayed silently. "I've made a mess of my life; please help me."

At that moment, Jason felt the Spirit of God fall upon him—He was all around, inside, outside; very real and very present.

The Presence spoke. "You've never had a relationship with Me, because you wouldn't give up your sin. You've never felt me near, because you weren't able."

Jason vowed that day to follow God with his heart, his mind, and in his actions. He had heard that Jesus Christ had died on the cross for his sins so many years ago, but had never taken responsibility for his part. Until that moment, he'd never understood that he needed to come to the point of repentance—confessing that he'd done wrong, and then believe that Jesus's death on the cross paid the penalty for his crimes.

As he did so, he felt free for the first time in his life.

Jason started making new decisions and choosing to live right. God was there, constantly reminding him, "Jason, I got you. You are a new creation—the old things have passed away, and a new life has come."

Jason also realized that even though he never felt like God was there, He was. He referred to a corny poem he'd read—Footsteps in the Sand—where there was only one set of footprints in the sand. The poet assumed God had left and the footprints were his own before realizing the footprints were actually God's. God had carried him through those times of hurt and grief.

The poem now resonated with Jason. God had protected him through all his rebellion—even from childhood. He'd smoked a few cigarettes in elementary school—but it did not become a lifestyle. He'd drank here and there—but it never grew to addiction. So many mistakes that didn't ruin him over the years. For some reason, God had protected him.

Now it was time to humble himself—to give God his life, and make Him a priority.

****

Sacramento
October 1, 2016

On October 1, 2016, Missy and Ryan were married in Sacramento. I had the honor of walking her partway down the aisle. When she asked, I'm not ashamed to say I almost cried. There are no words to express how much it meant to me. I was there to represent Danny. He would've been so proud. I imagined his huge smile seeing his little girl getting married. I walked her from the bride's room to the aisle. Susan took over from there, and I walked the rest of the way behind them.

It was a beautiful day and a beautiful ceremony. I hung out with the groomsmen and took pictures with them. I wore the same suit as the guys, which Susan had purchased for everyone. I really felt like part of the family. Missy asked Liz to spend the day with her in the bride's room (and Liz had been a guest at her bachelorette party, too).

Missy wanted the wedding to be a joyful celebration, and also wanted to honor her dad. She pulled it off with grace. There was a seat reserved for Danny in the front row. His uniform shirt was draped over the seat, along with a picture of him and a white rose with a blue ribbon. She also sewed an SSO patch into her dress so Danny could still "walk" her down the aisle. It was the perfect way to honor his memory.

****

Placer County, California
October 2016-July 2017

After a process that required a lot of effort, Moose was finally getting the help he needed. The first meeting with his new therapist took two-and-a-half hours to go through all the shit he'd experienced in his career.

His therapist used cognitive-behavioral therapy for seven months. This type of therapy focuses on thinking, behaving, and communicating in the here and now rather than on trauma-related or childhood experiences. It is a practical, rational therapy that helped Moose understand how his job was affecting him.

From the beginning, the therapist asked him, "Why are you going back?"

"This is what I do! I've been at this for almost 30 years," he reasoned.

The therapist thought that 30 years was quite enough—with all he'd seen, dealt with, and sacrificed. He encouraged Moose to move on.

About two months into therapy, Moose succumbed to the process. He told himself to quit being stubborn and stop holding on to improper thinking. No more blame, no more guilt. He was ready.

Toward the end of those seven months of therapy, he quit smelling blood.

And on July 8, 2017, he retired.

****

Rocklin, California
Winter 2016

"Jason, I want you to pray for Luis Bracamontes. I need you to pray for your brother's killer."

He heard it plain as day, but no one was around.

Jason asked God how to pray for someone like him, but there wasn't an audible answer. He knew God was telling him to just pray. For Bracamontes.

Jason took it seriously and started praying every night for his brother's murderer. Although at first it was awkward, it slowly became natural. He prayed that God would save Bracamontes's soul. That was strange at first, because he didn't want Bracamontes to find salvation in Christ. He didn't deserve it!

But the more Jason prayed, the more he realized—he didn't deserve salvation, either.

****

Ramada Inn, Sacramento, California
August 30, 2017

SSO Deputy Robert "Bobby" French was the first officer to arrive at my shooting—the one who pulled me from Danny and administered first aid until the ambulance arrived. We will forever be bonded together because of that traumatic day.

Bobby was one of the many deputies who attended Police Week 2015. I have pictures of him at the Law Enforcement Memorial Wall in front of Danny's name and at several other events that week. I have a photo of Bobby signing the SSO cruiser door at Kelly's Irish Times.

Little did we know then that he would be the next Sacramento Sheriff Deputy to be put on the law enforcement memorial wall in DC.

Bobby was murdered on August 30, 2017 by a thug in the parking lot of a crappy motel only a few miles from where Danny lost his life.

Bobby was a well-liked and seasoned veteran. Everything seemed good when he was around. Bobby was good for calm when shit went down, good for professional perspective, and good for laughs. He was well-respected by not only those in our agency, but others as well.

The last few months before he was killed, Bobby sat at my desk in the CID Property Crimes Unit. He volunteered his time to get experience doing detective work, because he wanted to move to our division.

The last time I saw Bobby was mid-August 2017. I was on my way back from conducting an interview when I pulled up next to him at a stoplight. I stared, waiting for him to look at me so I could do something silly and speed off.

But Bobby had target lock on a guy walking down the street, and I knew he was on a call. When the light turned green, I pulled in behind him. When he turned his lights on to stop the guy, it looked like the suspect was considering a run for it. But he thought twice, and Bobby detained him without incident as I covered him. Apparently, the man had just robbed someone down the street.

After the arrest, we stood around for a minute or two catching up. I gave him crap for leaving his damn chew cup on my desk for me to find when I returned to work. I think once he knew it bothered me, he did it on purpose! I had a suspect turning himself in shortly, so we arranged to meet at CID, where a transport unit met us to take our guys to jail. We turned our suspects over to our transport unit and said goodbye. I never saw Bobby again.

The incidents that killed Danny, Michael and Bobby were eerily similar. Besides being killed in a motel parking lot with assault rifles, Danny and Bobby were close to retirement. There were other cops who were wounded by gunfire, barely escaping death. Both incidents included several departments, multiple scenes and a high-speed pursuit. Several cops were traumatized from aspects of each.

Michael Davis was killed on the same day as his dad 26 years apart. Bobby was killed the same day his parents died in a plane crash ten years earlier. Both Bobby and Michael died by the same type of bullet wound that ripped through vital organs.

All three funerals were held at Adventure Church. The place was standing room only at each.

As we waited for Bobby's memorial service to begin, cell phones suddenly went off around the auditorium. Personnel from Sacramento Police Department discreetly scrambled out of the auditorium. It was another OIS in which a suspect who had murdered two people exchanged gunfire with officers, wounding two. Officers returned fire, and the suspect was killed.

It was tragic to be back in DC the next May, three years after our previous visit, to etch Bobby's sacrifice into stone. I got a rubbing of his name on the wall and signed the SSO car door for him at Kelly's, just as Bobby had signed for Danny three years earlier.

All too familiar. All too soon.

For those of us who were still struggling with Danny's loss, this was more grief piled onto grief. Bobby's death was devastating not only to our department, but to our Sacramento law enforcement community as a whole.

****

Greater Sacramento Region
2017-2019

The deaths continued.

On November 10, 2017, Danny's father, Bill, died after a long illness. He passed on Veteran's Day. We remembered his service as a Marine who served in the Korean War and was stationed at Marine Corps Air Station Kaneohe Bay. This was difficult for me, as I had grown close to him and Jeri, and loved him dearly.

When Bill was dying of cancer, Jeri called me to the house to be with Bill and the family in his final moments. It was a high honor, and I was blessed that they wanted me there. I also felt an enormous amount of sadness, because I knew how much Danny loved and respected his dad. I would've much rather been by his side, helping him through his grief.

I attended Bill's funeral. Jeri even asked me to accompany her and say a few words if she wasn't able. She did just fine, and Bill was buried with all the honors of a Marine.

On Christmas morning of that same year, we were saddened to hear of another local CHP officer who was killed when his patrol car was struck by a drunk driver. His car partner was injured both physically and emotionally. Officer Andrew Camilleri had been with the CHP for barely a year. He left behind a young wife and three children.

During our trial, one of our K-9s died suddenly in March. Nikk was a large German Shepherd assigned to Deputy Ramie Folena, whom I often worked with on graveyard shift. Often Nikk joined us in briefing, trotting around to say hi, sniffing us, and making friends. I found that he liked chasing a rolled-up piece of paper. We would play catch for a while, and then he would lay down to destroy the paper ball, leaving scraps everywhere. I remember Ramie looking at me and saying, "You know you're cleaning that up, right?"

With his hairy paws, Nikk had a hard time stopping his big body on the smooth tile in the office. I used to throw the ball under someone's chair and wait for Nikk to crash into him or her. More than once, I threw it toward the sergeant's desk.

After Danny was killed, Ramie and Nikk stopped by our house. They couldn't stay long, because they were on duty, but my boys got to play with Nikk and took a few pictures. It did my heart good to see the big K-9 goofball and was grateful for the support.

Nikk's death was a very sad loss for all of us, especially Ramie.

On the dark night of March 18, 2018, Sacramento Police Department officers encountered Stephon Clark in the backyard of a residence, following a short foot pursuit. Clark had been smashing windows of cars and residences in his neighborhood. The officers thought he was armed and shooting at them, but he was not. When Clark extended his cell phone toward them, they mistakenly and tragically thought it was the flash of a gun. They shot and killed him before realizing he was unarmed.

Via Clark's text messages and a search of his computer, it was later determined that he had committed suicide by cop.

This tragedy touched off weeks of protests led by Clark's family and Black Lives Matter Sacramento. On March 22, BLM briefly took over Interstate 5, which is the freeway that runs through downtown Sacramento. It was a huge mess. I took my turns downtown on the line for weeks, managing the protesting with other agencies. At times, the protesters became very nasty.

Bracamontes's trial ended April 25, and we had a short reprieve from tragedy through the summer. [37]

On August 10, 2018, Solano CHP Motor Officer Kirk Griess was killed on a traffic stop by a driver who was driving erratically.

Just three weeks later, on Labor Day, CHP Officer Brad Wheat killed his wife, shot her lover, and then took his own life in nearby Amador County. This was a big blow to our law enforcement community—just months earlier, they had seemed a happy family and active in the community. So tragic.

Two weeks later, on September 17, 2018, SSO Deputy Mark Stasyuk was shot and killed while responding to a disturbance at a Pep Boys store. Mark was a newer member of our department, and at the time, he was working with Rancho Cordova Police Department, which is a contract city through the Sheriff's Office. He and his partner, Officer Julie Robertson, arrived, and immediately, the suspect started shooting at them. Julie was wounded in the arm but continued to engage in a gun fight until the suspect fled and was caught shortly after another gunfight with deputies. Julie recovered from her physical injuries. Mark, who attended our church, had been married for only six months.

Danny had been considered the "brother" of the department. Bobby was the "big brother," and Mark is now considered the "little brother." This is the way we see those we work with—as brothers and sisters in the Blue Family.

Officer Robertson and I found much in common after that, and I look out for her. She's become like a little sister to me.

Three weeks after that, on October 23, CHP Officer Sean Poore in South Sacramento left briefing in full uniform and drove to an underpass

---

[37] More on the trial in later chapters.

on Interstate 5 in a remote area. He texted his wife, Samantha, goodbye, and then shot himself in the head, leaving her and three young children behind.

The next morning, we mourned the fourth anniversary of Danny's death.

Exactly two weeks later, the Camp Fire broke out in Paradise, California, just under two hours north of Sacramento. It was the deadliest fire in California history, causing an entire community to leave everything and run for their lives. The fire also left 88 people dead and over 30,000 homeless.

There was a massive law enforcement response. Hundreds of our Sacramento area officers were put on tactical alert (all days off revoked, mandatory 12-hour shifts) for the next month. Those working long hours in thick smoke and devastation were the same who had lived through the incidents I've described.

Liz was very instrumental in coming alongside the 146 law enforcement families who lost their homes in the fire. Through her involvement with our spouse association and How2LoveOurCops,[38] she spent weeks working with the Butte County Sheriff's Office helping field phone calls and aid requests for the families. Liz then led several organizations and people in putting together a huge Christmas relief event in Chico on December 23rd for the families. She and I stayed up all night together finishing up the details.

It was a huge success. She received a Chief's Commendation from the California Highway Patrol for that work a month later.

Yet 2018 wouldn't be complete without one more line-of-duty death. On Christmas night, Newman Police Officer Ronil Singh kissed his young family goodbye and was shot dead just hours later, in the wee morning of December 26, 2018. Singh, a legal immigrant from Fiji, was murdered by an illegal immigrant. President Trump tweeted, "*There is right now a full-scale manhunt going on in California for an illegal immigrant accused of shooting and killing a police officer during a traffic stop. Time to get tough on Border Security. Build the Wall!*" He also brought up Officer Singh's family on stage at the Police Week Memorial Service the following

---

[38] Liz started our SSO Spouse and Family Association, and joined the Board of How2LoveOurCops, a nonprofit dedicated to LEO Family wellness. More on these organizations in later chapters.

year, representing the 185 officers who had died in the line of duty in 2018.

Two weeks later, on January 10, 2019, rookie Davis Police Officer Natalie Corona, the beautiful young lady who took pictures in a blue dress wrapped in a blue line flag, was gunned down by a bicyclist while conducting a vehicle collision investigation. Once she was down, he continued to shoot her at close range.

Liz attended her funeral, as she was a UC Davis graduate and had connections in Davis. She went with Christina Chellew, a CHP widow with whom we spend time. At that point, I had to take a break. I could not attend Natalie's funeral. It was … Just. Too. Much.

But it still didn't stop.

On June 19, 2019, Sacramento Police Officer Tara O'Sullivan, another beautiful young officer new to the profession, was ambushed while conducting a domestic violence standby. Several officers heroically retrieved her while under heavy fire from the suspect. Tara was transported and pronounced dead after receiving additional and extraordinary medical effort to save her at UC Davis Medical Center. The funeral was held at Bayside Adventure Church and thousands attended. There wasn't an extra seat in the auditorium, overflow rooms were full, and there were still officers who stood outside.

Several months later, as the five-year anniversary of Danny's death approached, we made our plans to come together again at East Lawn Cemetery to honor him. The night before we were to gather, tragedy struck again.

An illegal immigrant shot and killed El Dorado County Deputy Brian Ishmael on October 23, 2019, as he responded to a marijuana plant theft. An off-duty deputy with nearby San Joaquin County who was on a ride-along with Ishmael was also shot, but he survived. At least one of the suspects was an illegal alien. It was the county's first line-of-duty death since the 1800s.

And what can be written about the year 2020? It was very hard on everyone, but especially difficult for law enforcement officers and their families. The anti-cop rhetoric, ambushes, targeting homes and police stations, having rocks, blocks of cement, bags of urine, and frozen water bottles thrown at officers during the riots, extreme hate speech on social media, news media, and government, and finally the "Defund Police" movement all have been brutal. Many officers have retired, others have left the profession, some have moved to more conservative and rural areas/states. Recruitment of new officers is down. Having less cops on duty leads to more crimes—and nobody wins with that.

At the time of this writing, our last line-of-duty death was SSO Deputy Adam Gibson, who was shot and killed on January 18, 2021. We also had another deputy critically wounded in the same incident, and his K-9 Riley was shot and killed. It was one of three shootings that week, leaving an additional deputy wounded.

For me, each death reinjured the wound of my own soul … especially Bobby's, because he was a friend. As a law enforcement community, we were buried—trying to come up for hope, but pushed back down with discouragement over and over and over again.

In the middle of all of this was the three-ring circus of a trial that would make national news.

And because of it, I would face the evil that had been haunting my dreams for three-and-a-half years.

My tattoo in honor of Danny.

From the Brown album.

16

CIRCUS

"Scotty took the brunt of the bullshit from Bracamontes."
—Placer County Detective Mike "Moose" Simmons

Sacramento County Courthouse
January 16-17, 2018

My subpoena for the Oliver/Davis murder trial showed up in my email inbox in December 2017.

Leading up to the trial, I grew anxious about testifying. Word was that Bracamontes was acting out in court appearances, saying terrible things to people. I hadn't seen him since the day he shot Danny, three-and-a-half years prior, and I wasn't looking forward to facing him again.

I tried to lean on my friends. I asked people to pray for me. I also asked for passages from God's Word that would calm my soul.

I met with Rod Norgaard, the lead prosecutor, on January 15, 2018. Norgaard was the Assistant Chief Deputy District Attorney for the Sacramento County District Attorney's Office. He is a soft-spoken, thoughtful, seasoned prosecutor. His approach was methodical and gentle, not political. Danny's trial was not the first or last officer-involved death he'd prosecuted. He treated me with compassion and made sure both Liz and I were educated on the process by ensuring our questions were answered. I felt like he truly cared for us.

In preparing for my testimony, we watched my videotaped statements and looked at photographs. I was on TBN (To Be Notified) for January 17th. Norgaard's investigator, Derrick Greenwood, shared that I would most likely see the courtroom on Thursday the 18th, but to be prepared before then just in case.

Bracamontes's case was eligible for the death penalty. There are four stages in a capital case: pre-trial motions, guilt trial, penalty phase trial, and appeals. Because Monroy's plea deal kept her case from the death penalty, she and her jury went through pre-trial motions, criminal trial, sentencing, and appeals.

First are the pre-trial motions. Common motions made before the trial begins include the exclusion of certain evidence, preventing witnesses from testifying, and case dismissals. A couple of the motions filed in this case were: 1) A change of venue, which means the trial does not take place in the county where the crimes occurred. This is done when the defense feels the jury pool is tainted by the impact of the event, so a fair trial cannot be attained. This motion was denied. 2) The defense tried to get Bracamontes deemed insane and therefore incompetent to stand trial. This motion was also denied.

The guilt trial phase includes jury selection, opening statements, witness testimony, closing arguments, jury instruction, and verdict.

In the capital case, the penalty trial phase argues aggravating circumstances, which are facts that make a crime worse or more serious, and mitigating circumstances, which are facts that may reduce the degree of moral culpability, and thereby reduce the penalty. Aggravating circumstances in Bracamontes' case were that he killed more than one person, and those persons were police officers. After those arguments, the jury hears victim impact statements, and then, they recommend a sentence. After considering the jury recommendation, the court formally pronounces punishment on the defendant.

Presiding over Bracamontes's trial was Judge Steve White, who has had a long and distinguished legal career since the mid-1970's. He was elected as Presiding Judge in 2009 and served two years. As Presiding Judge, he was the chief administrator and spokesperson of the court. He oversaw 59 Superior Court judges, 800 court employees, seven referees, and five-and-a-half commissioners who work in seven facilities.

I respect Judge White. I admired the way he handled the courtroom, the circus that came with the trial, and even Bracamontes himself.

Guilt Trial
January 16, 2018

The trial began Tuesday, January 16, 2018. There were two juries—one for Bracamontes and one for Monroy. The juries were separate, because Bracamontes was up for the death penalty, whereas Monroy was not.

The first day consisted of opening statements by Norgaard,

Bracamontes's Public Defender Jeffrey Barbour, and Monroy's lawyer, Peter Kmeto.

The next day, ten witnesses were called to testify, beginning with Hugo Monroy, Bracamontes's brother.

A friend of ours gifted Liz and I a movie date to help distract us while waiting for my court appearance. The theater featured reclining seats and served food and drinks during the movie. She wanted us to relax.

The kids were taken care of, so Liz and I headed to the theaters in Folsom for a little "us" time. We made contact with the manager, ordered drinks at the bar, and then walked to the theater. At 12:45 p.m. on a Wednesday, we were the only two in the place. We relaxed into our nice, comfortable chairs in the middle of the theater. Once situated, I checked my phone one last time before the movie started.

I saw a text from Derrick Greenwood and returned the call. He apologized profusely, but said he needed me to be ready to respond to the courthouse within one hour should the call come. Since we were about that distance away at the theater and would need to change into appropriate court attire should they call, the movie would have to wait.

Luckily, the theater manager was very gracious. We returned the untouched drinks, ordered food to go, and went straight home.

Once there, Liz gave me a wide berth so I could get ready in my own way. She notified a few people, including our parents, to be ready if they wanted to go to the courthouse. I shaved, showered, and laid my suit on the bed.

I changed into my suit. My mother-in-law Catherine arrived, and Liz and I piled into my car and left. As we drove, I grew progressively calmer, which was not what I was expecting. I believe God laid His Hand on me at that moment, and it gave me peace. I knew He had my back.

Once we arrived at the courthouse, I signed in and locked up my gun in a small closet that contained safety deposit box-like drawers. The closet is to the right of the entrance metal detectors and manned by two deputies. Then, we were escorted to a waiting area upstairs where my parents joined us. I was nervous but composed, and mentally reviewed my testimony.

Liz, family, and friends wanted to be in the courtroom when I testified. We had previously agreed that it might be too hard for me to see Liz, especially if she got emotional. I also didn't want evil to make eyes at her. She, on the other hand, wanted to experience it with me, and there would be fewer questions later.

After some thought, I concluded that I felt steady and more confident than expected. I also didn't want anyone to have regrets or feel left out. Despite worries of my family hearing the story and seeing pictures from that day, I wanted them to heal as well. After some discussion, we decided they would go in, sit in the back, and if it became too much, they'd leave.

Greenwood then appeared and informed us that I wouldn't testify until first thing the next morning.

God works in mysterious ways. The whole afternoon turned out to be a decent practice run for the next day. I was confident I'd be able to keep my cool, and that comforted me. It was important to honor Danny and Michael, my family, my department, and most importantly God, as I told my story.

I expected no more than ten minutes of sleep that night but was happily surprised when I woke up after a good six to seven hours. I had coffee and ate a bagel even though I wasn't hungry. Liz sent the kids in their respective directions, Catherine arrived, and we headed out again. My parents and CHP Chief Brent Newman met us at the courthouse. Liz, Catherine, Brent, and my parents were taken into the courtroom to reserved seats in the back.

****

Sacramento County Courthouse, Sacramento, California
January 18, 2018

The first-floor courtroom was a relatively large, dark-paneled chamber, and on January 18, 2018, it was packed. Upon entering, the gallery was about 15 rows deep with approximately 12 seats per row, and all were taken. The juries were on the right; Bracamontes, Monroy and their lawyers were seated on the left. The witness stand was to the right of the judge. There was a large table in front of the gallery facing the judge for the prosecution. Behind the defendants was a door that led to a holding cell downstairs.

There were 24 jurors plus alternates. There was a media section as well, where reporters took notes and cameras rolled.

The Oliver and Davis families were present. Officers were permitted to attend, but wore suits, not uniforms, at the direction of the judge (uniforms may intimidate witnesses). There were law students from several area law schools in the gallery, as well as families and friends of victims.

****

As I waited in the hallway, I sat down, folded my hands, and prayed. I asked God to help me carry myself in a way that would honor Him and Danny. As I finished my prayer, Jason Davis hurried through the metal detector. He said a quick "hello" and rushed inside.

Shortly thereafter, I walked into the courtroom. I refused to look at my family.

It was the first time I had faced Bracamontes since we exchanged gunfire in the Motel 6 parking lot on October 24, 2014 … three years, two months, and 25 days before.

As I approached the witness stand, the jury sat stone-faced, and Judge Steve White nodded. Bracamontes sat at a table to my left between his two court-appointed attorneys. Monroy was three seats to his right, seated between her attorneys.

When I looked at Bracamontes, he grinned at me and winked. He also muttered some things under his breath. I ignored him, as I had a job to do.

The court reporter swore me in and asked me to spell my name. I hesitated.

Do I spell both first and last, or just my last?

I covered all bases by spelling both.

"Coward," Bracamontes blurted out. "Danny Oliver was a pussy." He said this loud enough for everyone in the courtroom to hear.

Gasps could be heard throughout the gallery.

"Be quiet!" Judge White warned. He then ordered the courtroom cleared of the juries and the gallery.

"You have the right to attend court, but you cannot continue to disrupt proceedings," he admonished Bracamontes. Judge White then had him removed.

While people exited, Bracamontes's lawyers approached me and apologized for his behavior. They said they had no control over what he did or said. They also reassured me they would ask me only minimal, easy questions. I took that with a grain of salt, but appreciated the gesture.

Bracamontes was placed in a room downstairs with a closed-circuit monitor to watch the trial. Everyone else was re-admitted to the courtroom and returned to their seats.

Back on the stand, Norgaard began to question me. I began to recount the morning of October 24, 2018, describing it in vivid detail. About the time I went into the details of the actual shooting, Bracamontes was allowed back into the courtroom. Once he sat down, I continued.

"As soon as her backside hit the seat, that's when I heard multiple gunshots," I testified.

"How many shots were fired?" Norgaard asked.

"About five, I believe." I answered.

"Please continue," he coaxed.

I recalled every detail, like it was happening all over again.

At the point of my calling for backup, they played the recording of my radio traffic.

"Shots fired! Shots fired! Motel 6, Arden Way … Officer down!"

The voice didn't even sound like me. I wondered how anyone could understand what I was saying, because it was so amped. This part bothered me—it was really difficult to listen to. The other really difficult part was hearing Bobby's voice—his deep, southern drawl coming through on the radio was disconcerting. No one could have imagined as he came to my aid that day that he would lay down his life less than three years later.

I continued my testimony after the radio traffic was played. "I knew if Danny wasn't hit, he'd be in the fight, and he wasn't."

I described the gunshot I heard and my reaction: "Holy shit, he just executed Danny!"

I recounted how Bracamontes then ran Danny over with the car. It felt like it happened just yesterday. "I remember watching the car bounce, like it hit a speed bump. Knowing the hotel like I did, I knew there were no speed bumps. I knew the vehicle had run Deputy Oliver over."

Norgaard introduced a photo into evidence at that point. It was an aerial shot of the crime scene that showed a large puddle of blood where Danny had fallen. I had not seen it before, and it hurt to view.

Susan, and several others, began to cry.

But Bracamontes laughed out loud. All eyes went to him.

"Bailiff, please remove Mr. Bracamontes from the courtroom," the judge ordered, and the jury was immediately excused. As they filed out, Bracamontes became vocal again.

"Fuck you all," he shouted as they led him away shackled. "Fuck Danny Oliver! Fuck Michael Davis!"

He continued to scream obscenities, seemingly directed at Susan, who was seated in the first row of the gallery, not ten yards from him. He continued to spew hate all the way down the stairs.

Nobody else said a word, seemingly stunned by the filth spilling from his mouth.

Monroy sat with her head against her hand. I didn't see her exhibit any emotion whatsoever the entire two-and-a-half hours I was on the stand.

After about ten minutes, the jury returned. The judge carefully instructed them to disregard Bracamontes's outburst as they weighed the testimony and evidence.

I wondered, *how can they not consider it?*

As the trial resumed, Norgaard asked me to describe what I saw when I approached Danny after the suspect's vehicle sped away.

"He was lying on his back, gun still in his holster," I said, the emotion beginning to leak out. "There was blood coming from his forehead … he had a gunshot wound to the forehead. His eyes were open, and he wasn't breathing."

The questions continued for a few more minutes, and then Norgaard rested. The cross-examination consisted of maybe three questions from each defense team. They kept their word, as none were very challenging or controversial. Thank God, because I was in no state to take a beating from them at that point. Norgaard had speculated that they wouldn't ask many questions, because it would make them look bad to beat up a witness like me, but you never know until the time comes.

I tried not to look at my family in the back of the room, but I couldn't help it. They appeared to shed tears here and there, but everyone remained poised. I was so proud.

After I finished testifying, I was excused from the stand. Everyone went to lunch.

I had no appetite.

****

Jason Davis hadn't understood why God prompted him to pray for Bracamontes, but he was faithful in doing so for almost two years. Once the trial started, the reason became clear to him.

Jason was surprised to find that he had little emotional attachment to the trial, no hatred toward Bracamontes, and no reaction to his outbursts … even when the monster yelled at his mother.

This man was Satan personified. He was vulgar. He was a coward who didn't want to face what he'd done, so he pulled stunts and said things to deflect. He was truly pure evil.

And that is why God had asked Jason to pray—so that he was ready, calm, and unemotional in the courtroom. God was protecting him once again.

Jason wanted to be mad—he even felt guilty for not being angry. But he realized Bracamontes was not worth the emotional investment.

The prayers weren't for Bracamontes. They were for Jason.

****

Sacramento County Courthouse
January 18, 2018

The afternoon session continued to be a circus, with Bracamontes playing the creepy clown. As soon as the victims' families were brought in, he smiled, then made lewd faces at the women. A bailiff stepped up and blocked his view.

The six witnesses who were present at Motel 6 testified. The last of the day was Adam Holst. He recalled how Bracamontes approached him as he sat in his car.

"He said, 'Give me your car,' like he's serious," Holst testified. "I'm like, 'Man, I don't know you!' I tried to start my car up, and he just shot me in my head—my ear."

Holst said Bracamontes smirked as he pulled the trigger. "Yep, like [the one] he got right now," he pointed out.

When Holst was cross-examined, they asked if Bracamontes appeared "off in any way."

Holst cut him off. "Man, he was trying to kill me! Man, he's not crazy, I'm telling you. He's trying to act like he's crazy."

As Holst left the witness stand, Bracamontes bellowed, "You're lucky I didn't kill you!"

"Fuck you," Holst replied.

"Black lives don't matter," Bracamontes shouted. "Monkey!"

****

When I walked out of the courtroom that afternoon, my friends and family were waiting for me. Finally, I let myself cry. I wasn't upset; I was relieved.

Liz and I went home, packed our bags, got the kids squared away, and left town. We had prearranged a few days at a cabin offered to us by our pastor. It was located at Lake Almanor, about a three-hour drive north. Liz and I talked about a lot of things on the drive there, but we avoided trial talk most of the way.

Over the next three days, we ate, read books and the Bible, fished, and spent quality time with each other. It was incredible. It allowed us to decompress as the stress drifted away.

One of the nights, Jason and Traci Davis joined us, and we got a chance to talk about the trial and how it was affecting both our families. Jason and I sat together by the lake talking while we fished. Our conversation connected us on a deeper level.

By the time the weekend was over, neither Liz nor I wanted to leave, but knew we had to rejoin the real world. I can honestly say that during that weekend, I got closer with my wife, the Davises, and God in a way I couldn't imagine.

One of my main goals for that trip was to deflect any internal reaction I had to Bracamontes's rants and insults. I wasn't about to give him the satisfaction. Despite how venomous and painful his words were, I felt successful in accomplishing my goal, because I didn't let him take anything else from me. While I wanted to rip his head off, I of course didn't.

For over three years, I had been working up that moment of facing Bracamontes in court in my mind. For what I knew at the time, it was finally over.

But it wasn't over.

****

January 19, 2018

After Judge Steve White warned Bracamontes once again to refrain from speaking, the defense asked him to allow them to enter a "not guilty by reason of insanity plea."

Judge White denied the motion. He suspected that it was all a show. In doing so, the judge said, "These are unforced errors. These are things that Mr. Bracamontes does to himself. He goes off when I expect him to go off."

****

The trial progressed, with almost 100 witnesses for the prosecution. Bracamontes continued to put on his show of gleeful-yet-evil comments and facial expressions designed to get into the heads of those who testified.

On Wednesday, January 24, 2018, it was Liz's 40th birthday. She celebrated by going to the trial to support Moose as he gave his testimony.

Later, Placer County Deputy Jeff Davis was on the stand, describing the shootout on Ridgeview.

"Fuck it, I don't wanna be here no more," Bracamontes exclaimed. "Fuck the jury, too. And the dead cops, and their stupid fucking families, too!"

Judge White once again cleared the courtroom, then ordered deputies to take him to the video-equipped cell downstairs, which he had been to so often. The judge told him he wouldn't be back during the guilt phase.

"Fuck you, judge," Bracamontes replied over his shoulder.

****

The prosecution rested on the morning of January 31, 2018. The defense began and ended their case on February 5, 2018, as Monroy was the only one who testified. Bracamontes waived his right.

I guess he'd already said enough.

****

The closing arguments occurred on February 8, 2018. To my surprise, I was allowed in the courtroom. I was not permitted to attend any of the earlier phases of the trial other than my testimony since I was listed as a "victim." I missed Monroy's closing argument, because no one told me I could go. I planned on hanging out in the hallway just in case they came back with an immediate verdict; I didn't want to miss that. So when Greenwood told me I could come in, I did.

My dad showed up to keep me company, so we sat together in the back. We listened to Placer County Deputy District Attorney Dave Tellman lay out all the facts in the case and how the evidence had shown that Bracamontes was guilty. It was rough learning a few things I hadn't known. Seeing my picture projected on the screen as a victim of attempted murder was difficult, as well.

The defense attorney stood and told the jury they did not dispute any of the facts in the case and everything happened as the trial had laid out for them. He then made the excuse that Bracamontes was so high on methamphetamine that he could not make any rational decisions, therefore taking away the premeditation aspect of the crimes.

After the lawyers were finished, Judge White proceeded with jury instructions for all 16 counts against Bracamontes. There were two counts of murder in the first degree, four counts of attempted murder, two counts of carjacking, two counts of attempted carjacking, one count of vehicle theft, and multiple possessions-of-weapons charges. There were also five special circumstances the juries were to decide upon.

The jury was then released for deliberations. Because it was very late in the day, everyone was sent home.

This memorial for Michael Davis was erected under the oak tree in the cul-de-sac where he was murdered.

Photo from the Brown album.

17

OVERCOMING EVIL

"Do not be overcome by evil, but overcome evil with good."
Romans 12:21

Sacramento County Courthouse
February 9, 2018

The next day, word came that the jury for Bracamontes had notified the judge that they had arrived at a verdict. Liz and I returned to the courthouse. On arrival, we learned the jury actually just had a question for the judge about the jury instructions—that they hadn't arrived at a verdict. We then waited in the hallway with many others until word came that his jury had reached a verdict on all counts. Phone calls began fast and furious, as anyone who wanted to be present had one hour to get there.

A lot of people were getting nervous about Susan maybe not making it to the courthouse on time. She had to drop off Jenny and was coming from a distance. Luckily, she and Missy, along with Jason Davis, made it just in time.

We all shuffled in. I tried to sit in the back, but Susan called me up front to sit with her and Darrell Amos.

Over a dozen deputies from Placer and Sacramento counties entered the courtroom. Bracamontes was escorted in, wearing a white dress shirt over his orange jumpsuit. He was smiling and laughing with his lawyers. There were cameras from about 15 news stations pointed at him, waiting for his reaction.

I was a little nervous. Although we were pretty confident he'd be found guilty, there's always a chance that one gullible, bleeding heart could complicate jury decisions. We took the quick verdict as a good sign.

The jury filed in, and the formalities began.

Then, the first verdict: Guilty of first-degree murder of Danny Oliver.

I breathed a sigh of relief.

Bracamontes smiled at Susan, and softly said, "Yay!"

The verdicts continued:

Guilty of first-degree murder of Michael Davis, Jr.
Guilty of special circumstance of a police officer in both cases.
Guilty of special circumstance of killing police officers to avoid arrest.
Guilty of special circumstance in killing Davis while carjacking.
Guilty of attempted murder of Scott Brown.
Guilty of attempted murder of Adam Holst.
Guilty of attempted carjacking of Adam Holst.
Guilty of carjacking the owner of the white Mustang.

Bracamontes sat there smiling.

The verdicts continued:

Guilty of carjacking the owner of the red Ford F150.
Guilty of attempted carjacking of the owner of the BMW.
Guilty of attempted murder of Charles Bardo.
Guilty of attempted murder of Joseph Roseli.
Guilty of stealing a patrol car.
Guilty of attempted murder of Jeffrey Davis.
Guilty of possession of 9mm handgun, .380 handgun, assault rifle, and shotgun while a felon.
Guilty of possession of an assault weapon.

Luis Enrique Monroy Bracamontes was found guilty on all 15 counts and five special circumstances. He was eligible for the death penalty.

He smiled at us as if he knew something we didn't. I think it was the devil smiling through his own face, but that's just me.

"Congratulations," he offered.

Bracamontes was led away in shackles. "I'm going to kill more cops soon!" he called out as he was escorted from the courtroom.

****

I left the courtroom feeling an odd sense of relief and confusion. Although happy for the verdict, it felt weird to be happy about a man convicted of killing two people and trying to kill several more, including me.

The sense of peace I was hoping for wasn't there, but at least that part was over.

****

Sacramento County Courthouse
February 15, 2018

Monroy's jury took more time. We waited for over a week, not entirely sure how it would go.

On February 15, we finally got word that the jury had reached a verdict. The circus started up again as everyone rushed to the courthouse and gathered outside. Eventually, my family and I were ushered into the courtroom and took our now-familiar seats. Not as many cameras this time, but plenty still.

Monroy waddled in accompanied by jail deputies and her attorneys. The jury entered and took their seats without looking at her, and the judge took the bench.

Monroy did not say a word as Judge White silently reviewed the verdict forms that had been handed to him. Her charges did not include Danny's killing nor my attempted murder, but she had been charged as an accessory to everything afterward.

Judge White read, "guilty of first-degree murder of Michael Davis Jr." The gallery let out a collective sigh. There were even a few fist bumps. I found this odd, because the Bracamontes' verdict was met with silence. We were so confident he would be found guilty, it was not a shock; with Monroy, we just weren't sure.

The verdicts:

Guilty of attempted murder of Adam Holst.
Guilty of attempted carjacking of Adam Holst.
Guilty of carjacking of the owner of the white Mustang.
Guilty of carjacking of the owner of the Ford F150.
Guilty of attempted carjacking of the owner of the BMW.
Guilty of attempted murder of Charles Bardo.
Guilty of attempted murder of Joseph Roseli.
Guilty of attempted murder of Jeffrey Davis.

Guilty of unlawful possession of assault weapon.

Janelle Monroy was found guilty on all ten counts including any special circumstances related to her charges. She sat in her chair without any apparent reaction.

Most of us gathered in the lobby to hug and congratulate one another on the guilty verdict. It felt awkward, so I stood back and watched. It was good to see Danny's mom, Jeri, happy and hugging people. I was sad that Bill had died before seeing justice for his son's killer.

While we were standing around, I noticed the Monroy jury exiting the elevators. They walked toward the Davis and Oliver families. Most began crying and hugging family members. Jurors apologized for taking so long. They told them they had no doubt of her guilt, but wanted to make sure they did it right. They went on to say how encouraging it was to see the family in the audience every day throughout the trial. I enjoyed watching them love on the family.

The jurors still had business at the DA's office. I was asked to escort them across the street, since I knew where it was. As we moved in front of the DA's office, one of the jurors realized who I was and gave me a big hug. The others joined in, and I received another and another. I had never been a part of anything like that as a cop, and I'm willing to bet I won't ever again. They cried, thanked me for my service, and eventually left Liz and I with Jason Davis.

The three of us talked about the trauma the jury goes through with a case like this. They view photographs, witness the families' emotion, listen to testimony, and in this particular case, listen to Bracamontes's vile outbursts, all while having no outlet. We agreed that they should be offered some sort of counseling afterward, but none of us knew if they were.

I pray that God is with them. I hope they know they are warriors and can consider themselves heroes.

****

Penalty Phase Trial Begins
Sacramento County Courthouse
March 1, 2018

Unbeknownst to me, I wasn't even close to finished with the trial. I thought I was done with all the bullshit, believing I would not be required to testify during the penalty phase of the trial.

I was wrong.

When I was asked to come back and testify again in front of Bracamontes, it was a hard pill to swallow. But I figured if it meant putting him behind bars for the rest of his life, it was worth it.

I had not been part of a penalty phase before, so didn't know what to expect. I met with Rod Norgaard, who went over the rules of testifying in this phase. He advised me to keep my opinion of Bracamontes to myself.

I hated the guy with very fiber of my being. I believed he was evil from his head to his toes. If the devil ever resided in someone, it was him. I had been struggling with these types of thoughts. I knew I should forgive—that it wasn't godly to hate, but I couldn't help it.

Based on the charges, Bracamontes had two options:

1. Life without the possibility of parole, or
2. The death sentence. (Although California doesn't actually carry out the death sentence, it remained an option.)

Norgaard told me to abstain from telling the jury how I wanted Bracamontes punished. I informed him that I had no intention of voicing my opinion. Did I feel like he deserved to die? Hell yes! But I also didn't feel like it was my place to say; that was God's choice. I had my chance to end him in the parking lot, and I failed. It was strange to want someone dead and not dead at the same time. My main hope was that he never got an opportunity to hurt anyone again. But his real judgment would come from God, not me.

Norgaard explained their plan to focus on Danny as a deputy, partner, and friend. He had obviously done his homework, because after asking me questions about work, he inquired about Danny's nickname, "Teddy Bear." I smiled and recounted the story I shared in the prologue of this book.

Norgaard then asked me to gather pictures, videos, lists of memorials, and anything else that would paint the picture of who Danny was. It took me the next couple of days to gather what I could from many sources. I'll admit, it was a fairly painful process. But if it would help, I was willing.

****

Sacramento County Courthouse
March 5, 2018

Unlike the previous time I'd testified, I had an idea of what to expect. So, I was a different nervous this time.

When I testified during the criminal phase, I worried about getting facts right and not showing weakness. This time, I was concerned about how the family would receive my testimony. I worried about saying something offensive or not adequately explaining Danny's character. I also expected Bracamontes to say something, and I didn't want him to get a reaction out of me.

Everyone gathered just outside the courtroom. Liz had invited a bunch of people for my support. She said she wanted to fill the courtroom with good to overpower the evil. Several friends and family showed up, and I felt a lot of love. But when we went in, I sat separately so I could concentrate.

Rod Norgaard opened with a short opening statement; he would let the family describe their loss.

The defense's opening statement spoke of Bracamontes as a product of his environment—an alcoholic father and living in poverty. They then named contaminated water as a contributing factor as well. They described his illegal journey into the United States, his multiple deportations, and his arrest for selling drugs as "desperate." They concluded by blaming methamphetamine-induced psychosis for his crimes, and therefore, he did not deserve the death penalty. They wanted him to live to get help.

They took a good 90 minutes to detail this. I think I saw at least one juror doze off.

I understand they were just doing their jobs, but it made me sick.

There was a short break after the opening statements.

Next, it was time to hear from the victims. When we were situated, the jury re-entered and took their seats.

As it turns out, Bracamontes didn't want to be in the courtroom during the penalty phase of the trial, but the judge decided to bring him in to listen to the victims. If he acted up, he would be removed.

I hoped if Bracamontes was going to act out, he would do it while I was on the stand, since I was going first. I preferred he said things to me rather than any other member of the family, especially Missy.

Bracamontes was brought up from the holding cells below. As soon as he entered, the feeling in the court changed. The air seemed heavy. That devilish grin was on his face again, and once he sat down, he scanned the courtroom. He looked at the families for a bit but then fixated on me. We locked eyes, and he did not look away. He smiled, even winked. I abstained from saying or doing anything to provoke him, but also did not look away.

I was called to the stand and was reminded by the judge that I was still under oath from my previous testimony.

"I understand."

Norgaard asked me where I currently worked. Then, where I worked when Danny was killed. He asked me to explain what POP was and its duties. As I did so, Bracamontes began.

He started out softly, but gradually increased his volume until everyone could hear.

"You're a coward. You ran like a little bitch."

Judge White ordered him removed from the courtroom. He also cleared the jury.

"You didn't *protect* your partner. You *killed* him!"

The bailiff stood him up and unlocked his legs.

"You and Danny were dirty! I'm glad I killed him!"

The deputies escorted him down the stairs and out of the courtroom.

"Do you want to know what his last words were? He blamed YOU! And he cried like a little bitch!"

I didn't give him any satisfaction by responding. After a moment, Judge White was about to have the jury brought back in. I asked, "Judge, can I have a moment?"

He granted my request, and I went to a small office near the judge's chambers. The tears flowed. The anger was so pent up, I felt as if I would explode. I then punched a metal desk as hard as I could. The bang was heard in the gallery.

After a short time, Derrick Greenwood came in to calm me down. I had to literally bounce up and down for a few minutes just to release the energy. After about five minutes, I composed myself and went back to the stand.

While they escorted the jury back in, I went to take a sip of water from a tiny Dixie cup. My hand was shaking so bad, I had to put it back down. Apparently, I hadn't gotten all my pent-up energy out.

Judge White informed the jury that although they had to previously ignore Bracamontes's outbursts, the penalty phase of the trial allowed their consideration. Several jurors looked relieved, shaking their heads up and down at the news.

I testified for a little over an hour about POP, the Teddy Bear story, and what it was like telling Connor why Daddy was sad. The jury laughed and cried. I felt I had communicated who Danny was and what his loss cost me. More importantly, the family felt the same, and even thanked me for "taking one for the team" in regard to Bracamontes and his outburst.

When court was done for the day and everyone was out front, the public defenders again approached and apologized for my having to endure the outbursts. They clarified they didn't have anything to do with it. I appreciated the effort and respected their apology, because they didn't have to offer it.

Liz and I spent the next two days in that courtroom watching family, friends and victims testify as to the destruction Bracamontes caused during his day-long crime spree.

Missy talked about walking down the aisle without her father, and how Danny had missed her college graduation.

Susan talked about Danny's love for his daughters and dogs.

Moose described the loss of his career.

But it was Jason Davis's testimony that hit me hardest. He talked about losing his father in a Riverside PD helicopter crash when he was a kid on October 24, 1988. Michael had practically raised Jason and his younger brother.

Jason then shared how his younger brother had committed suicide with the gun that had been issued to Jason while going through the police academy. When he heard about his brother Michael's death, he wondered how to tell his mother she had lost another son.

It was powerful, and I was blown away by his strength and perseverance.

After three days of witness testimony, the prosecution rested. We were all exhausted after hearing so many sad stories. I had nothing left.

****

Rocklin, California

Throughout the trial, Jason listened, supported his family, and prayed.

God was still speaking, and he was willing to listen. He thought through his life before Christ and remembered all the people he'd hurt or let down.

Bracamontes killed Michael, a good man he had never even seen before. But Jason had hurt people he knew and loved. In his heart, he considered his own actions worse than what Bracamontes had done to his brother.

Jason continued to ask even deeper questions … why did God protect him? Why were his brothers and father gone—and why was he the only man left in his family? What did God have in store for him?

By working through his grief via those questions, thoughts, and prayers, Jason realized something.

He'd lost his brother on October 24, 2014, but he gained his salvation through the work that Jesus Christ did on the cross. Losing Michael caused him to really look at his own life—and realize how much he needed God.

Jason and I: we've developed a friendship despite all that has happened.

Photo from the Brown album.

18

JUSTICE

"What is the fair punishment for a man who can do this? What would be a fair and fitting punishment for someone who can reap such harm on these people, these families, and these communities? The only just verdict in this case is death."
—Placer County Deputy District Attorney Dave Tellman

Sacramento
Spring 2018

The penalty phase of the trial was difficult.

There were several things I knew going in. I knew I wouldn't feel any sense of justice, no matter what sentence Bracamontes received. There was no sentence that could return Danny to us or heal the pain and suffering caused by his death. True justice for Bracamontes would come from his Maker.

Many people had asked me how I felt about the death penalty, what I wanted for Bracamontes, and if I would attend his execution should there be one. My thoughts on the death penalty are heavily influenced by California law and my faith in God. I felt Bracamontes should be given the maximum sentence allowed by law, which in California is the death penalty.

But the reality is, California has about 744 inmates currently on death row, and the average time spent there is 25 years, as numerous automatic appeals consume time and taxpayer dollars. It is entirely possible I could die before Bracamontes does.

In my mind, the death penalty is more of a formality signifying the horrific nature of his crimes. I just wanted to make sure he would never be out on the streets to hurt anyone again.

I know that God is just. Bracamontes will answer for his sins. I also believe that sins are forgiven through Jesus Christ's substitutionary death on the cross for those who believe in Him and repent of their wicked ways.

If Bracamontes makes this change in prison, he will be saved. I just know that I don't have it in me to lead him there. If God chooses to perform that miracle, I will rejoice in God's glory.

But I won't be the one to usher him into new life.

If this sounds contradictory, it is. That's what makes it so difficult. I despise Bracamontes and want all the fires of hell to rain down on him for what he did. But God loves all people, and I pray for salvation for all. I don't get to decide someone's eternity.

****

Sacramento County Courthouse
April 25, 2018

The end had finally come. It was the last time I would have to face evil and put up with his devilish smile and hateful comments.

I was invited to provide a victim impact statement. I had gone back and forth as to whether I would, well aware that no matter what I said, it would not bring Danny back. It wouldn't change how I felt. And I really didn't want to face evil again. The first three times were plenty.

I seriously doubted Bracamontes would care or suddenly experience remorse. It would just give him another chance to get under my skin, and I didn't want to give him that satisfaction.

But after listening to the victim impact statements given in Monroy's case, I had a change of heart. Monroy was not charged with anything against Danny or me, so I wasn't a victim in her case. As I listened, I realized the statement isn't for the defendant.

It wasn't for Bracamontes; it was for everyone else. I could have an impact on the jury, the judge, the families, my partners, and possibly the community, since it would be televised.

I met with District Attorney Rod Norgaard, and we decided I should go first again. We knew Bracamontes would most likely go off on me again and get kicked out of the courtroom, which would make things easier for others. I wasn't looking forward to it, but took on the responsibility of protecting others. I knew what to expect, so prepared myself emotionally and mentally.

As the day drew closer, Liz and I talked about how to deal with it. We decided together to handle it one day at a time, and when the time came, we would play it by "feel." We figured I would need to take time off afterward to wind down from the trial. I didn't want to be all keyed up at work, and then have someone say the wrong thing and set me off.

The week before, Liz and I attended the C.O.P.S.' Coworkers/ Couples Retreat for partners of fallen officers in Missouri. I had written a statement by that point, and previously asked a few people to review it. But none had been partner to a cop who had been killed. So, at the retreat I asked other survivors to read it and provide their feedback, since they had gone through similar circumstances.

I also read it to a few of our therapists to see if they could offer some insight. One of them was Denny Conroy, a retired officer turned therapist. He said I had written a great essay, but not an impact statement. He advised me on how to change the wording to drive home the impact of my loss. He also told me to lose the touchy-feely, nice stuff and shout-outs. Although what I wrote was true and accurate, my main goal was to make sure the jury knew the pain Bracamontes caused.

After a few more attempts, we worked it out. The statement was short, to the point, and conveyed my message well. I sent the finished product to Denny, and he approved. I was so grateful for his mentorship in the matter.

The day came, and I was slated to go first as planned. This time, I wore my uniform—I wanted Bracamontes to see me as an officer. He could not break me.

At the last minute, it was decided that Adam Holst would deliver his statement first. He was to basically tell Bracamontes off, and then walk out. Holst wanted to look him in the eye.

Holst walked to the podium and then turned to the audience. He thanked them for coming and offered some nice comments for the Davis and Oliver families. He then turned to Bracamontes, flipped up his middle finger, and said, "Fuck you!" He turned and walked out of the courtroom.

No one said a word.

Bracamontes let out a little laugh. Judge White told him to be quiet.

When it was my turn, my heart was pounding. I wasn't nervous about Bracamontes, but prayed I would say the right things without upsetting either family.

I stepped to the podium and read my statement:

"The events of October 24, 2014 changed my life forever. I will never be the same. There are scars that will never heal completely. I have memories that haunt me and visions I will never forget. I have shared many of them during this trial. As I thought about what to say and how this affected me, I realized there is no way to adequately express the sense of loss to myself, my family, my department, and my community.

"This event has broken my heart as well as the hearts of the rest of my family and friends. After Danny was murdered, I didn't sleep more than an hour a night for a long time. I had panic attacks, stomach problems, couldn't be in crowds, and jumped out of my skin at loud noises. I got angry easily and had a hard time finding joy in anything, including my family and friends. I was broken. Over time, these things have faded, but I would be lying if I said they were completely gone.

"Before the shooting, I knew what I wanted to do with my life. I knew what course my career would take. I had the confidence needed to make all of these things happen. When Danny was murdered, all of that was shattered. For a short time, I wasn't even sure I wanted to be a cop anymore. I have worked through most of these things, but it has taken time and caused those around me immeasurable pain and sorrow.

"I struggle with survivor's guilt. I carry the burden of feeling responsible for everything that happened that day. I felt guilty for not being able to keep my partner safe and protect my friend. I thought if only I had stayed in the fight longer, Danny would still be alive. If I had kept firing when I saw the assault rifle instead of taking cover, Michael would still be alive.

"If only I had gotten a couple of rounds off at the car as it sped away after running over Danny, Adam Holst would not have been shot in the face. I felt responsible for Michael's death, because in my mind, if I would've stopped the defendant in Sacramento, Danny might not have made it, but the Davises would still have Mike. I felt like every person in Placer County hated and

blamed me for Michael's death—because I blamed myself. There are a lot of "if onlys" in my life.

"I felt guilty for living. Why am I still alive? Why Danny and not me? Why do my boys have a dad, but Missy and Jenny are without a father? Why is Susan without a husband? I couldn't understand why Susan didn't hate me. Over the past three-and-a-half years, I have convinced my head that almost all of these things were either out of my control, or not true. I am still trying to convince my heart.

"My family has suffered more than you can possibly imagine.

"I had to tell a six-year-old why Daddy was sad. I had to tell him that a man he just went camping with was murdered. He continually reminds me how this event affected him. Just recently, he asked me how long it will be until I retire. I told him a little over 10 years. I asked him why he asked. He said because he wanted to know how much longer he would have to be scared of losing me. I had to hold back my tears, assuring him I wasn't going anywhere. But we both knew I lied. I couldn't make that guarantee.

"That day changed my wife Liz and our marriage. Liz was with Susan from the time she stepped off the plane that day all the way to the morgue. Being with Susan reminded Liz of how close she came to being in her shoes. She stayed strong while I fell apart. Liz felt a rollercoaster of emotions, but didn't show them because she didn't want to burden me. She has suffered greatly. Liz is as much a victim of Danny's murder as I am.

"I am a man of faith, and even the defendant can't rob me of my faith in God. I know it's a cliché, but it is true; you don't know how precious life is until you almost lose it.

"In the words of Romans 12:21, 'Do not be overcome with evil, but overcome evil with good.' The defendant succeeded in murdering Danny and Michael. He has not taken my life, my faith, and my family, but he has changed them forever.

"The defendant murdered my partner and friend, Danny. He murdered Michael and tried to kill me and several others. He has shown no remorse for his actions. He has spewed forth the most

wicked, vile, and hurtful things every time I was on the stand.

"My faith tells me to forgive the defendant. For the longest time I struggled with this. How do I forgive him? I came to realize that I wasn't forgiving him, or his actions. I was giving myself permission to not think about him anymore.

"To not hate you. Not have you be a poison in my heart and mind for one moment longer.

"Thank you, Prosecution, for your work in this case. Thank you, Jury, for enduring the horror of this trial and finding the defendant guilty. Thank you, Judge White, for presiding over these proceedings with dignity and professionalism. I know this will shock a few people, but thank you, Defense Team, for treating me and most of the other victims I was able to witness you question with respect.

"Now with all of this said, I want the court to sentence you to the maximum punishment allowed by law. My only goal is that the defendant never again be free to kill another person, be it a civilian or law enforcement.

'May the Lord judge between you and me. And may the Lord avenge the wrongs you have done to me, but my hand will not touch you. As the old saying goes, "From evildoers come evil deeds, so my hand will not touch you.' 1 Samuel 24:12-13.

"Thank you."

I had expected Bracamontes to chime in with his bullshit. Instead, he made a couple comments under his breath with a few little chuckles. Judge White told him to be quiet, and that was that.

Why didn't he go off this time?

It was Chuck Bardo's turn. Every time I'd seen him throughout the trial, he looked very angry. I had a feeling his statement would be the same, and Chuck did not fail to deliver. Most of his statements were aimed at Bracamontes, but he tucked in a few jabs at his department, too.

That was fuel to Bracamontes's fire. Eventually, he and Bardo got into a shouting match that continued until Judge White cleared the courtroom and had Bracamontes escorted out.

"And in the true fashion of a coward, he retreats," Bardo threw out.

Once Bracamontes was gone, Bardo finished his statement without fanfare.

Susan was angry. Knowing Bracamontes was watching the statements from another room via video, she added a little something she'd learned in Spanish at the end of her statement. I imagine that felt good.

Danny's mother Jeri, Michael's mother Debbie, and Moose talked about their grief. They described how Bracamontes had changed their lives—and not for the better.

The carjacking victim of the Ford F-150's statement was short and sweet. He thanked God to be alive, then expressed how sorry he was about what happened.

Cheryl Robbins, the Mustang owner who was carjacked, was still traumatized from the incident. She did not attend. A victim advocate read her statement. We were disappointed she wasn't there, as we wanted to thank her. She was the first person to identify Bracamontes. I never saw his face—only the gun.[39] Adam Holst had been shot in the face and was unable to give a description. Cheryl saw him, and had talked to him briefly. Her description and photo lineup were crucial to catching him.

Then, Sergeant Jason Davis stepped to the podium in uniform.

> *"Good morning, Your Honor.*
>
> *"I thought long and hard about what I would talk about, and I don't want to reiterate whatever everybody said. I feel the same way. I was hoping Luis would be in the courtroom, because I would like to look him in the eye when I tell him this:*
>
> *"There is a message of hope. In all things, God works for the good of those who love him, whatever the call and according to His purpose.*
>
> *"Having experienced the sudden and unexpected deaths of my father and my two brothers, along with the many death investigations I have conducted throughout my career, there's always the underlying, seemingly unanswerable question loved ones want to know: why, God?*
>
> *"On January 21st, 2015, I believe God answered this for*

[39] While being shot at, cops tend to focus on the gun, not the person shooting. I was not able to identify Bracamontes in a photo lineup.

me. See, Michael was my older brother, but to simply describe him as 'my older brother' would not nearly or adequately state the impact he's had on my life. Michael always looked out for and protected his two younger brothers. Michael genuinely loved and sacrificed for us. He was the first person I have ever known who taught me about love and sacrifice. I could always count on him in a time of need and stand before you wearing this uniform today because of Michael.

"Two months after the death of our younger brother, I moved 500 miles to a place I did not know to work for an agency I had only heard of. My family had worked here before, but I didn't know much about it—simply to be with Michael.

"Making my situation even better, Michael and I both started working for the Placer County Sheriff's Office in 1999, the greatest agency in the world. Sorry, Sac County, but I believe that.

"We had an opportunity to be be partners at various times throughout our careers, and I will forever cherish the memories that took place on those nights when we'd meet and have conversations. I'm so grateful for the opportunity to work with Michael and continue our legacy our father had started so many years before.

"Luis Bracamontes—he can hear me, right?"

The judge nodded, and Jason continued.

"I have spent a tremendous amount of thought and prayer over the past few years about what I would say to you when and if I got the opportunity.

"As I thought about the pain your actions caused, an anger would rage inside me. God would gently remind me of the pain my sins had caused and the grace He and those I loved had for me.

"When I was 14 years old, I accepted Jesus Christ as my Lord and Savior, or at least I thought I did. My pastor told me I was saved because I said the salvation prayer, but what the pastor nor I knew at the time was I was not relinquishing myself to God. I was gonna hang on to certain sin.

"Over the next 25 years, I claimed to be a Christian,

having read my Bible cover to cover twice and shared passages throughout, said my prayers on a nightly basis, went to church, while indulging in sin and never experiencing a relationship with Jesus that had been described in the Bible and by so many other Christians I knew. I couldn't understand. 'God, if I believe in You, wouldn't You be there for me?'

"A couple years before Michael was killed, I had all but given up on God. I said, 'I never felt You, never heard You, never saw You as people described.' *So, I started to pursue this sin, but I couldn't totally give up on God. I needed an insurance policy, because I knew He was there.*

"After Michael was killed, I totally abandoned God and continued this life that I was living, with the belief that God was full of grace and mercy just as everyone had always told me. He would forgive me.

"On January 18, 2015, God exposed my sin, and all aspects of my life were turned upside down. My personal life, my career, and most importantly, my spiritual life was in extreme turmoil.

"On January 21st, three days later—three days is key in Christian faith—I was standing in church, and I said, 'God, I'm done. I'm done with this sin. It's ruined my life. Jesus, please forgive me.' I'll never forget… at that moment, the Holy Spirit entered me.

"Over the last two-and-a-half years, I've had a daily relationship with my Lord and Savior, Jesus Christ, and it's the greatest gift I've ever been given.

"My marriage has been restored only because of the grace of my beautiful wife. My career is on a correct path, but that's not important. My faith in God and my family are my priorities.

"Luis Bracamontes and my sin will be with me for the rest of my life. The consequences of my actions will be with me for the rest of my life. That's the natural consequences of sin. And, like you, I imagine the judge is gonna reach the proper sentence. You will be sentenced to death, but so am I. We all are. The only man to defeat death is Jesus Christ. He's the One that defeated death 2,000 years ago.

"As I prepared for this, I spent a lot of time in prayer, hours and hours and hours. I can't get enough of my Lord and

Savior. It's amazing! I can't believe in 25 years I didn't have any idea what this relationship was like.

"See, Luis, what you meant for evil, God turned again. That's what He does for those who love Him.

"Jesus was tortured on a cross. He was tortured, ridiculed, mocked, spit upon, and nailed to a cross 2,000 years ago. I was the one who did that. I spit on Him. I mocked Him. I walked away from Him, and what did He do? He pursued me, and He found me at my lowest point, and He restored me.

"After receiving God's grace, one of the first things God asked me to do was pray for Luis and Janelle. I remember thinking, 'What should I pray for? That they would spend the remainder of their lives in a cage?' And God told me to pray for their hearts. As I started praying, I realized I would be praying for the exact same mercy and grace that God had given me. And in all honesty, I didn't want to do that. I didn't want him to receive this gift.

"See, I know our God is gracious and merciful. I know that He would forgive any sin if a person earnestly asks it. God again gently reminded me of the grace and mercy He poured out on me. And so, I began to pray for you and Janelle, and I continue to do so on a daily basis.

"When I arrived for my first court appearance, I thought you and Janelle would be changed people, because I know that God does not ask us to pray for those He's not going to answer. When I heard your evil outbursts, my initial thought was, 'This doesn't make sense, God.' *As I sat in my chair, I asked God,* 'Why did you have me pray if You weren't going to answer that prayer?'

"He gently told me He did answer that prayer. He said, 'Examine your heart, Jason.' *And I realized there was no bitterness. There was no anger.*

"I must admit, I was pleasantly surprised when I heard your evil outburst, because I knew God was not a part of that. Therefore, God was not a part of you! It didn't take me long to sin in a godly moment.

"Evil comes in many forms, but rarely does it broadcast itself so openly. Satan would rather work in the dark using deception, because that attracts more people, fools people, even

people who don't believe in Satan, despite his evil.

"So, as I pray for forgiveness, God put on my heart to make you and Janelle my top prayer. So, before I pray for my wife and kids or anything else, I pray for you.

"Michael and Danny sacrificed their lives protecting our community. Law enforcement officers put on their uniforms every day fully expecting to go home at the end of their shifts, with a little part of them knowing that might not happen.

"I wear this uniform with great pride. But this morning, as I put on this uniform, I took some extra time to reflect on the honor it is to wear it. My father wore it before me. Michael and I had the opportunity to wear it together.

"I also had time to reflect on the thousands of other officers who have made the ultimate sacrifice while protecting their communities. As I stand here, there are ongoing protests over the way the police are doing business. I will not judge those people, as I have not walked in their shoes, but I know lawlessness is not the answer. California is leading the nation in lawlessness, and God will not honor that. We are trying to find solutions to major problems. As a community services officer, I meet with so many schools about active shooters. Banning guns is not gonna solve this problem. It's only people's heart changes that are gonna solve this problem.

"As I said, Michael sacrificed his life protecting our community. Michael sacrificed many things throughout our lives for me and our younger brother. But his greatest sacrifice, he did unknowingly. When he died that day, he saved my eternal life, and I will forever be grateful for Michael.

"I love him. I miss him. Thank you."

****

It was amazing to watch Jason speak. I don't know how many heard his speech, but it was powerful to see this man in uniform proclaim he had forgiven Bracamontes. He proclaimed that he, too, was a sinner saved by Jesus. His remarks were like a beautiful sermon and went on for about 20 minutes. I ate up every last word.

It made an impact on me. I could not forgive Bracamontes. But Jason stood in uniform and proclaimed it to thousands, not only in the courtroom, but via live recording.

****

Sacramento County Courthouse
April 25, 2018[40]

I didn't think it would be hard to wait for sentencing, but it was. We strongly suspected Bracamontes would be sentenced to death, but doubt crept in. Each time I convinced myself it was just the devil messing with me, doubt would reappear.

After the victim impact statements, there was a break. Bracamontes was brought in for the reading of the sentence. His devilish grin never left his face, but he didn't say much.

Judge White went through the procedures and said his own peace about the matter. He read every count and the sentence for each. In summary, Bracamontes received:

Two death penalties.

Three 15-years-to-life sentences, one of which was for my attempted murder.

375 years added for all other crimes committed.

It was strange, the way the sentence handed down for the crime against me played in my head. I thought about what my life was worth to the State of California. Had Danny and Michael lived, Bracamontes would still go to prison for the rest of his life—unless they found a reason to parole him. With the death penalty, there's no chance of that.

Despite her claim of being a victim, Monroy got 75 years for her involvement. She is eligible for parole around her 80th birthday. Did she need to be punished for her part? Yes. Was I worried about her getting out

[40] It should be noted that on this day, the Sacramento news media was buzzing with the arrest of the Golden State Killer, a serial rapist and killer California law officers had been chasing since the mid-1970s.

and hurting others, like I was with him? No, but she's the kind who would hook up with another bad guy and help with his crimes.

Everyone was pleased with the outcome of the case. As we were leaving the court, I gave my first interview with the media. It was short and sweet, and the reporters were respectful.

Sacramento Bee reporter Sam Stanton and I chatted briefly. He covered the entire trial and had been present for all of it. He did a great job of reporting—not expressing personal feelings... other than that Bracamontes was very, very bad. I thanked him for his honest articles and hard work. He said he wasn't sure how I was able to sit quietly while Bracamontes said the horrible things he did. He commended me for being a true professional on the stand.

We waited for the jury. Liz and I thanked them for their service, because they'd been through a lot. I wish I'd had more time with each individual. We made a few inquiries as to whether counseling or debriefing had been offered to them. Seems the answer was that it was not. What a shame. We take citizens who've probably never been exposed to anything like the cases they're told to decide on and then flood them with images and sounds that are beyond traumatic. It has to have an impact. I pray they have good support networks and seek counseling if needed. (If anyone on the jury or involved in this case in any way is reading this, please reach out to me. I would love to have a cup of coffee and talk.)

Walking away, I felt a weight lift off my shoulders. Liz and I had spent three-and-a-half years looking forward to the next step in the process. There was always one more thing, one more trauma to endure, one more Band-Aid to be ripped off. It was difficult—because it just didn't stop.

But on April 25, 2018, it finally all came to conclusion. By the end of that day, Bracamontes was firmly planted on death row where he belonged.

It was over.

Now, it was time to fully heal.

PART THREE

AFTERMATH

"After you have suffered for a little while,
the God of all grace who called you …
will Himself restore you and make you strong,
established, and settled."
1 Peter 5:10, NASB

I visit Danny's grave often.

Photo from the Brown album.

Results of my glass art "therapy."

Photo from the Brown album.

19

SURVIVOR

"The soldiers that didn't come back were the heroes.
It's a roll of the dice. If a bullet has your name on it, you're a hero.
If you hear a bullet go by, you're a survivor."
—Bob Feller

In the days, months, and years following October 24, 2014, I experienced a variety of emotions, phases of grief, and seasons that affected my family and career. Perhaps it was when I learned I was considered a victim of attempted murder by the courts that I realized I am also a survivor.

Survivors are those who have been through something traumatic. Survivors escape death. Survivors are those who live. But the near miss can have lots of consequences.

Survivor's Guilt

The American Psychologist Association Dictionary of Psychology defines survivor's guilt as "remorse or guilt for having survived a catastrophic event when others did not or for not suffering the ills that others had to endure. It is a common reaction stemming in part from a feeling of having failed to do enough to prevent the event or to save those who did not survive."

It's not hard to see why I suffered tremendous survivor's guilt over Danny's murder. The traumatic event part of the definition is self-explanatory, and well, he died—and I survived.

Cops are rescuers. We think we are indestructible. We save people from harm and watch our partners' backs. Our partners are not just people we work with; they are friends. They are family, and they are brothers and sisters-in-arms. You don't get much closer to someone than the one you entrust your life to on a daily basis.

Up to the point of losing Danny, I assumed if we did everything right tactically, we would be okay. Up to that point in my experience, it was true.

But then, there were so many questions:

> What if I had done something differently? Would Danny be alive?
>
> Was there something I missed—a sound, something out of place, a clue as to what was about to happen?
>
> Most importantly, why did I live, and Danny die?

These are unanswerable questions, but they've haunted me. I probably won't know the answers this side of heaven.

But there were things that have helped me work through survivor's guilt.

First, Susan and the girls didn't place blame on me for what happened. That made all the difference in the world. I know not everyone is that lucky. Grieving families sometimes place blame on partners, whether they deserve it or not.

Learning what happened at the scene and the suspect's mindset helped me settle on the fact that it was going to play out the way it did, regardless of anything I did or didn't do. There was nothing I could've or should've done differently. I was part of something horrific—and I've learned that it's okay to feel shitty about something so terrible. My wishes for a different outcome have no bearing on reality.

Interacting with other survivors like Susan, Bill and Jeri, Jason, Jessica, and Moose has been helpful, as well. They've embraced Liz and I as part of their lives, and we've grieved together.

Talking through these feelings has helped—with Liz, trusted friends and family, cops who've been through something similar, and a therapist. When toxic thoughts are trapped in the brain and unprocessed, they tend to take on a life of their own. Once I voiced my thinking to others who care about me, they lost momentum.

Lastly, my faith in Jesus Christ has been key. I may not know why I didn't die that day, but I do know there is a reason. I have a purpose in Him that has not been accomplished yet. I don't know exactly how the rest of my life will play out, but knowing that God is present and creating good things from a terrible situation is all I need.

Liz has felt survivor's guilt, too. She was thankful I was alive, but felt guilty because Susan lost Danny. We talked about it often. Although we are so grateful and happy that I am still around for her and the boys, we also felt guilty for being happy. Fun felt wrong, as did relaxing, complaining about stupid stuff, or even smiling. If Danny couldn't smile or relax or have fun, neither should we.

No one can live like that for too long without becoming a miserable mess. So, as time passed, I focused on three F's: faith, family, and friends. I realized not only do I owe it to Danny to live the best life I can, but I owe it to myself. I wasn't about to let the monster who took his life continue to hurt anyone else, including me. He had taken enough already.

Glass Art

When I was a senior in high school, I participated in sports year-round and needed something chill at the end of the day to ready me for practice. One of the popular electives was an art class in stained glass. It was taught by a hippie named Connie Hutler.[41] She was a little eccentric, but everyone really liked her and the class. I fancied myself a bit of an artist, so I signed up.

We made some pretty cool stuff, and I loved it. So, after graduation, I bought basic tools to continue to make windows at home. I made a few throughout the years. Later, my dad made me a work bench with slots for glass and a power strip for my tools. Eventually, life, marriage, work, and kids became the priority, and my work bench gathered dust.

A couple years after Danny died, I went back to making windows. It became my escape from, well, just about everything. I retreated to my work bench in the garage, turned on my music and focused on a project. The boys didn't come out because of the glass shards. Liz understood when I was at my bench, I needed alone time. She only came out to announce dinner or say goodnight.

Glass art is something I could concentrate on that was as far from work as possible. It is a near-perfect distraction. On more than one occasion, I cried alone while working on a window, which was therapeutic. I made windows for charity events, fixed broken windows for others and have made several pieces of art for friends and family.

---

[41] This is a pseudonym.

I encourage others to find something that is healthy and gets your mind off work, even for an hour or two each week.

Danny Days

Shortly after Danny was killed, I was lost in thoughts of his death as I mowed the lawn. Suddenly, a horrible feeling came over me: I couldn't remember anything I used to think about before Danny.

What permeated my thoughts before? What was my frame of mind? That one event had invaded every fiber of my being. It lived on in my heart and mind. I couldn't remember a time when it wasn't there.

Would it always be this way?

It has gotten better over the years, but honestly, Danny is always in the back of my mind. Some days are harder than others. Sometimes, the trigger is obvious, like memorials, dedications, and every October 24th. Other days, I have no idea what triggers a melancholy or somber mood.

Liz became very attuned to it. She always asked if I was okay, and I would answer, "It's a Danny Day." After a while, she'd just look at me and ask, "Danny Day?"

As the trial drew closer, it got worse. On those days, I was more irritable, but mostly, I was just sad. I didn't want to be around anyone or do anything. On those days, glass windows were a great distraction and a way to isolate temporarily. For the most part, I withdrew for a while, but occasionally, Liz didn't give me the option. She forced me to participate and be part of the family. This was exactly what was needed to get out of the funk. It's hard to be sad around three little boys who want nothing more than to play with Dad.

These days come less often now, but they haven't completely disappeared. They've become part of my normal. Occasionally, I just need time to work out my thoughts. As a family, we have learned to recognize and move through them easier.

I later learned that Darrell Amos has what he calls "Danny Moments" as well. Similar feelings, similar circumstances. We were amazed to learn we both refer to our grief in this way.

Spring/Summer 2019

Healing comes in layers. In the weeks after the shooting, I was overwhelmed with guilt, grief and Danny's loss—the effects of trauma. Many people who loved and supported me through it—first and foremost, Liz.

Through the losses, the trial, and learning how to navigate a new, different life, I'd healed here and there in many different ways over the first four-and-a-half years.

By early spring of 2019, there were a few issues I still needed to deal with. I was great at taking care of others (as a cop, I'm a rescuer and a fixer first), but had neglected myself, my family, and more specifically, Liz. To add to that, I soon realized that, although I had dealt with Danny's death and what transpired in the Motel 6 parking lot, I had not dealt completely with the guilt I felt around Michael's death. I held on to a belief that I directly caused the death of Michael Davis, Jr. I never really shared it, and it was eating me alive from the inside.

My conduct at work suffered. Nothing too drastic, but it was noticed. My work was still good, but I had started to make small errors. I forgot things at home. I didn't bring equipment with me to the field that I should have. For the first time in my 16-year career, I was written up—three times in the span of six months.

Then one day I found myself in the captain's office and was informed that my services as a detective were no longer needed. He said I was no longer a reliable teammate. As someone who lost a partner and was still holding onto the guilt from that day, this was a gut punch.

I was given two transfer choices: jail or patrol. He needed my decision by the end of the day.

It hit me like a ton of bricks. Issues still sitting in my gut were forced to the surface.

The jail is where my career started, and certainly not where I wanted to end up. As for patrol, the thought of stopping cars and making contacts for the next nine years scared me. I was a shit magnet—and convinced I would end up in more shootings. Liz and the boys were well aware of the dangers and my past history, which added more stress and fear. Plus, without the detective status, my pay would decrease, my schedule would suck, and I'd lose my take-home ride (which meant we'd have to buy another car).

My reaction was to panic—way stronger and more emotional than it should've been. Liz immediately contacted my therapist.

I had been seeing Joy for over a year. The moment I walked in, she knew something was wrong. It didn't take long for her to realize I needed to work out some things, so she put me on leave. She helped me see that I harbored blame for Michael's death. If I had taken care of Bracamontes in the Motel 6 parking lot, Michael would still be alive. Others, including Moose, said that was nonsense. But I just couldn't let it go.

Based on Joy's assessment and the recommendation of the department therapist, Liz and I searched for a post-trauma retreat or seminar I could get into as soon as possible. We were looking at the West Coast Post-Trauma Retreat (WCPR) in northern California, but the wait time was five months. Liz called our friends at Warrior's Rest Foundation, and they invited us to attend a Post Critical Incident Seminar (PCIS) in Oklahoma City. The retreat was approved by the department and worker's compensation.

Two weeks later, Liz and I attended the three-day retreat and were blessed to make new friends and pick up some new, helpful tools. Much of the retreat was similar to the C.O.P.S. retreats, the main difference being the absence of a line-of-duty death. Most people at the seminar were dealing with cumulative stress or a major incident where they or a partner barely escaped death.

As Liz and I listened to the conversations and spoke with other couples, we felt more and more blessed about our own relationship. Many of the cops there had held onto their feelings and kept them buried. Some had been suffering for a long time, and it was affecting their lives in many hurtful ways. Many had been divorced at least once, and some were headed toward another.

One of the attendees in my small group breakout was a state trooper, cross-sworn as a US Marshal, and military veteran. He looked like he could rip your head off, spit down your neck, and keep walking without breaking a sweat. He and I were veteran cops who had been through several shootings, and we got along really well.

I loved his outlook on enjoying the little things. This big, tough guy loved to bake—yes, I said bake! He lit up when he talked about it being his stress relief. For him, the job was temporary—his family was number one in life and decision-making.

Evidently, this attitude had not always been the case. That spoke to me.

The PCIS experience was an affirmation of the work I had already done at the C.O.P.S. camps and elsewhere. Those who had not been to anything like it went home with new perspective, new tools for mental health, and hope. We created friendships with like-minded people. Warrior's Rest staff have become friends, and their organization is an incredible resource for wellness training and peer support.

I took three months off that summer, attending counseling and seminars while trying to figure out the next step in my career path. More importantly, the time off enabled me to hit the reset button as I re-invested in Liz and the boys, which was so needed. Finally, we had time to spend together as a family. I attended church day camps with the boys and even led their groups—which I had never had time to do before. I went to several scouting events, as well. Liz and I also cleaned and re-organized the house, which reduced my stress significantly.

When I returned to work, I was assigned to the jail, making less money in a position I wasn't happy with. It was a humbling experience, but I also realized I could pass on what I'd learned in my career to the new hires.

From there, I was transferred to patrol for a short time of re-entry. I'm happy to report I wasn't involved in any shootings!

I was then transferred to serve at the Sacramento International Airport on graveyards. The Sheriff's Office is contracted to provide services at the airport—mainly, law enforcement support at the TSA checkpoints. We respond to the checkpoint if people are uncooperative or if there are suspicious packages or luggage. We also patrol the parking lots, deal with transients, lost customers, thefts, vehicle accidents, and anything else we can help with on duty.

Then, COVID-19 hit. As air travel diminished, there wasn't much to do at night, and I didn't complain.

After several months, an airport POP position opened up, and I was chosen for the job.

The POP team at the airport is similar to regular patrol. Our primary function is to cover the K-9 units while they perform their duties. K-9 officers never work without a cover officer. While the handler is focused on the door, the signs and the signals, the cover officer keeps a watch for threats. We patrol at the Sacramento International airport, but also routinely patrol Mather, a former air force base, and executive airfields. We conduct more in-depth investigations into crimes and attempt to work on long-term solutions to problems such as homeless camps, illegal dumping, crime, and customer safety. We work with the airport administration, the Sheriff's Office administration, and various stakeholders at the airport.

C.O.P.S.' Retreats

One of the most helpful organizations for Liz and I throughout our journey is Concerns of Police Survivors (C.O.P.S.). Near the end of our first National Police Week in Washington D.C., we heard about debriefings for survivors at the host hotel. C.O.P.S. hosts debriefs for wives, husbands, parents, siblings, and kids, but they also consider co-workers as survivors. Because of this, they hold debriefs for co-workers of all kinds and their spouses. Liz, who is smarter than me, signed both of us up. I attended the debrief for partners of officers killed by felonious means, and she attended the Co-worker Spouses Debrief.

I was the last to arrive. There were 15 officers, a counselor, and a few peer support personnel sitting in a circle. I had been to a few debriefings, so I had an idea of how it would go. Each told their story, and I noted one was from California. I went last. I thought it was good to be in a room of guys who understood without having to say a word. They knew how shitty I felt—the guilt, the "what ifs," and the sorrow.

I also realized that I was the only one on scene when the incident happened. I didn't realize it at the time, but I needed to find another guy who was there, like I had been. One who had seen it, smelled it, felt it. That is not to take anything away from the other scenarios or the experiences those guys went through. It was just something I needed, because I felt very isolated and alone. It seemed no one completely understood the trauma of being there when it happened.

When we finished, I picked up some pamphlets for the C.O.P.S. Coworkers Retreat and the Coworkers and Spouses' Retreats, which are held every year in Missouri. As usual, I passed them to Liz and completely forgot about them. I left Police Week wishing I had participated more at the C.O.P.S. conference.

In addition to the Police Week conference, C.O.P.S. holds annual retreats for survivors. There's a retreat for everyone—parents, siblings, spouses, kids, co-workers; if you've lost an officer in the line of duty, they have a retreat for you. The retreats are an opportunity to get away from the chaos and focus on you. The venues are beautiful. Most importantly, the retreats give survivors a chance to meet others who really get it. They understand. And knowing you're not alone is reassuring. The people you meet become family—not a family you asked for, but one you truly need.

One day, Susan asked me if I planned to attend any of the C.O.P.S. Retreats. I told her we had thought about it, but didn't have the money or the time. She shared that she had just returned from the Kids' Retreat with her daughter, Jenny. It's for children whose parent was killed in the line of duty. They provide seminars, support from peers, and resources for grief and coping skills. Although the retreat was not for widows specifically, she spent all week hanging out with other widows, and she said it helped a lot. Plus, the retreats are FREE.[42]

She then ordered me to go, guilting me shamelessly. I couldn't tell her no, but we really didn't have the money to pay for the flights, even if C.O.P.S. reimbursed us afterward. Susan felt so strongly about our going that she bought our plane tickets. Even though the registration deadline had passed, we were enrolled in the first annual Co-workers Couples' Retreat in August of 2015.

Truth be told, I wasn't looking forward to it. I imagined sitting around with a bunch of people I didn't know crying, hugging, wearing sandals and singing bad campfire songs accompanied by a guitar. It didn't sound like my idea of fun. But I couldn't anymore say no to Liz than I could to Susan. I was going whether I wanted to or not.

California had limited flights to St. Louis, so we flew in a day early. It was a good excuse for Liz and me to have some extended time together. We stayed at a casino hotel, then boarded the bus the next day for the lodge, which was a few hours away.

The bus ride was pretty quiet. Most of the ladies chatted with each other, and most of the guys kept to themselves.

We arrived at the lodge and checked in. We were told to gather in one of the large rooms for an orientation and a get-to-know-each-other

---

[42] The generosity of donors provides for these retreats.

type thing. Great! Stupid games that would force me to talk to people—just what I didn't want.

At orientation, they laid out how the next few days would go. We were told the food wasn't great, but there was plenty, so no one would go hungry. Each morning was a therapy-related event, and in the afternoon, a fun activity like shooting, zip-lining, fishing, kayaking, horseback riding and more. Liz and I signed up for horseback riding and shooting.

There were 14 couples. The first morning, officers and spouses were separated and went to different rooms. We had a debriefing led by one of C.O.P.S.' psychologist "mentals" as we affectionately refer to them. As others told their stories, I was comforted. I was with guys who understood me. I also started to worry, because no one who had spoken had been present when their co-worker was killed. I was really hoping to find someone there who fit that description.

I was to go last, but just before I spoke, a guy named Matt Hanlin told his story. Matt was a deputy with a sheriff's department in Florida. When he told his story, the heavens opened up. I found my guy! He shared how his partner was killed as they served a residential search warrant. A suspect shot down the hall and through the door with a .45. His partner was hit in the head and died on scene. Matt was hit in the upper arm, but didn't tell anyone right away, so he ended up almost bleeding to death. The suspect ran out the back, was shot several times by perimeter deputies, and died on scene.

It was a horrific story. Yet, finally, there was someone who would get me and my scene! I shared my story last, and Matt and I talked afterward. We have been friends ever since.

Liz connected with his wife, Anita, in the spouse debrief for the very same reasons. This was the first time the spouses were asked, "Where were you when you got the call?" They shared their stories for the first time and realized they were not alone in their feelings.

Spouses usually take the supportive role when we go through our incidents—they step up and take care of life while we get our heads back on straight. We realized that spouses go through a lot as well, but are overlooked. Sometimes a spouse is simply exhausted from taking up the slack in the aftermath of trauma. Other times, the spouse develops secondary trauma. This is stress that is caused by helping a person who's been through trauma. Symptoms include sleeplessness, withdrawal, physical illness, emotional exhaustion, intrusive thoughts, sadness and anger, fear, detachment and shame.

We learned about Eye Movement Desensitization and Reprocessing (EMDR) therapy, which I will explain in the next chapter.

I also learned what trauma and stress do to the body. Attaching a clinical explanation to my anxiety, stomach problems, and sleeping issues meant I wasn't crazy, and all my crap was *normal*. Sweet!

We also no longer felt alone.

Liz and I made great friends with participants and the staff, who were all incredible. After that first year, most of us vowed to return the next—not just to continue the healing process, but simply to see each other again.

We returned for the Co-worker Couple's retreats in 2016 and 2018, and the experience was different each time. In 2016, we got a ride to camp from a couple we met coming from Minnesota. Once we arrived, instead of awkward silence and small talk, it was hugs and laughing from the start. The general structure of the retreat was the same, but we were more relaxed and ready to hear what was said.

We were in a different part of our healing process, as well, so what didn't resonate the first year hit home the second. As "veterans," we got a good laugh watching the first-timers looking and acting like we did the year prior. By the end of the retreat, we all felt like family.

They call the C.O.P.S. Family the best family you never wanted to be a part of. We are so glad to be a part of it.

It is amazing to watch the transformation of individuals and the beginning of relationships. Each arrives weighted down by grief or guilt. A few days later, most look like new people. They walk a little taller, look up instead of at the ground and began to hold hands with their spouse/significant other.

For the 2018 retreat, Liz and I had two specific goals. The trial was underway, so we were hoping to connect with those who had been through a trial. Several couples and mentals fit the bill. We also were there to process Bobby French's death.

The next year, I attended the 2019 C.O.P.S.' Co-Workers Retreat (without spouses). This one held a special meaning for me, because I brought along three people from my department and one from CHP. I knew what to expect and was hoping the others would glean as much from their experience as I had every time I attended a C.O.P.S. Retreat. It played out exactly as I hoped.

Two of my co-workers were involved in the incident that took Bobby's life and the third was on the scene when Deputy Mark Stasyuk was killed. The CHP Officer was nearing the end of a 30-year career and had been through many line-of-duty deaths and suicides, both as a co-worker and supervisor.

Since I had talked up the retreat to each, I was hopeful and concerned that it would live up to their expectations. It did. Not only did we bond with each other, but we made new friends. Each got something they could take home to improve their situations. I did miss Liz, though. Things are so much better when I share them with her.

Liz and I will continue to attend these retreats, whether it be for our own benefit or for that of others.

I wish more officers and couples took advantage of them, as they provide education, therapy, relationship help, and understanding. The biggest barrier to attendance is ourselves. The help we need to be healthy and heal is there. The macho "I-don't-need-to-ask-for-help" mindset is strong in our law-enforcement community. It's not helping. We all need something, even if it is simply knowing we are not alone.

About Him

How I feel about Luis Bracamontes is a little more complicated than one might think.

Many people I've arrested have told me, "I'm not a bad person." Many have also said, "I know you hate me."

Fact is, most of the people I've arrested are *not* bad people, and I surely don't hate them. They are individuals who made a bad decision, and it is my job to call them on it so they don't hurt themselves or others. I sincerely hope the consequences a person receives are enough to ensure they never make the same mistake again.

I, too, have made mistakes. I have no right to judge anyone for anything. It is my job, however, to arrest those who break the law and to stop those who are putting others in danger. There should be consequences appropriate to the actions—breaking the law requires accountability. If we don't hold lawbreakers responsible, there will be more crime. This is human nature.

There are serious, horrible crimes committed. In these cases, the guilty have not made one bad decision, but a series of many. Pedophilia, child abuse, animal cruelty, rape, and murder are evil deeds committed by people who have invited evil into their souls. There are a few suspects that I won't ever forget because of the depth of evil in their deeds.

That said, I have gone back and forth in how I feel about Bracamontes and Monroy. I can't say I don't hate them. The pain and suffering they caused the Olivers, the Davises, my own family, and many others, is real and a definite source of anger. Bracamontes's conduct in court showed how truly evil he is. Unremorseful. Callous. Hateful. Manipulative. It's hard not to hate someone like that.

I also know that hate isn't good for the soul. Over time, my hatred for him has faded. I thought it made me feel better to hate him, but in truth, it just made me bitter. And bitterness has a tendency to spread. I realized that hatred is poison.

Bracamontes is an evil man. He met innocent people with violence without hesitation. He killed without remorse. The way he acted out in court is evidence. We felt it when he walked in the room. We heard it in his words. We saw it in his eyes and evil smirk. His teeth might as well have been fangs and his tongue forked!

As a man of faith, I know there is so much good in the world. I also know this world has plenty of evil. I've seen it. I've faced it. And some of it resides in Bracamontes.

I just need to make sure the evil within him doesn't find its way into me.

Liz and I have been through the journey to healing together. We are blessed.

Photo taken by Sarah Caponera of Blue Crew Photography.

20

GETTING HEALTHY

"I can rest in the fact that God is in control. Which means I can face things that are out of my control and not act out of control."
—Author Lysa Terkheurst

I faced evil during the gunfight in the Motel 6 parking lot. I survived that encounter, but it devastated me.

I faced evil again in the courtroom. He tried to get under my skin, to make me feel like I was a coward. I clung to the truth, and refused to respond to his taunts nor believe his lies.

When I faced evil the third time in the penalty phase trial, I was able to protect others from his words and actions. He was given a fair and just penalty—execution. He will stand before God on that day and reap the consequences of his deeds. My Bible tells me that vengeance is God's.

Bracamontes now resides in San Quentin prison, hidden from the world.

This evil has been overcome.

I am now learning how to thrive as a husband, a father, and a cop. Now that this evil has been vanquished, I am healing, one layer at a time.

Therapy

It is hard enough to talk about the need for therapy with the general public, but put a bunch of cops together to have this conversation, and it's even more difficult. To some cops, the word "therapy" might as well be a four-letter word. You'd generally have better luck getting one of them to open up about impotence than talk about emotions.

I've said before that those at C.O.P.S. call therapists "mentals." I think it's because if they call them "therapists," some cops would run screaming for the hills! We as a law enforcement culture look at ourselves as tough, hard, and emotionless.

Things we say to ourselves and others:

I've seen worse.
Nothing I haven't seen before.
I'll just suck it up and move on.
It's the job …
And my personal favorite: "I'm fine."

F-I-N-E stands for F'd up, Insecure, Neurotic, and Emotional!

Many of us think that if we admit something really got to us or that we're having a hard time, it means we are weak. We don't see others talking about it, so we assume they must be okay, and therefore, we should be, too. Some cops believe their department will take their gun or label them as "incompetent" if they need time off or to see a therapist after a traumatic event.

I totally get this, because it's what I used to think, too. I also firmly believe this mindset has destroyed many good cops. It has ruined marriages, leveled careers, and taken lives.

And it needs to change.

Until October 24th, I had been in car accidents, lost track of how many dead bodies (including babies) I'd seen, and never once thought I should talk to someone. I was "fine"! And if I actually wasn't, I was absolutely going to suck it up and be a tough guy like the rest of them.

That was all well and good … until it wasn't.

Recall that after Danny's murder, I could not sleep for more than an hour at a time. Mix in constant fatigue with grief, stress, guilt, and the waking images of Danny in the parking lot, and I was a mess. I had no idea how to fix it.

Honestly, I was at a breaking point. Against every fiber of my being, but feeling desperate and fearful for my future, I finally went to see our department therapist and asked for help. She knew about the incident. I told her what I was feeling and that I was not sleeping. She encouraged me to write my thoughts in a journal to help my mind process the event. That journal evolved into this book.

I saw the department therapist a few more times. As helpful as it was, I needed to find a therapist for both Liz and me. After all we'd been through, we needed some marriage counseling. I wanted someone familiar with a cop's life and who shared my faith. I needed the clinical side mixed with a heavy dose of God.

One day, someone much smarter and wiser than me pulled me aside. I knew his history, and we had talked a little bit about counseling, but nothing too deep. He asked how I was and offered some advice—to not settle for a therapist I didn't truly connect with. He went through four to five himself before he felt comfortable baring his soul. I took that advice to heart.

At our first C.O.P.S.' retreat, we got to know Dr. Kathy Thomas. She was exactly what we were looking for! She lives several states away, though, so we kept looking. We tried several who were qualified and said the right things, but after leaving, Liz and I would look at each other and say, "no." We found another one we both liked, but she was not on the county's list of approved therapists, and we couldn't afford her. We thought about trying to go through the church counseling program, but quickly realized they were missing the law enforcement aspect.

We eventually received a recommendation for a therapist named Joy Graf. After our first session, Liz and I knew she was the one and we have been seeing her ever since. We have spoken to her as a couple and as individuals. We've talked about the incident, trial, loss of positions, the kids, our marriage, and just about everything else.

At first, it was weird. But the more I went, the more it helped, which in turn got me to open up even more. I soon realized that it felt better to put feelings into words and get them off my chest. I left each session feeling a little lighter and usually with a tool to use in my struggle.

Joy and I worked through most of my difficulties in the traditional "talk therapy" method. Another technique we used was EMDR—Eye Movement Desensitization and Reprocessing. Joy described it to me like this:

The shooting was stuck in a part of my brain that would not process. Normally, our memories move to a different part of the brain, where they are stored and eventually forgotten. The vivid images of that day were stuck in the here-and-now part of my brain. As a result, nightmares constantly interrupted my sleep.

EMDR is a technique that stimulates both sides of your brain while talking about an event, which helps it move into the appropriate part of the brain. EMDR simulates REM[43] sleep—which reflects the normal

---

[43] Rapid Eye Movement

processing of thoughts while we sleep.

Originally, EMDR therapy involved following a finger back and forth with your eyes while talking. Therapists have since realized that the bilateral stimulation can occur in a number of ways. Some therapists have you tap your hands on your knees in an alternating rhythm. Some use headphones to transmit alternating tones. I used a ball in each hand that alternated a quick vibrating rhythm while passing between hands.

Long story short, when Joy worked me through an EMDR session, it made a tremendous difference. The emotional trauma that came with recalling my story subsided. It didn't take the memory away, but my brain was able to process it better.

Over the years, I have come up with a list of things that have worked to help me through the tough times. It includes traditional talk therapy, couple's therapy, EMDR, journaling, medication for sleep and heartburn, group therapy, and going to church for a heavy dose of God's Word—the ultimate therapy. I also added scuba diving, fishing, playing with my kids, making stained glass windows, and reading to the list.

Everyone is different, and I can't promise the ideas on my list will work for all. Every person should be encouraged to try something new or out of their comfort zone, though, especially when recommended by a competent mental health professional. Find what works and stick to it.

If it weren't for therapy, I would not have made it through the first year, much less the last six. It helped my mental health, my marriage, and with things at work.

I went from a skeptic to a strong believer. And I'm not the only one. There are countless people, cops or otherwise, who say it saved their lives. So, let's ditch the stigma, and start a new trend of cops being healthy inside and out. After all, being "half-healthy" is just no good.

Family and Friends

Through these years since Danny's death, I have not journeyed alone. God has placed people into my life who have stood beside me, listened, and supported Liz and I through very dark times. While some of these important relationships occurred after Danny's death, many already existed. All were crucial to my survival and well-being.

First and foremost, Liz and the boys have been nothing but amazing since day one. My folks and siblings were strong and supportive at every turn. This holds true for my in-laws, as well. I have been a part of their family since I was eighteen, and they treat me like blood. They have attended almost every event and supported Liz and I in every way. If it were not for the support of our families, Liz and I would not be able to help others as we have. They take on the burden of watching three boys for several days at a time with generosity and love. If you ask most people to watch three boys under twelve for more than a few hours, they will quickly come up with an excuse. Not my family! They jump in and help make it work, and I am so grateful.

Our Marriage

Life as a cop is very hard on a marriage.

On 10/24, we learned that the divorce rate in our department is 80 percent. 80 percent!!! The shift work, stress, and risks wear on a person—and it can break a marriage apart. Add in a critical incident, and it's even worse. It can make or break you as a couple.

Liz and I decided the day it happened that we wouldn't let it break us.

We have changed and grown through this journey as individuals and as a couple. It has been a series of ups and downs, sorrow and laughter, fighting and making up. We have made good decisions and bad, and are learning from both.

I learned how strong Liz is. I admit that I took her for granted and have treated her like shit at times. I have learned how to let her help me, and in turn, how to support her.

Over the last seven years, we have learned one VERY important thing: Without communication, we are doomed.

When we assumed things or got upset about something but held it in, we unraveled. I've also learned that sarcasm is not constructive communication.

In February 2020, Liz wrote me a letter. The short version is that I was not treating her well. She felt unloved, disrespected, and unwanted/unneeded. She felt I would be happier without her, because all I did was point out her faults and complain.

Her letter was a wakeup call. I had no idea she felt that way, let alone that I was treating her that way. We had stopped communicating and neglected each other while taking care of others at each other's expense. Evidently, that happens a lot in cop marriages.

When the career is in the rearview mirror and the kids are grown, it'll be just us. If Liz and I don't keep our relationship strong, we won't have much left. I know a life without Liz is a very grey and lonely world. I would hate to enter retirement and not have her to enjoy it with. Not worth it.

We know how things can happen in an instant. One moment someone you love is there—the next, he isn't. We can't prepare for it. Yet we shouldn't live in fear of it.

We *can* make the most of every moment.

Liz and I take trips, have date nights, and make love as often as we can. If I go to work and never come home, I don't want her to ever doubt how much I loved her.

The Boys

Our boys are more aware of how the world works than many kids their age. They have attended law enforcement memorials, watched me cry, and overheard me talking about things most adults can't tolerate. They live with someone who checks the doors twice before he goes to bed. They have a parent who assumes one lie means they will end up in jail—and he has one hell of lie detector built into him.

More importantly, though, I hope they see a dad who stands up for what he believes in. I hope they see a man who isn't afraid to show his faith and love for God at work and in front of the world. I hope they see a dad who coaches every team and attends all the scouting events he can. One who makes time to play, helps with homework, tells them he loves them every chance he gets, and hugs the crap out of them before he goes to work. I hope they not only learn right from wrong, but also how to be great husbands and fathers someday.

I know Connor worries about me. Brandon thinks I'm a hero, and Tyler wants to be a cop (and Batman) when he grows up, which scares the hell out of me. Before Danny, I'm not sure I ever thought about how I'd feel if the boys decided to become cops. I think about it all the time now. I would of course be proud of them for following such a noble calling and profession, but I would also worry all the time.

Over the years, I have met many parents of fallen officers, and I see the pain it has caused them. No parent should outlive their kids. The thought of losing one of my boys that way keeps me up some nights.

My family has given up so much for this career they really didn't ask for. It boggles my mind, how they still stand with me. They've seen me angry, yell, shut down, and cry. They have seen the public go from praising the police after 9-11 to what it is in 2021. I have gone from thinking how cool it would be to have the boys follow in my footsteps to praying they don't.

Men's Group

I have been a part of a men's Bible study. We meet once a week to study and discuss curriculum geared toward being a man of God. I attend with my dad, my brother and his son Mason, and my son Connor. My brothers-in-law have also popped in from time to time.

When Danny was killed, this group rallied around me. They've understood when I can't make it, given ample hugs, and on one occasion, bought plane tickets out of their own pocket, so Liz and I could get away for a weekend.

This group not only gave me the opportunity to share my story, but it helped me grow as a Christian. Prior to Danny's death, I didn't talk much about my faith. I didn't share with others, would never have taken a leadership role in my church, and never prayed out loud in a group. After Danny's death, I had several wakeup calls—one of them around my relationship with God. I couldn't wait *until later* to share my faith anymore. I decided I would say "yes" to God even if it made me uncomfortable.

This group allowed me the chance to do that in spades. I was a table leader[44] for a while, and then became a leader of the whole group and the emcee for our weekly meetings. I not only talked about God in front of these guys, but I shared my story with them and prayed for them. Then, I started sharing my faith all over the place. And the more I did, the more I loved it. I knew God was using me.

---

[44] A table leader is responsible to lead discussions, make sure everyone gets to share, and to communicate with the rest of the men during the week.

While my faith grew, I made a lifelong friend and battle-buddy, Woody, whom I could confide in. He was a former army ranger who was going through the army chaplaincy program. I am so grateful for his friendship, and I owe it to my men's group. They gave me opportunity to connect with likeminded men and set a great tone for my week by focusing on God and others.

Small Group

Liz and I joined a small group Bible study in 2018 with other law enforcement couples. Getting into God's word with a group of people who know the unique struggle of being a Christian in law enforcement is priceless.

Each couple has a unique dynamic that offers new perspective. Liz and I now have a sounding board for problems, and just knowing we're not alone in our struggles has been very helpful.

Jason Davis is a part of this group, too. He has shown me true strength alongside vulnerability. The views he shared with the court about October 24th have challenged me spiritually and become a source of healing.

Brent and Vicki Newman are not only the host couple of our group, but they have become mentors to Liz and me. They are a loving, caring, godly couple who exemplify how to nurture a strong marriage and parent as cops and Christians. I love how they share their successes in these areas, but also their failures, to help others hope, learn and grow.

Brent is a skilled communicator who enjoyed a long, successful career as an officer. He makes even a complicated concept make sense, and his work advice and wisdom are priceless.

Vicki is an amazing woman I am blessed to have in my life. When she reads that sentence, she'll probably cry; with a heart that big, she wears her emotions on her sleeve. Without her, this book would not have happened. Her vision and heart have inspired me and many others. I love that Liz has Vicki to talk to and lean on when she is in need. Vicki's mentorship to Liz has benefited me more than I will ever know.

I love my small-but-mighty group, and I look forward to going through this life journey alongside them. I pray that every cop finds a group like mine to support them along the way.

Faith in God

The sacrifices of cops are not just personal, but emotional and spiritual. Cops see more death, violence, suffering, and tragedy in a year than most people will see in a lifetime. No one calls 911 to report they're having a great day and ask the cops to come by for lemonade. They call asking for help on the worst day of their lives. We're expected to make it better—to stop someone from hurting another, get property back, stop the bleeding, bring someone back to life, make a death notification, help raise a child, rescue a child from abuse, and much, much, more. If you don't think that sticks to a soul, you're sadly mistaken.

There have been times I've questioned God. How can He let such bad things happen? How can He let kids die? Why did He let that girl get raped? How can He let that man beat his wife? But then I realize God didn't commit those heinous acts—humans did.

The Bible is clear. All humans have sinned. What is sin? Not obeying God's commandments. He's given us a book that spells out how we are to live—and we don't do it. Then we wonder why our world is so screwed up.

My faith has grown stronger since facing Bracamontes. I never got mad at God—not sure why. I am alive for a reason, and God has been revealing that to me in His time. I know my guardian angels worked overtime that day. I know God keeps throwing miracles in front of me as well as the ability to recognize them.

I also came to realize that I don't have all the time in the world to show my faith and love for God to my boys. I now feel a sense of urgency to invite my friends to church, so they can begin to hear how much God loves them. I am no longer worried about what people think, feel, or say about me being a Christ-follower. I pray, believing in God and talking about it wherever and whenever I feel moved to do so.

When I do finally meet my Savior, I want to walk up to the gates of heaven and hear, "Well done, my good and faithful servant," as referenced in Matthew 25:21.

A New Career Perspective

I am called by God as a police officer to protect the weak, stand in the gap between good and evil, and bring peace to chaos. I try to do it with integrity. Compassion. Discernment. And yes, even love.

But being an officer for any length of time changes people. We are not the same cops we were when we graduated the academy. We've been there, done that, and seen it all.

Getting healthy also means accepting that cop culture actually plays against emotional wellness.

We are trained to do the opposite of what will actually help us the most emotionally. We aren't supposed to ask for help. We think we are to depend only on ourselves, shut down emotion, and isolate. It took several years for me to get that through my thick, bald skull.

At Danny's funeral, Captain Dave Torgerson said it best:

> *"How many times have you heard, 'I wouldn't do your job for all the money in the world?' I have, many times. Cops don't do it for the money, fanfare, or rewards. Cops suit up every day because they are special. They have made a significant commitment to serve and protect the communities they serve, including those who try to hurt and sometimes kill them.*
>
> *"At times like these, we feel helpless and wish to God there was something we could've done to prevent the situation or to protect one of our brothers or sisters. As cops, we're expected to have all the answers, be able to reason, mediate, and negotiate any situation to its successful conclusion. Cops are the gladiators others call when they need protection and assurance. Cops don't call 911.*
>
> *"At times like these, we ask ourselves 'Why? What if? How could this happen?' But in reality, we may not always get the answers we seek, or truly understand why to give us the ultimate closure we seek.*
>
> *"In times like these, whether privately or publicly, we feel pain and sorrow. We sometimes lose the knack of having all the answers and feel helpless. Some of you may be angry, experience great sadness or rage. Know that you are normal. While others may be unemotional or still in shock at this point, know that you are normal. Grief and the grieving process affects each and very*

one of us in various ways and at various times. For one person, a single event may have significant impact emotionally and physically, while for another, a series of events or incidents over time may take its toll and manifest itself during what some may say was a relatively minor incident.

"As you move through the grief process, you may be the rock to support others, but realize there may be a time when someone else will be your rock."

My career has changed me. I loved my job and couldn't picture myself doing anything else. I realized I left a lot more of myself in that Motel 6 parking lot than I cared to admit.

I still like my job and can't picture myself doing anything else. I will give my all to every assignment and would give my life for others. The difference is now, when I chase that bad guy or pursue a car, I think about the danger and weigh the cost.

Do I still get a thrill out of it? Hell yes! Do I search for it? No!

Do I get an adrenaline rush when a guy takes off on foot, and I catch him and throw cuffs on him? Yes, I do. Do I stop a guy hoping he runs? Nope. Now, I make assignment decisions based on how it will affect my family, not my career. If given the choice of overtime or time with family, I will pick my family every time.

I haven't gotten close to a partner since Danny was killed. Not sure if that's intentional or not. I speculate that I keep myself from getting close to partners out of fear of losing another close friend. I have made several good friends since Danny was killed, but have not found an on-duty partner I can confide in, invite on vacation, or have over to the house for a beer and BBQ.

I sincerely hope that changes before I am done with this career, but only time will tell.

October 24th has changed every aspect of my life. There has not been a day since I lost Danny that I have not thought about him. Some days more than others—I am better at working through it now, so that it doesn't take over. I don't see this ever changing, for the rest of my life—and I am not sure I'd want it to.

The pain and suffering my family and I have been through have made us into who we are now. We are stronger as individuals and as a family. We are closer, because we no longer take our time together for granted. I have learned to put God and my family first in my life. All decisions—including around my career—are made for the glory of God and the benefit of my family.

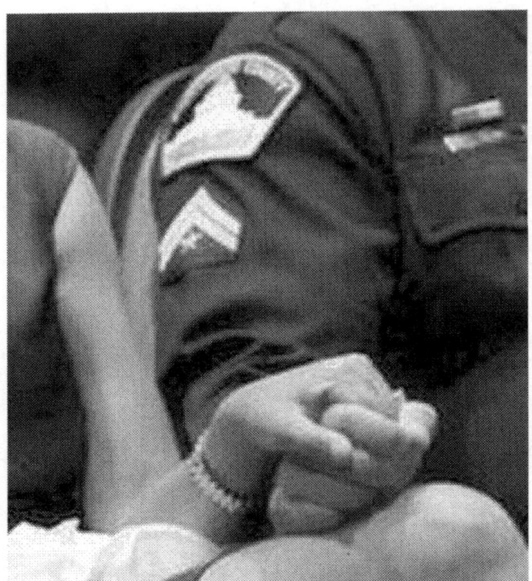

Susan and I held hands during the funeral. One of the lessons I've learned is to hold onto good friends—never go it alone.

Photographer unknown.

21

LESSONS LEARNED

"Bravery is not the absence of fear, but action in the face of fear."
—Mark Messier

October 24, 2014 changed many lives. In the years since, our Sacramento community has been through so many losses, disasters, and protests.

There were marriages that suffered afterward as trauma and grief affected officers and their families. There were several early retirements from the effects as well, including Deputies Chuck Bardo and Jack Hickey, Detective Mike Simmons, and CHP Paramedic Jim Hendrix.

Not every peace officer experiences an incident as big as this one. Many suffer a number of smaller incidents over a long career, which have a tendency to attach together to significantly affect the officer at some point. More recently, officers are experiencing multiple critical incidents as they work crime-laden areas. Still others survive their careers only to find past incidents haunting their minds in retirement.

Stress and exposure will manifest themselves—cops don't leave this job without its imprint on their souls.

Yet there is still an expectation that officers remain unscathed by the violence they see and experience, the human suffering they witness, the criminal coldness they encounter, and the threats they endure. "Old school" mindsets around law enforcement are still present, and they can be devastating.

For years, families and those who work in and with law enforcement have been sounding the alarm. But there is still a stigma—if you ask for help, you're weak. You're done. And you're abandoned.

So, cops suffer silently, and suicide becomes an option for some. It needn't be this way!

Thanks to people who really care, we now have great understanding about the emotional toll policing has on a soul. We now have therapies and protocols that have produced incredible results, including getting cops back out on the street even stronger and more resilient than they were before. There are retreats for officers and couples that open a whole plethora of programs, people, and education that otherwise might not be found.

There is still work to do in getting officers over the stigma. There are many who have no idea what is available to them, and that there is indeed hope. We talk with cops and families who've been suffering for years, unaware that help is just a phone call away.

All of this is exactly why Liz, Victoria, and I felt this book was worth the work. Our story documents what help looks like in the aftermath of a horrific incident.

Below, we're sharing a list we've compiled summarizing the lessons we've learned over the last seven years[45] , so you can use it as a resource in your own healing:

Work:

- Have a current End-of-Watch packet filled out and in your file at work. If you don't have this provided through your agency, C.O.P.S. has a downloadable copy on their website.[46]
- Make updates to your personnel file and End-of-Watch packet yearly, especially your beneficiary information, perhaps at your annual evaluation. There are heartbreaking stories of estranged family members receiving death benefits, leaving current spouses and children with nothing.
- When choosing who you wish to notify your loved ones, consider a chaplain. It is a difficult thing for close friends and partners to shoulder, and they will be struggling themselves should something bad happen. Chaplains are trained, apart from the incident, and readily accessible.
- If you've been in a serious incident, consider going to a hotel for a couple days immediately afterward while getting your bearings.

[45] These suggestions and more are part of the presentation Liz and I give during the Traumas of Law Enforcement class provided by Concerns of Police Survivors. For information on this free class, including dates in your region of future trainings, visit https://www.concernsofpolicesurvivors.org/traumas-of-law-enforcement-trainings.

[46] https://www.concernsofpolicesurvivors.org/digital-materials

- Attend a critical incident debrief. If a spouse debrief is offered, encourage your spouse to attend.
- If your department takes good care of you, make sure you thank them.
- If you are command staff, welfare checks on involved officers is huge—days, weeks, months, and anniversaries after the incident.
- Disability insurance should be mandatory—you're more likely to be injured than killed in the line of duty. If you don't have it, get it.
- Remember that others are feeling similar feelings as you are. You are not alone. Reach out!
- Your family, friends, co-workers, and the public rely on your physical, mental, and emotional well-being.
- Carry on with your life in a positive way to honor the sacrifice of those who've fallen.
- Helping others helps you heal!
- If you would like to talk with someone and don't have anyone to call, contact How2LoveOurCops, Warrior's Rest Foundation or call COPLINE.

Marriage:

Liz was an absolutely brilliant asset in the aftermath of my incident and remains unselfishly so even today. She shared my pain—helped me carry it. And I allowed her to help carry my pain, even leaned into her. Her strength and love led me to hope ... and then, she walked alongside me to help me heal. Your spouse could be your greatest asset!

- Think "we," not "me": You are a team through thick and thin.
- Give each other grace in tough times—make room for grief, loss, stress, and effects of trauma.
- Have patience during the healing process. It's a marathon, not a race.
- Grieve together. Celebrate service and sacrifice.
- Go to Police Week with your spouse.
- Learn to communicate. Then, relearn how to communicate. Then, learn how to communicate even better.
- Get couple's counseling with a therapist who understands the

law enforcement culture.

- Find a mentor couple. Ask the hard questions. Watch their lives and follow in their footsteps.
- Talk it out: co-workers, therapists, clergy, family, peer support, trusted friends.
- Get to a retreat, and take your spouse!
- Build your support system—those you trust and want what is best for you.
- Get educated on stress, trauma, the associated red flags, and resources available. This book is a great start.
- Take time in quiet, beautiful places.
- Eat healthy food and take walks.
- Be involved in each other's lives—home, work, play.
- Accept help from others, and pay it forward.
- Take time off from work!
- Have a stress-relieving, non-police related hobby, and return to it regularly.

Kids:

- Kids are more aware than we realize. They see it, hear it, and feel it.
- Keep kids in the loop and informed according to maturity. There's power in learning information from the parent first, instead of from friends, outsiders, or social media.
- Involve them in functions, memorials, anniversaries, and the cool things that come with your job.
- Ask questions—how do you feel? What do you want to know? Any questions?
- Be ready for a child's honesty and innocence.
- They'll only be small for a few short years—soak in the innocence.
- Teach your kids to be aware and smart.
- Listen, talk, and then listen some more.
- Always believe the best in them, even when they're teenagers.

Here's a list of healthy perspectives and practices I've incorporated into my life:

- It's ok to ask for help—it is not a sign of weakness.
- Don't waste mind time on "what ifs". It won't change the outcome, and that kind of thinking isn't based on reality.
- Have faith and work on keeping it.
- TALK! Talk to your spouse, a friend or a counselor. Don't keep it inside.
- Learn to forgive yourself as well as others.
- There is no timeline on grief and mourning. Don't let anyone else dictate when it's time to move on.
- Make God and family top priorities.
- It's healthy to be happy and enjoy life after a tragedy. You don't have to feel guilty.
- It's okay to cry, smile, hug and express emotion like a normal human being.
- I am not alone. You are not alone.
- Don't wait until tomorrow to implement changes needed today.

Throughout this book, I've also highlighted some of the amazing programs that exist to help our law enforcement and their families. Others include the use of therapy dogs, EAP (Employee Assistance Program), the Cordico app, regular health screening, exercise and stretching, adequate sleep, and practicing mindfulness. For information on these and more, go to the resource section of www.how2loveourcops.org. There, you'll find a content library of articles, videos, and blog posts that speak deeper to the emotional wellness of officers and their families.

Please see our website, www.scottandlizbrown.com.

If you would like to contact Liz, Victoria, or myself, here are our email addresses:

Scott & Liz: ScottandLizBrown@gmail.com
Victoria: victoria@how2loveourcops.org

Our family today.

Photo taken by Sarah Caponera of Blue Crew Photography.

22

A NEW MISSION

"I want to look into the puny face of the enemy of our souls and see him squirm when I hold it out and declare that everything he took from me, from my family, and from our futures here on this earth is nothing in comparison to what I will take from him with and through the power of God. Because I Will. Not. Stop."
—Vanessa Shepherd, *The Good in the Awful*

Since October 24th, 2014, I had been looking for the reason I was spared that day. Over time, I realized I have been called to help officers that have been through trauma, and Liz and I have been called to help law enforcement marriages and families. It has been a slow road, finding this new mission, but I have had help along the way. The help came through C.O.P.S., How2LoveOurCops, The Danny Oliver Foundation, Warrior's Rest Foundation, speaking engagements, SSO peer support, and writing this book. My experience is uniquely my own, and yet that experience relates to others.

Perhaps the most redeeming thing about October 24th is the new calling, purpose, and mission that was born. As a knuckle-dragging Neanderthal, there was much I didn't know about the emotional toll of policing. Each incident takes a small toll, and in my experience, there were many incidents. I just sucked it up. Filed it all away. No problem.

But after Danny, I couldn't function as before.

I needed help, and in seeking it, a whole new world opened up to me. There are organizations, individuals, therapies, and people who have found ways to help cops through trauma—all kinds of programs and treatments just waiting for cops to embrace.

I also felt like I had been spared for a reason, despite not knowing what that reason was.

In the end, I've been able to use the entire experience I've described to answer a new calling.

Right now, the law enforcement community is trying to solve the problem of police suicide. There are far too many cops who are killing themselves, or in my case, suffering with different types of post-trauma bullshit. Peace officers are under incredible and increasing stress since 2014. As of 2021, that stress has escalated to inconceivable heights. Cops are leaving the profession en masse after the George Floyd incident and the fallout. Our profession is suffering in unbelievable ways.

My calling, now, is to help my fellow cops. Liz's calling is to help law enforcement families. This comes from our hearts, and we're united in it. We're not perfect, we're just transparent. We've been there, and we want to stand alongside others who are there now.

Telling Our Story

The first time I felt a pull toward this new calling was when I was invited to share my story at the 2017 Nor Cal C.O.P.S. Annual Black and Blue Ball. This formal event is held each January to raise money for the services they provide. The program includes a speech from a survivor, and I was to be the last speaker before outspoken Sheriff David Clarke from Wisconsin. Over 700 people were in attendance. I let them know that I am not a polished public speaker; I am only capable of being me. That's what they were looking for, though, so I accepted the invitation.

While preparing, I realized I don't like when presenters read a speech from a page without eye contact. They don't seem genuine. Realizing I couldn't just wing it, I developed an outline to keep me on track during the speech.

The event took place at the Hyatt Regency Hotel in downtown Sacramento. Liz rented me a tuxedo for the night so I would look good, despite my mild protests. She looked amazingly beautiful in a blue gown.

We checked in and found our table. In true-Liz fashion, we said hello to just about everyone in the room. Those who knew I was speaking asked me if I was nervous; I lied, saying, "Just a little." Their well-intended questions didn't help the butterflies swirling in my stomach, though. I had been in fights, pursuits, shootings, and a hundred other crazy scenarios, but this took the cake.

Why would anyone want to listen to me? What do I really have to say? How much of an idiot will I make of myself?

As I was introduced and walked to the stage, sweat poured through my shirt, jacket, boxers, pants, and even my socks. The ballroom was maxed out at 750 people, but it felt like a million. To make matters worse, I noticed Jessica Davis, Michael Davis's widow, sitting at a table in the front. How would she respond to my story? It was too late to back out, despite my fear of upsetting her.

I told my story in some detail, pausing to compose myself a few times. I spoke of what happened at Motel 6, the survivor's guilt, and some of the ways I'd gotten through it. I spoke of the C.O.P.S. retreat, and the ways Concerns of Police Survivors had been there for us.

The crowd gave me a standing ovation as I stepped off the stage, although it was probably out of pity.

Needing some air, I made a beeline for the lobby area. Tears of mourning and relief began to well up. My best friend, Mike Putnam, and Liz followed me out, and we talked a bit. My wife told me I did great, but I admit, I was just glad it was over.

As I re-entered the ballroom, I was rushed by people who wanted to talk. People hugged me, shook my hand, and bought me drinks the rest of the night.

What meant the most to me were the cops from all over the state who told me I said things they needed to hear. They thanked me for being so open and honest. One guy I'd never met gave me a hug, started crying, and then said, "I know how you feel." To this day, I have no idea who he was or what agency he came from, but I remember the pained look on his face. He was relieved that someone else understood. He wasn't alone.

That night lit a fire inside of me to help people.

I began speaking to recruits during the health and wellness section of the academy. One shared her amazement at how open I was about my faith in an educational setting. It had not occurred to me that it was a big deal.

This was affirmed again after speaking to a different class. A recruit who looked like he was really hurting asked if he could speak to me outside. We went to a private place, and he confided in me that a relative of his had died, and he didn't know if that person was in heaven or not. I was caught off guard and had no idea what to say. After a moment of silence, though, I shared that although he might not have known what was in his relative's heart, God knows … and that is what really matters. I referred him to someone at his church for a more educated, biblical answer, having no idea that my belief in something would have such an impact. It was an honor to me, that this person felt he could open up to me after just a short interaction.

Eventually, Liz and I were invited to speak together as a couple. One of the first times was at a conference called Breaching the Barricade Conference in Indiana. We had met the host of the conference, Jim Bontrager, when in Washington D.C. for Police Week the year after Bob French was killed. Jim is a former Marine and a bold Christian. He was at Police Week reaching out to cops, and we met through the Newmans.

The conference speech went great! Officers expressed regret that their spouses had not attended, because Liz said things they had never thought about before. We realized that Liz had a unique perspective that could help fill another void.

The next day was a law enforcement appreciation day at a farm across the border in Michigan. We had a great time doing a few things that would not have been legal in California, like shooting guns with oversized magazines, handling a 50 caliber Gatlin gun, and shooting air soft guns at targets from a dune buggy going 30 miles per hour.

After we had been to a couple of the C.O.P.S. retreats, we were asked to become speakers at the Traumas of Law Enforcement (TLE) class. The three-day course covers topics such as line of duty deaths, cop trauma, mental health, and suicide. We speak on Day One as an injured officer and spouse. Since some injuries are not physical, but invisible injuries of the heart and mind, we tell ours from both perspectives, sharing specific lessons we've learned along the way.

The feedback has been amazing. Officers thank me for being open and ask good questions. The recurring theme is that they now know they are not alone in their thoughts. Some want to share their story, and I am honored to listen.

There is something healing about putting your thoughts and feeling into words to someone who gets it.

Many also thank Liz for her part of the story and wish their wives had heard her speak. Some say they will have a conversation with their spouse they might not have had, were it not for our story. And that right there is why we speak.

We now speak at a spouse's conference called Home Watch, hosted by How2LoveOurCops. Other agencies are asking us to speak, as well. And each time we do, I feel we are genuinely helping people. Something good happens every time, and sharing my story helps me, too.

We're on the road when we speak, and I love the time alone with Liz. With three boys, it is rare to just be together. After each speech, we get to hang out with the local officers, and we are filled with hope and motivation as we interact with them. This is the opposite of isolation, and it speaks to our nature as humans to seek out community and support in order to thrive.

How2LoveOurCops

The combination of doing life with Brent and Vicki Newman, telling our story, and our calling to help law enforcement officers and their families led to our involvement with a national non-profit that serves law enforcement families. How2LoveOurCops (H2LOC) helps families thrive relationally, emotionally, and spiritually by creating resources to help families in all aspects of the career—from rookie to retirement.

H2LOC's founder, Victoria Newman, authored A CHiP on My Shoulder, which is a book about how to survive and thrive while being married to a cop. Liz met Vicki at our church and was invited to join a book club with other LEO wives. This happened in 2014, months before the shooting. The book club created a community that was there for us when we went through our incident later in the year.

In 2017, Liz was invited to be on the H2LOC Board. She serves as the Community Liaison and does an incredible job in support of law enforcement families. I also volunteer—sometimes speaking, but more often lifting boxes, setting up and cleaning up at events, and sometimes pulling all-nighters with Liz to finish whatever the latest project brings.

Sacramento Sheriff's Office Spouses' & Family Association

We view it as providence that Liz joined Vicki's spouse book club. She loved meeting with the other wives from several agencies in the area. After we lost Danny, it was on her heart to do something else—perhaps start a Facebook group for law enforcement spouses. She talked with our local head chaplain, Mindi Russell, and her response was, "When you're ready to put together a group, I'm ready!"

When Liz opened our home to the other wives involved in our incident, one of the spouses said to Liz, "If this would've happened to me, I don't have support. I would be alone."

This is what drove Liz's inner mission to create a non-profit that would ensure families would have the support they need in crisis. She first spoke with SSO Sheriff Scott Jones, and he loved the idea. Then, she talked with SSO Peer Support Leader Gordon Smith, who said "This is the missing piece in our support." She met with our Association President, Kevin Mickelson, along with Kim Tarabetz, Founder of the PCSO Spouses Association, and PCSO Lieutenant Andrew Scott, seeking guidance on how to begin. Sheriff Jones put her in touch with Janine D'Agostini, wife of Sheriff John D'Agostini and leader of their family association, Thrive 10-35. Janine took Liz under her wing and guided her through the process of setting up the organization. Liz was also introduced to a SSO (retired) spouse, Kathy Rogers, who had experience with nonprofits, business, and finance. The two ladies assembled the non-profit paperwork, and the Sacramento Sheriff's Office Spouses' & Family Association (SSOSFA) was born in 2018.

When Deputy Stasyuk was killed that same year, SSOSFA gathered community support to provide a lunch for those who were involved in the incident. Held in the parking lot of the California Highway Patrol Communications Center, Liz and her team provided ample food and drink for over 100 officers in honor of their assistance. The event was a complete success, having provided a respite for all who attended in the aftermath of another horrible incident.

Since then, Liz and her team have been the go-to for the department when needs arise. They've provided peer support and partnered with the chaplaincy during debriefs for other spouses, meal trains for injured and overwhelmed officer families, blue memorial ribbons after LODDs, and connections to services provided by our department. The favorite event of families is the annual Milk and Cookies event with Sheriff Jones and Blue Santa at Christmastime.

In January 2021, our department experienced three shootings in one week, and the subsequent loss of Deputy Adam Gibson and K-9 Riley in the line of duty. Two other deputies were also wounded by gunfire but survived. Liz and her team were involved in caring for these families, a critical incident debrief for spouses, and a night of food and peer support at the Newman home.

The Danny Oliver Foundation

In 2015, Susan approached me with the idea of starting a non-profit in Danny's honor. I was all in!

Our goal was to bridge the gap between the community and law enforcement and to help out law enforcement in times of need. Since Danny was a POP Officer, we wanted to involve the community he served, and to be there for those who supported us in our grief.

Danny grew up in a community that doesn't traditionally produce officers. So, we decided to create a scholarship for recruits at the academy to help alleviate some of the financial burden. Students are evaluated based on criteria and selected by the Academy Staff. In our short time of existence, we have given away thousands of dollars in scholarships and are now working to expand to other academies in the Sacramento area. Our hope is that it will provide students putting off academy training for financial reasons a chance to fulfill a calling.

Our annual fundraiser is a poker tournament. Susan had previously owned a property management company, which hosted employee appreciation nights with a poker tournament. Danny loved it, so it was only fitting to make a tournament our annual fundraiser.

More recently, we expanded to support families of fallen officers in our area, remembering anniversaries and sometimes offering financial support. We have sponsored Eagle Scout projects and other community-related events, as well.

I love that we honor Danny's service and keep his memory alive through the Foundation.

SSO Peer Support

Peer support is a program through which cops support and listen to other cops. Because talking to a therapist is a big risk for some, it's often good to start with someone who's been there. Someone who understands. Sometimes, peer support is all that is needed; other times, peers can refer the officer to a culturally competent therapist. Peer support members have been trained in Critical Incident Stress Management (CISM) and given specific resources to refer others to. Gordon Smith, a retired captain with our department, is the team leader of approximately 65 members who've gone through a week of training to be peer support members.

Before October 24th, I heard about peer support but had no idea what it entailed. The day of the shooting, the SSO Peer Support Team came alongside Liz and me. They checked in with us often afterward.

There were few people who had practical experience in what I went through, and even fewer on our support team. Cops are cynical and cautious—even amongst themselves. Unless someone has been through it, we don't put much weight into what they say. So, if a records officer came alongside me and told me all the right things in the best possible way, I wouldn't listen, because he or she hasn't been in my shoes. Now, if a hardened street cop who has seen it all says the exact same things, I will take it to heart. That's one thing that makes the peer support group so powerful.

I really connected with Gordon. As a former SWAT operator and commander, Gordon was involved in a nationally known incident at a Good Guys store in Sacramento on April 4, 1991. Several hostages were taken by multiple suspects who had automatic weapons. During the final moments of the standoff, several hostages were killed by one of the suspects, and cops took out all suspects but one. Gordon has his own demons. That is why we connected so well.

A little over a year into this journey, I felt a pull to become a member of the peer support team. I wanted to help others, should this type of incident happen again. Little did I know how soon that would be.

The week of CISM training was rough—it included testimonials and scenarios, and it was intense. But Gordon and a few others kept their eyes on me, and I managed to get certified on April 15, 2015. I then took a 13-hour Assisting an Individual in Crisis class that concluded in 2017. The training consisted of lectures, testimonials, and scenarios. We learned how to talk to someone in crisis and techniques for being a better listener. We don't try to solve the problem, but listen for how the person in crisis is responding to the problem. We learned some of the signs and symptoms of trauma, what to say, and what not to say. We give referrals when needed.

Deputy Scott Padgett gave his testimony. Padgett lost his partner, Deputy Larry Canfield, in an on-duty motorcycle accident on November

12, 2008. Canfield lost one of his legs and bled to death on the scene. Padgett talked about the incident, how it affected him at work and at home, and why he joined peer support, which was to help others go through the loss of a partner. I remember thinking to myself how we had joined for the same reason. His talk was very emotional and brought back a lot of my feelings. I had to leave the room at least once, and when I returned, I stood in the back. Gordon Smith and Chaplain Mindi Russell were right there with me.

Listening to the scenarios was tough mostly because I was like an exposed nerve. The role players did a good job of acting like they were truly in distress, too, and I was worn out. In retrospect, I should have waited a little longer to train.

I asked Gordon if I could help specifically with officer-involved shootings and LODDs. A few months later, Bobby French was killed. I talked with several deputies afterward. I listened, referred them to culturally competent therapists, told them about C.O.P.S., and provided other resources.

When Mark Stasyuk was killed in the line of duty on September 17, 2018, there was a great need for peer support. These officers were younger—and several had heard me speak at the academy. My role this time was driving a chaplain to Mark's parents' house to notify them of his death. Tragic, but I was honored to be a part of it. I also was able to come alongside Mark's partner, Julie Robertson. She and I had very little in common personally, but in the shared tragedy, we bonded immediately. She has been very strong through her grief, injuries, and trauma.

It was and continues to be an honor to help others who are suffering.

Although Liz is not a member of peer support, her role with the spouse association has allowed her to come alongside spouses and significant others over the years. When Mark was killed, she passed along support and insight to his widow, Amy. When CHP Officer Lucas Chellew was killed, she came alongside his widow, Christina. She continues to share her love, experience, and wisdom with others through practical help and a listening ear.

Finding My Purpose

If I can help one cop stay healthy and happy through their career, it's worth it. If I can help an officer through a trauma because we have a shared experience, it's worth it. If Liz and I can help heal a marriage and keep a family together it is worth it. If by writing this book and helping out with each of these amazing organizations I can do just one of those things, then I feel like I accomplished my purpose.

"If a man has a hundred sheep and one of them goes astray, will he not leave the ninety-nine on the hills and go out to search for the one that is lost? And if he finds it, truly I tell you, he rejoices more over that one sheep than over the ninety-nine that did not go astray."
Matthew 18:12-13

While I can't personally save anyone, I can offer tools to cops to save themselves. Through sharing my experiences, I hope others find a nugget of useful wisdom.

I look forward to finishing up this career as a Deputy Sheriff, so I can start a second career. What that looks like, I don't know. But I will give my all to wherever and whatever God has for me.

What Bracamontes and Monroy meant for evil, God has made good.

Evil comes to steal, kill and destroy.

Jesus Christ said, "I came so that you would have life, and have it abundantly."[47]

Glad I'm on the right side.

[47] John 10:10, NASB

EPILOGUE
WHERE ARE THEY NOW?

Facing Evil is a true story that continues to this day. Although the incident took place years ago, that fateful Friday lives on in the memories of dozens of people. It lives on in nightmares in the middle of the night. It lives on in the empty chairs of loved ones missed. Broken relationships. Early retirements. Anger. Tears.

But survivors are strong and have taken life one day at a time. This is where they are today.

Susan and Jenny Oliver

Susan sold her company and the home she shared with Danny. She now lives happily out of the state of California. She remarried a wonderful man who treats her amazingly and is great with the girls. She's taken up cigars and hunting, and she can shoot the wings off a fly! After starting The Danny Oliver Foundation, she turned over the reins to Missy.

Jenny Oliver graduated high school in 2021. She has a pet lizard and is planning to head to college and then on to the rest of her life. Through it all, she has had some great friends by her side.

Missy Oliver

Growing up, Missy felt like she'd been in a protective bubble, and was therefore a bit naive. The day her father died, that bubble burst, and she felt exposed to the crazy world all at once. It hit her hard. The dad who'd always listened was gone. She felt like she had to be strong for her mom and sister, and carried that weight on her shoulders. She had a choice to make—let the darkness swallow her whole and go down an unhealthy path, or listen to the voice of her Superman: "Pick yourself up, move forward, and live your life to the fullest."

In the days that followed Danny's death, Missy and Michael Davis' daughter, Samantha, became very close friends. "Samantha and I met under terrible circumstances, but she was and still is someone I can call day or night. She just gets it, She's become one of my best friends, and no matter how long we go without speaking, we always pick up right where we left off. She will always be a part of my life."

Missy began a career in 2019 working for the Department of Consumer Affairs, developing and validating licensing exams for various professions across California. She is now in the last semester of a master's program for Industrial-Organizational Psychology. She became the President of the Danny Oliver Foundation, and has purchased a home with her husband.

She says, "I believe my choice to return to college only three months after losing my dad is what got me through to this point. Through it all, my dad's voice was pushing me. He was there for all these special moments in my life—not physically, but emotionally. I always felt him on those special days. He's gone, but I believe he lives through me every day."

SSO Deputy Darrell Amos

When Darrell placed the Honor Flag into the case in which it came, he felt a sense of finality. "It was, 'See ya later, Danny,'" he says. "It gave me peace to carry that flag. It was a link to Danny. My final service to him."

Deputy Darrell Amos now works for the civil division of Sacramento Sheriff. He is a strong family man, and he and Becky and their two children make the most of their lives together. Darrell coaches his kids' sports teams, volunteers in their classrooms, and teaches them strong values.

In the aftermath of 10/24, Darrell went through grief therapy. He realized he didn't have to be directly involved in the incident to be affected. The relationship he had with Danny was enough. He's grateful for the time they served together.

Darrell hears Danny's voice often. People, places, and situations bring him back. At work, Danny's voice coaches him. "Danny used to say, 'Don't sweat the small shit,'" Darrell shared.

Adam Holst

After surgeries, severely injured civilian Adam Holst recovered from the five gunshot wounds to his head and arms. At times, he still experiences residual nerve pain while doing simple movements, like reaching to open the door. His emotional injuries remain, although they have lessened over time.

He lives in Northern California with his girlfriend and has moved on with his life.

PCSO Deputy Chuck Bardo

Deputy Bardo developed Post-Traumatic Stress Disorder after the shootout with Bracamontes. Over the years, he has been able to manage it through diligence, hard work, and prayer. He has not shied away from help and credits his faith in Christ and his family as the key to his survival.

"I fought/fight PTSD through therapy, counseling, EMDR, Rx medications, medicinal cannabis, and a post-trauma retreat for first responders," he says. "Most recently and effectively, I had a stellate ganglion block procedure which has enabled me to be medication-free for the first time in six years."

Shortly after the shooting, Chuck was contacted by a local group of military vets called Welcome Home Vets in Grass Valley, California. They welcomed him into their weekly group therapy sessions free of charge. Six years later, they still do. They told Chuck that whether in uniform overseas or at home in community, combat is combat. They saw the parallels between the growing public anti-law enforcement rhetoric and the anti-war protests of the Vietnam era and wanted to help. "They saw a need," he says. "I thank God they did. These brave men helped save my life from suicide."

Bardo also struggles with the government's role in this case. He sees the rise of Kamala Harris, California's Attorney General, to Vice President as dangerous to the public and to officers. "She embraced sanctuary city laws and is no friend to law enforcement. I watched her walk out of Michael Davis' funeral as his brother, Sgt. Jason Davis, asked for punishment to the full extent of the law for his brother's murderer. This divisive behavior by elected officials must stop. It is a cancer."

Chuck retired from law enforcement in 2016 and is living in

Northern California with his wife of 25 years and two children. PTSD has not allowed him to return to the work force, but he says it will not rob him of God's gift of life.

"The very nature of the job of deputy, coroner, and marshal will change you. No one is impervious. Add in the evil of that day, and for some, it's more than they can handle. Just look at the growing number of law enforcement suicides. Agencies and law enforcement themselves need to be more vigilant in their self-care."

PCSO Deputy Joe Roseli

Joe Roseli is now a detective with Placer County Sheriff's Office. He has continued to serve on the SWAT team. He is a firearms instructor and a field training officer, and works with his department's Explorer program, which he loves. He lives in a beautiful area of Placer County with his family.

What has struck Roseli is the fact that the incident affected so many people, even those not directly involved. He overheard a conversation in a restaurant involving a person who transported Bracamontes to the hospital, who was considering not ever going back to work because of how it affected him.

Roseli has given much thought to 10/24 and the way it changed his own life. His girls exhibited a lot of fear afterward when he was called out for SWAT. He's faced nightmares and dealt with the effects of trauma. "I have a really good excuse to be a fuckin' asshole every day, and not engage in the way I should. I could drink too much, or not PT (physically train) like I should, or not do what I need to do to be a good husband, father, and friend," he says. "But for me, it's the opposite. Because of folks … who actually give a shit about the mental state of those of us who have a cumulative amount of negativity and garbage that we take in, we continue to do it. Not because we love doing what we do, but because at the end of the day … we want to help people."

PCSO Detective Mike "Moose" Simmons

On October 1, 2017, Moose was in his room in the Mandalay Bay Hotel in Las Vegas, Nevada. He was there to lead a training for POST[48] the next morning. Unbeknownst to Moose, a man named Stephen Paddock open fired from another room in the same hotel on a crowd attending the Route 91 Harvest music festival. Sixty people were killed, and 411 wounded by gunfire. The ensuing panic increased the number of injuries to almost 900. In the aftermath, Moose's son called to make sure he was alright, and that is how Moose was notified of the incident. Even in retirement, Moose is a shit magnet!

As a certified instructor for Nevada POST, Moose spends the first hour of the training sharing his October 24th story. He tells officers to leave old-school thinking[49] in the past—if a cop doesn't talk about the stuff he's seen, he or she will implode. "Pay attention to yourself and your partner," he warns. "If you see something, SAY SOMETHING!"[50]

Moose is now retired and lives on a nice piece of property in Tennessee. He enjoys the quiet life, riding his Harley on long trips. He has finally found some peace.

PCSO Sergeant Jason Davis

Jason Davis has continued his service as a sergeant with Placer County Sheriff's Office. He is working on a degree in Criminal Justice and manages a nonprofit called Placer Sheriff Activities League.

He and Traci live in the hills of Northern California with their three growing children.

Jason continues to give powerful, moving speeches on behalf of law enforcement and the policies that affect them.

---

[48] Police Officer Standards of Training

[49] The belief that law enforcement officers aren't supposed to be affected by trauma, and therefore don't talk to anyone about it—not spouses, other officers and certainly not a therapist.

[50] If you see changes in behavior or attitude in your partner, ask them about it!

PCSO Deputy Jeff Davis

Jeff Davis went through months of physical and occupational therapy to get the use of his right hand back. He experiences lingering pain, weakness, and some slight numbness from the injury, but has otherwise fully recovered. He was cleared for full duty and returned to work in late October 2015. Jeff now works for court security, but he misses patrol.

Getting shot wasn't the most difficult part of 10/24 for Jeff. What bothers him the most was watching Michael die just feet away. "I can't get his face out of my head," he says. "It broke my soul. My only solace is that I like to think he knew Jimmy and I were there, and I hope it gave him comfort knowing he wasn't alone."

Jeff was diagnosed with PTSD and underwent therapy for several years. He also attended the West Coast Post-Trauma Retreat (WCPR), a week-long residential program for first responders. In addition, he took Rx medication for two years before choosing to go medication-free.

Jeff credits his recovery to the support of his wife and daughter, friends, family, and coworkers. "It's extremely healing to speak with a combat vet, either military or law enforcement, and fortunately, I have some in my family and at work. They provide understanding, the camaraderie of shared experience, and acceptance."

Jeff joined the Placer County Peer Support Team. He loves the feeling of helping others in need, and his soul continues to heal as others heal. Although he laments that he has changed through the experience, he can finally say he's happy again.

CHP Paramedic Jimmy Hendrix

The events of 10/24 were traumatic for Jimmy, too. He'd been a first responder and military medic for 20 years at that point, so he had accumulated many incidents leading up to the "final straw." With his wife, Becky, by his side, Jimmy went through therapy, including brainspotting and EMDR, took medication, and attended WCPR. In the pursuit of getting healthy again, he realized, "I love my job. But it's killing me." He finally made the difficult decision to medically retire. Jimmy chose November 11, 2019—Veteran's Day—for his last flight. It was followed by a barbecue to honor Jimmy as everyone celebrated his meaningful career of dedicated service.

On the five-year anniversary of Michael's death, Jimmy penned a poem that recounts his experience that day. It ends with, "Those eyes will never leave me, it's one more set I see. They're added to the list of things that I cannot unsee. It's one more trauma added, compacted over time. In 25 years of service etched in my timeline. But here it is, five years ago today … I get to sit here quietly and ponder on the way Mike Davis changed my life on that unforgettable day.

"Quieter is the noise now, the race is in my mind, giving me serenity in its splendid, ugly way. Gone is the chatter ringing through my head. No more calls to action. No more sleepless nights. No more fits of fear remembering all those flights. For today, you see, is different. For today, you cannot see … there is a peace that's swelling, rising up in me. Stillness, quiet is a storm residing in my head.

"Peace is what I want. Peace is all that's dear. Peace at last is what I've found, knowing that I won't have to face another hero down."

Jimmy now manages 70 acres of generational property in Placer County. He, Becky, and their three boys live nearby.

SSO Sergeant Randy Winn

After 30 years of service that included nearly 18 years as a SWAT team member and leader, Randy Winn retired from law enforcement in July of 2018. Building on a passion for aviation and all things flying, he pursued a second career as a commercial airline and corporate pilot. He and his family now reside in the foothills of Placer County, just a couple miles from the scene of the Davis shooting and the spot where he handcuffed Bracamontes.

Sergeant Winn lost a tremendous amount of faith in the criminal justice system as a result of this incident, particularly in California. "The officers who responded to this incident did everything humanly possible to track down, locate, isolate, and detain Bracamontes without additional injury," he said. "It is extraordinary that a suspect who had deliberately and intentionally murdered two police officers and seriously injured a third would eventually crawl out on his belly and surrender without an ounce of resistance. Many were surprised … many were disappointed.

"Personally, I believed that Bracamontes had earned what would ultimately be a life sentence of agonizing and tortuous incarceration on

San Quentin's Death Row. While prepared for anything, I was somewhat relieved that Bracamontes did not come out shooting or commit suicide when confronted by officers, thus granting him the tranquility of a certain and immediate death. That was too good for him. After having to watch and endure the years of pretrial motions, spontaneous outbursts in court, and the excruciating testimony of the survivors, I was relieved that Bracamontes was convicted and eventually sentenced to death.

"That gratification, however, was short-lived. Less than a year later, while many people attempted to put the pieces of their lives back together, a politician with a personal agenda, without any consideration for hundreds of victims and survivors, signed an executive order banning the death penalty and giving an unjustifiable reprieve to 737 convicted killers. It was then, at that moment in the spring of 2019, that I became disenchanted with our criminal justice system, and I wished Bracamontes had actually died on that day in 2014."

Motel 6

The Motel 6 hotel had been purchased by another company prior to October 24, and there were plans to tear it down along with the theatre next door. Following the Oliver murder, the timeline was expedited. On January 30, 2015 the motel was razed to the ground. Today, the property boasts several buildings and stores, including Home Goods and Nordstrom Rack.

Janelle Monroy

Janelle Monroy was sentenced to 25 years to life. On March 23, 2018, she arrived at the Central California Women's Facility in Chowchilla, California. She will be eligible for parole in July 2040.

Luis Enrique Monroy Bracamontes

Bracamontes is sitting on Death Row in San Quentin Prison.

VICTORIA'S THOUGHTS

After hearing about the events still unfolding on October 24, 2014, I followed updates on the news, hoping and praying for a good outcome. I eventually sent texts to the cop wives in our winter small group to check on them. Several ladies said their husbands were indeed involved or friends with one of the deputies killed. Liz responded that Scott was on scene.

Feeling the sorrow for my friends, I shared a Facebook post that night:

> *"As I prepare for bed, I wonder at the day's happenings. It weighs heavy. I think of two women who will cry themselves to sleep, knowing that there are cold sheets an arm's length away, and as they reach for his pillow, drinking in the scent of him, knowing that, too, will fade away in time. I think of six children who will grow up without their father, and in that is profound sadness.*
>
> *"In that moment, I am overcome with thankfulness that my Chief is nestled next to me, worn by the day, but safe. Yet there is a sense of guilt for that thankfulness as I mourn for Mike, and I mourn for Danny, two men whom I've never met, but will attend their funerals, and cry, and feel the loss to our Blue Family.*
>
> *"I also think about the female officer I saw on TV today who was crying while trying to fill out her report. And I think of Danny's partner and his wife, who I've come to know and love, and wonder how many nights they will be awake replaying October 24, 2014. And I think of Mike's mother, who 26 years ago TODAY, lost her husband in an LODD. I wonder at the tragic irony and can only imagine the depth of her grief.*
>
> *"I know the risks of this career, and I've felt and dealt with my fears through the years. But it doesn't mean that I ever get used to it. So, I will allow myself to shed some tears, and come alongside those left behind in the days to come, and we will never forget."*

I had no idea how true that last line would become five years later. Scott and Liz are now intertwined in our lives. They introduced us to Jason and Traci Davis, who we've also come to know and love deeply. This book guarantees that we will never forget the sacrifices of Danny Oliver and Michael Davis.

Every book I write is a journey of discovery and learning. I immerse myself in the story and engage my mind and heart in every interview. I have taken part in some very intense conversations with incredible men and women who serve.

Facing Evil has been this and so much more. As I listened, researched, visited affected neighborhoods, and interviewed those who were involved, this story imprinted itself on my soul. I endured many sleepless nights, knowing those I interviewed were probably awake, as well.

I saw the demons. I heard the pain. I felt the impact of one evil couple on many lives. I then took the advice provided in this book and sought therapy for the way other people's trauma affected me.

I am blessed to already see healing through the process of writing this book. Scott, Liz, and others have let me know they, too, have worked through the trauma they've experienced. At least two marriages have been saved, and the conversations that have occurred have really drilled down on the truth of what this job can do to the human soul. We've learned firsthand, too, of the plight of secondary trauma, and are moving forward in addressing it in a real and healing way.

Some of those I interviewed are not mentioned in the story because we had to cut back to keep from confusing the reader. There were many more officers involved than we included. El Dorado County Deputy Jason Bloxsom was on the doorstep of the yellow house while supposed to be on vacation. SSO Detective Scott Swisher trusted me with his personal experience through all of this, and every deputy and officer I interviewed went deep in their stories. Dozens of other officers were involved and affected as well—Scott, Liz and I have been amazed at the magnitude of this one day. There was simply no way to interview every single person involved.

As tragic as this day was to so many, I love what Scott's story teaches:

- To overcome evil, implement both humility and the courage to face it in whatever form it comes in.

- Don't let go of tragedy, but use it as a stepping-stone to healing and growth.
- Understand that bad things happen, but good can come out of it.
- Grieve loss, but embrace the lives that were a part of our own and take them with us into the future.
- And lastly, move forward with an outward mindset, helping others who experience much the same.

Writing *Facing Evil* has challenged me as a citizen, a cop's wife and a support/advocate for police families, while giving me deeper understanding of our police officers and the sacrifices they make on our behalf.

My hope is that you see it, too, and be grateful for the role our police officers play in our communities.

If you are a police officer, may God bless you and those who love you, keep you safe, and bind up the wounds on your heart and soul. Thank you for your service and sacrifice.

AUTHOR PAGE

Scott J. Brown

Author Scott Brown has been a deputy with the Sacramento Sheriff's Office since 2002. In that time, he worked the jail and patrol, was a member of the POP Team, CERT Team for the jail, a Custody Training Officer, and a Field Training Officer. He's worked as a detective in the property crimes unit, was in charge of the bait property program, and was on the Animal Cruelty Task Force. He is a Silver Star of Gallantry recipient.

He has a degree in Psychology from California State University, Sacramento, with a minor in Criminal Justice. Scott earned a full-ride scholarship as a place kicker for the Sacramento State Hornets, still holding college records. He plays every year in the Sacramento Pig Bowl's Guns and Hoses game. He was awarded MVP in 2018.

Scott volunteers regularly with the Boy Scouts, Bayside Church, How2LoveOurCops, and is Co-Founder of The Danny Oliver Foundation. He is a member of the Peer Support Team with Sac Sheriff.

Scott likes to unwind and decompress by making stained glass windows in his garage and being out in nature, preferably fishing.

Scott and Liz have been married since 2004. They have three boys and live in the Sacramento area.

AUTHOR PAGE

Victoria M. Newman

Victoria Newman is an award-winning author of five books. She has spoken to law enforcement officers and their families all over the United States, Canada, and the Philippines. She is Founder and President of How2LoveOurCops, a 501(c)(3) organization that creates resources for law enforcement family wellness.

Victoria supported her husband, Chief Brent Newman (retired 11/19), through 31 years of service with the California Highway Patrol. His career included many high-profile events, LODDs, and coworker suicides, and Victoria came alongside not only her husband, but coworkers and their families. They now serve side by side, helping law enforcement officers and their families navigate challenges of the career. They reside in the Sacramento area, have four adult children, and one adorable grandson.

Other books written by Victoria M. Newman:

A CHiP on my Shoulder
A Marriage in Progress
Selfish Prayer (with SSG Emmett William Spraktes)
Unwrapped at the Edge of Grace
(with the late Carol L. Barron)
Coming Soon: *One Word* (with Dr. Raleigh Washington)

ACKNOWLEDGEMENTS

I thank God first and foremost. I believe He saved me on October 24th, and since then His strength has helped me to keep going. He hasn't left my side the entire healing process.

Liz and the boys have put up with a lot these past years and have supported me through this book endeavor. Liz is my rock and continues to bless me. She is the love of my life and will be for all time. The boys' smiles, laughter and joy keep me positive in the dark times.

To my parents, thank you for raising me with the love of God in my heart, a strong work ethic, and strong convictions that won't let me give up. Your emotional support and help with the boys has been instrumental. To Catherine and the Anderson family, thank you for your support. Without your help and care for the boys, Liz and I would not have been able to attend the events that helped us heal nor share our story with others. This includes the many meetings to write this book.

I thank both the Oliver family and the Davis families for their support with this project. Specifically I want to thank Susan, Jeri, Missy, Jessica, and Jason for their input into some very personal areas of their lives. This book would not be complete without them.

I thank Mike Simmons (Moose), Jeff Davis, and Adam Holst for their willingness to share. As victims, I know it was not easy to recount the events of that day. I appreciate you and know the readers will, too.

There were several others who made sure the content was not only accurate but personal. Thank you Scott Swisher, Randy Winn, Derrick Greenwood, Rod Norgaard, Jimmy Hendricks, Joe Roseli, Chuck Bardo, Darrell Amos, Eric Eastman, Dale Hutchins, and Jason Bloxsom. Thank you for your thoughtful additions. Thank you, Adam Davis, for your marketing expertise and a great website!

Thank you, pastors from Bayside Church—your support and care have meant so much to me. Thank you for your recollection of detail—I couldn't remember everything, but I certainly felt the care you've offered.

Thank you to Brent Newman, for content editing—your suggestions transformed the manuscript. Thank you Megan Yakovich, for your excellent editing skills and feedback as a civilian. Thank you to David

Eaton for a powerful cover and excellent interior design!

Last but certainly not least I want to thank my co-author, Vicki Newman. Vicki is not only a great author, but a great friend. She invested her time, body and spirit into this book. She knows more about this incident than anyone on the planet, including me. Thank you, Vicki, for all the hours, research, tears and sleepless nights you put into this. You are an amazing woman, and Liz and I are blessed to know you.

Scott

APPENDIX

List of Events

October 24, 1988	Michael Davis, Sr. Killed in Helicopter Crash on Duty
October 25, 2013	Roseville Shootout, RPD Officer shot in the face
October 24, 2014	Incident occurs, Oliver and Davis are killed
	Monroy Surrender and Arrest in Auburn
	Bracamontes Surrender and Arrest on Belmont Drive in Auburn
October 25, 2014	El Dorado Hills rock painted by Jenny's friends
October 26, 2014	Danny's Body moved to East Lawn
October 27, 2014	POP Team Debrief
	Home
October 28, 2014	Talk to Connor
October 29, 2014	Dutch Bros Fundraiser raises $96,597
	Sacramento Kings Honor Oliver/Davis
	Michael Davis' Birthday Party
	Told Liz' Family
	LECS Debrief at Bayside Church
October 30, 2014	Liz has SSO spouses over to the house
	Scott plays golf with coworkers
October 31, 2014	Halloween Parade with Boys, Trick or Treat
November 1, 2014	All Dept Debrief
November 3, 2014	Danny Oliver Funeral
November 4, 2014	Michael Davis Funeral
November 12, 2014	Sacramento Board of Supervisors issue Proclamation
November 25, 2014	Simmons responds to Bodies of Infants Found in Storage Unit
January 2015	Scott's Trip to Cozumel
	Susan Oliver Goes to White House,
	Attends State of the Union Address
February 1, 2015	Motel 6 demolished
February 2015	Scott returns to work
March 13, 2015	Old Foothill Farms Bench Dedication

May 2015	Department Memorial
May 2015	Local Memorial
May 2015	Candlelight Vigil
May 2015	California Memorial
May 12-16, 2015	Police Week, Washington DC to honor Danny and Michael
August 2015	C.O.P.S. Coworkers for Couples Retreat
October 11, 2015	Orangevale Community Park Dedication
October 24, 2015	One-Year Anniversary
November 7, 2015	Patriot Park Dedication
January 16, 2016	1st Annual Danny Oliver Foundation Poker Tournament
January 18, 2016	Simmons responds to Shooting at PCSO Loomis Substation
March 13, 2016	CHP Officer Nathan Taylor LODD
March 28, 2016	Preliminary Hearing
April 2016	CHP Motor Officer Mike Ericson Intentionally Run Over on Sacramento Freeway
July 7, 2016	Dallas Police Department Ambush & LODDs
July 10, 2016	Simmons responds to Homicide in Auburn, ends near Michael Davis' grave
August 2016	C.O.P.S. Coworkers for Couples Retreat
October 14, 2016	Simmons responds to Clown Hunting Bottle Throwing
October 23, 2016	Danny Oliver Foundation Punt, Pass, Kick Event
October 24, 2016	Two-Year Anniversary Service
November 13, 2016	Stanislaus County Deputy Dennis Wallace LODD
February 22, 2017	CHP Officer Lucas Chellew LODD
February 28, 2017	Jessica Davis and Susan Oliver Attend State of the Union Address as President Trump's Guests
March 17, 2017	How2LoveOurCops is Created
May 16, 2017	HR 2431 Introduced to Congress by Rep. Raul Labrador
May 20, 2017	SSO Deputy Dan Cabral dies of pancreatic cancer
June 27, 2017	SSO Deputy Alex Ladwig shot in the face
July 15, 2017	Michael Davis Freeway Sign
August 30, 2017	Bobby French LODD
September 2017	French LODD Funeral interrupted by Sac PD OIS
September 16, 2017	Second Annual Danny Oliver Poker Tournament
October 1, 2017	Mandalay Bay Mass Shooting in Las Vegas
October 11, 2017	Danny Oliver Freeway Sign Unveiled
October 12, 2017	Freeway Sign on display at Rancho Cordova Police Station

October 24, 2017	Three-Year Anniversary Service
November 10, 2017	Danny's Father Dies
December 24, 2017	CHP Officer Andrew Camilleri LODD
January 2, 2018	Scott turns 40 years old
January 16, 2018	Janelle Monroy & Luis Bracamontes Trial Begins
January 18, 2018	Scott Brown Testifies
January 19, 2018	Trip to Lake Almanor
January 24, 2018	Liz turns 40 years old, Moose testifies
January 31, 2018	People Rest
February 5, 2018	Defense Arguments Begin
February 7, 2018	Jury Deliberations Begin for Monroy
February 8, 2018	Jury Deliberations Begin for Bracamontes
February 9, 2018	Bracamontes Guilty on Danny Oliver's Birthday
February 15, 2018	Monroy Guilty on All Counts
February 24, 2018	Mission Park Dedication for Danny Oliver
	Scott & Liz' 40th Birthday Party
March 1, 2018	Penalty Phase of Trial Begins
March 5, 2018	Scott Brown testifies
March 6, 2018	Jason Davis and Mike Simmons testify
March 2018	SSO K-9 Nikk dies suddenly
March 18, 2018	Stephon Clark killed by Sac PD
March 22, 2018	Black Lives Matter Protesters shut down Sacramento freeway
March 26, 2018	Penalty Phase Closing Arguments
March 27, 2018	Bracamontes is sentenced to death
April 2018	C.O.P.S. Couples Retreat
April 25, 2018	Victim Impact Statements
May 2018	Police Week in Washington D.C. to honor Bobby
August 10, 2018	CHP Officer Kirk Griess LODD
August 18, 2018	How2LoveOurCops Becomes 501c3
September 3, 2018	CHP Officer Brad Wheat Murder-Suicide
September 15, 2018	3rd Annual DOF Texas Hold 'em Tournament
September 17, 2018	SSO Deputy Mark Stasyuk LODD
September 24, 2018	Spouses Host Lunch for Officers involved in Stasyuk LODD
October 5, 2018	Browns Speak for Breaching the Barricade Conference
October 23, 2018	CHP Officer Sean Poore Dies by Suicide On-Duty
October 24, 2018	Four-Year Anniversary Service at East Lawn
October 31, 2018	Trump Administration Runs Nationwide Ad Linking Bracamontes

	to Democrats' Policies, Trump Tweet
November 8, 2018	Camp Fire Breaks Out
November 9, 2018	H2LOC Gala @ Union Hall
November 2018	H2LOC/PCSO/BCSO Spouse's Camp Fire Event in Oroville
December 23, 2018	Blue Line Christmas Event in Chico
December 26, 2018	Newman PD Ronil Singh LODD
January 10, 2019	Davis PD Officer Natalie Corona LODD
March 2, 2019	Browns Speak for Home Watch Conference
March 2, 2019	Officers Not Charged in Clark Case; Put on Alert
March 13, 2019	Governor Puts Moratorium on Death Penalty
May 2019	Police Week in Washington D.C.
	—Liz attended to support Amy Stasyuk
June 19, 2019	Sacramento PD Officer Tara O'Sullivan LODD
July 21-24, 2019	Post-Critical Incident Seminar, Oklahoma City, OK
September 28, 2019	4th Annual Danny Oliver Foundation Poker Tournament
Early October 2019	COPS Coworkers Conference in Missouri
October 23, 2019	El Dorado County Deputy Brian Ishmael LODD
October 24, 2019	Five-Year Anniversary Service at East Lawn
April 2020	Virtual C.O.P.S. Couples Retreat
January 18, 2021	SSO Deputy Adam Gibson LODD, K-9 Riley LODD
April 2021	C.O.P.S. Coworkers for Couples Retreat
August 28, 2021	Fifth Annual Danny Oliver Poker Tournament

Officer Down
October 24, 2014

Flying in response, Call goes out!
Did they really say that? Did it really get put out?
Panic in the air, hurt heard in their voice
Trying to find the Officer, we need to get them out.
A racing in my heart, a fear within my soul
What if I can't hack it? What if I don't know?

Skids hit the ground, the engine's idled down.
Time to get to action, time to double down!
My pilot points to action, my head swivels round.
"Fuck" is what I thought; "Fuck" is what I said!
For what was coming, was another Officer dead.

The panic in their eyes, the anger in their heads
I can see they want me to save him, to make their Friend undead.

I put myself to action, I went to work that day
To save a Warrior stricken by evil in the way.
Time slowing down, my movements quick and swift
Acting under pressure by the frantic of his friends.

"SAVE HIM!" is what I hear. "SAVE HIM!" is what I feel.
Tension rises in me as Death lingers near.
Fighting back against it, keeping it at bay
Telling evil, "Fuck you! You aren't winning here today!"

Quickly, swiftly, strategically I whisk the Officer away
Working on him feverishly, to give him just one more day.

"Are his pupils fixed?" is spoken in the wind.
His partner frantically grasping at any kind of win.

The face I looked at then is the face I see today
Always looking at me, every time of day.
For lifeless eyes were staring back at me right then
How do I say it? It's a fight we cannot win!

"Fuck!" is a word his partner whispers then.
"I have to tell his wife," is how it finally ends.
A Husband, Father, Brother, Son is suddenly in my mind
How is it so likely that this world can be so unkind?

Those eyes will never leave me. It's one more set I see.
They're added to the list of things, I can never not unsee.
It's one more trauma added, compacted over time
In 25 years of Service etched in my timeline.

But here it is, five years ago today.
I get to sit here quietly and ponder on the way
How Mike Davis changed my life on that unforgettable day!

Quieter is the noise now, that races in my day
Giving me serenity in its splendid, ugly way.

Gone is the chatter ringing through my head.
No more calls to action. No more sleepless nights.
No more fits of fear, remembering all those fights!

For today, you see, is different. For today you cannot see
There is a peace that's swelling, rising up in me.
Stillness, quiet is the storm residing in my head.
After living through a moment of seeing one more dead.

Peace is what I want and cherish.
Peace is all that's dear.
Peace at last is what I found...
Knowing I won't have to face another Hero down!

Jimmy Hendrix
10/24/19

NATIONAL LAW ENFORCEMENT RESOURCES

Concerns of Police Survivors—www.concernsofpolicesurvivors.org

Programs for line of duty death survivors including a national conference during National Police Week every May, scholarships, peer-support, counseling reimbursements for children, camps and retreats. National Wellness Conference, Traumas of Law Enforcement Training, and other assistance programs.

COPLINE—www.copline.org

An international confidential 24-hour hotline answered by retired law enforcement officers who have gone through a strenuous vetting and training process.

How2LoveOurCops—www.how2loveourcops.org

A national organization that educates, encourages, and equips families to thrive amidst the challenges of a law enforcement career. They have programs, events, and in hand resources designed to help families relationally, emotionally, and spiritually.

PCIS/LEAP—www.scleap.org

Post Critical Incident Seminar (PCIS) is a three-day intensive seminar for officers led by culturally competent therapists. Designed to jump-start healing after trauma. Spouses encouraged to attend.

Survivors of Blue Suicide—www.survivorsofbluesuicide.org

Provides support for survivors and co-workers of law enforcement suicide while working with agencies to provide respect and dignity to families and law enforcement community.

That Peer Support Couple—www.cathyandjavi.com

As seen in the documentary, Officer Involved, Cathy & Javier Bustos's mission is providing peer support for first responders and their families. They are recognized national speakers on various first responder mental health topics.

The Wounded Blue—www.thewoundedblue.org

An organization dedicated to injured and disabled law enforcement officers. They provide peer support, education and assistance. They also work to propose legislation that supports those injured in the line of duty.

Warrior's Rest Foundation—www.warriorsrestfoundation.org

An organization dedicated to law enforcement and first responder wellness. They train peer support teams, provide wellness training, leadership training, and respond to departments in crisis.

SACRAMENTO AREA RESOURCES

Back the Badge Yuba Sutter—https://www.backthebadgeys.org/

Community and spouses who support law enforcement in Yuba and Sutter counties.

Blue Line Outdoors—http://bluelineoutdoors.org

Hunting and fishing trips for law enforcement who've been involved in a critical incident and need time to decompress.

C.O.P.S. Nor Cal Chapter—https://www.norcalcops.org/

Support for survivors of line-of-duty-death.

The Danny Oliver Foundation—https://dannyoliverfoundation.org/

Scholarships for those entering the law enforcement field.

End of Watch—https://www.eowf.org

Foundation that assists officers and survivors in time of need.

Frontline First—https://frontlinefirst.org/

Helping first responders, military and the community through trauma via training, compassion and faith.

Law Enforcement Chaplaincy, Sacramento—https://sacchaplains.com/

Community and law enforcement chaplains that assist law enforcement throughout the Sacramento County region in emergency situations.

Placer County Law Enforcement Chaplaincy, Inc. —https://placerchaplains.com

Field service ministry to law enforcement officers and their families and the citizens of Placer County.

Sierra Law Enforcement Chaplaincy—https://www.slec.us

Field service ministry to law enforcement officers and their families and the citizens of El Dorado and Amador counties, and the city of Folsom.

SSO Spouses Association—https://www.ssospouses.com/

Spouses and family members of Sacramento Sheriff Office who support one another in crisis, as well as ongoing training and support.

STAR 6 Foundation—https://www.star6.org/

The benevolent arm of the Sacramento County Sheriff Deputy's Association, providing financial assistance and services for their fallen and injured.

Thrive 10-35 Families' Association—https://thrivewith1035.org/

Assistance and support for the deputies and families of El Dorado County Sheriff's Office.

Made in the USA
Middletown, DE
26 November 2024

65082496R00172